How Our Lives Become Stories

How Our Lives Become Stories

_____ MAKING SELVES

Paul John Eakin

CORNELL UNIVERSITY PRESS

ITHACA AND LONDON

First published 1999 by Cornell University Press

First printing, Cornell Paperbacks, 1999

Printed in the United States of America

Library of Congress Cataloging–in–Publication Data

Eakin, Paul John.
How our lives become stories : making selves / Paul John Eakin.
p.   cm.
Includes bibliographical references (p.   ) and index.
ISBN 0-8014-3659-1 (cloth : alk. paper). — ISBN 0-8014-8598-3
(pbk. : alk. paper)
1. Autobiography.   2. Self-perception.   3. Identity (Psychology)   I. Title.
CT25.E25   1999
808'.06692—dc21   99-28793

Cornell University Press strives to use environmentally responsible suppliers and materials to the fullest extent possible in the publishing of its books. Such materials include vegetable-based, low-VOC inks, and acid-free papers that are recycled, totally chlorine-free, or partly composed of nonwood fibers. Books that bear the logo of the FSC (Forest Stewardship Council) use paper taken from forests that have been inspected and certified as meeting the highest standards for environmental and social responsibility. For further information, visit our website at www.cornellpress.cornell.edu.

Cloth printing   10   9   8   7   6   5   4   3   2   1
Paperback printing   10   9   8   7   6   5   4   3   2   1

To James Olney

Contents

Preface

This is a book about autobiography. Even more, though, it is a book about how we come to be the people we say we are when we write—if we ever do—the stories of our lives. Thus my concerns are both literary and experiential, for the selves we display in autobiographies are doubly constructed, not only in the act of writing a life story but also in a lifelong process of identity formation of which the writing is usually a comparatively late phase.

Autobiographical discourse tends to promote an illusion of disarming simplicity when it comes to self and self-experience. We already know, without having to think about it, how to play the autobiographical game if we have to: "I was born," we say, "I did things . . . I felt feelings . . . and now I write these facts of my story." Use of the first person—the "I," autobiography's dominant key—compounds our sense of being in full command of our knowledge of our selves and stories; it not only conveniently bridges the gaps between who we were once and who we are today, but it tends as well to make our sense of self in any present moment seem more unified and organized than it possibly could be. But who is the "I" who speaks in self-narrations? And who is the "I" spoken about? Are the answers to these questions self-evident? I once thought so, at least sufficiently to be willing to think of autobiography as in some fundamental way "the story of the self"; now I don't, but my thinking about autobiography and identity formation has evolved so gradually that I can trace the change only if I look back by decades.

Twenty years ago, for example, studying *The Autobiography of Malcolm X,* I questioned—along with Malcolm himself—whether any autobiography could keep pace with the biographical fact of "a ceaselessly evolving identity" ("Malcolm" 183). I argued nonetheless that motivating the writing of a story like Malcolm's was a belief that an "uncompromising commitment to the truth of one's own nature . . . will yield at the last . . . a final and irreducible selfhood" (193). Following this early profession of faith, my posture toward the self gradually shifted, such that ten years later on I spoke of the self more tentatively as "a mysterious reality, mysterious in its nature and origins and not necessarily consubstantial with the fictions we use to express it" (*Fictions* 277). I concluded, agnostically: "Whether the self . . . is literally dis-covered, made 'visible' in autobiography, or is only invented by it as a signature, a kind of writing, is beyond our knowing, for knowledge of the self is inseparable from the practice of language" (*Fictions* 278). Now, after another ten years, I find myself reluctant to speak of "the self," for the definite article suggests something too fixed and unified to represent the complexity of self-experience.

I mean to explain in the course of this book why I prefer to think of "self" less as an entity and more as a kind of awareness in process, a process I have sought to capture in the phrase *making selves* in my title. We don't, I think, pay much attention to this process, not only because we want to get on with the business of living our lives, but also because identity formation is not available for conscious inspection as it happens. We can never expect to witness the emergent sense of self as an observable event precisely because it is an ongoing process, taking place mostly beneath our notice from day to day—and indeed, physiologically, moment by moment. We never catch ourselves in the act of becoming selves; there is always a gap or rupture that divides us from the knowledge that we seek.

I believe nevertheless that we can with confidence say a good deal about the nature and origins of self-experience. The rapidly expanding literature of contemporary autobiography, protean in its forms and startling in the range of experience it now encompasses, can help us to do so. The plan of this book is comparatively simple. Using autobiographies as examples, I apply recent research in neurology, cognitive science, memory studies, developmental psychology, and related fields to the task of rethinking the nature of self-experience. As a starting point, Chapter 1 examines the ways in which our lives in and as bodies profoundly shape our sense of identity. Building on this substrate of somatic experience, Chapters 2 and 3 explore social sources of self, treating respectively relational and narrative modes of identity. Self and self-experience, I conclude, are not given, monolithic, and invariant, but dynamic, changing, and plural. Thus, to speak of "the story of the self," as I did for a good many years, oversimplifies the experiential reality that cognitive studies—"the mind's new science," in Howard Gardner's memorable phrase—has helped us to understand more clearly and complexly. We do better, I think, to speak of "registers of self and self-experience," for there are many stories of self to tell, and more than one self to tell them. In the final chapter, on the ethics of life writing, I test these findings about identity against the limits of a traditional privacy-based ethics centered on the autonomous individual.

Portions of this book appeared previously in somewhat different versions. "Relational Selves, Relational Lives: The Story of the Story" appeared in *True Relations: Essays on Autobiography and the Postmodern*, ed. G. Thomas Couser and Joseph Fichtelberg (Westport, Conn.: Greenwood, 1988), 63–81. " 'The Unseemly Profession': Privacy, Inviolate Personality, and the Ethics of Life Writing" appeared in *Renegotiating Ethics in Literature, Philosophy, and Theory*, ed. Jane Adamson, Richard Freadman, and David Parker (Cambridge: Cambridge University Press, 1998), 161–80.

I would like to thank the following people who variously encouraged, invited, read, and criticized this project along the way:

H. Porter Abbott, Jane Adamson, William L. Andrews, Patrick Brantlinger, Fred Cate, G. Thomas Couser, Roger Dworkin, Emily Eakin, Susanna Egan, Richard Freadman, Marianne Gullestad, Karen Hanson, Suzette Henke, Carol Holly, Joy Hooton, Michael Kiskis, Arnold Krupat, Peter Lindenbaum, Nancy K. Miller, David Parker, Jeremy Popkin, Oliver Sacks, Jeffrey L. Saver, Elaine Scarry, Daniel L. Schacter, Thomas R. Smith, Eugene Stelzig, Drude von der Fehr, and Kay Young.

Bernhard Kendler, my editor at Cornell, grasped the intent of this book immediately, and gave me wise counsel and support at every stage along the way. I thank John LeRoy and Candace Akins for their careful editing of the manuscript.

As always, Sybil S. Eakin prodded me to write as clearly and effectively as I could.

PAUL JOHN EAKIN

Bloomington, Indiana

How Our Lives Become Stories

CHAPTER ONE

Registers of Self

Possessing bodies is precisely what persons do indeed do, or rather what they actually are.

—Paul Ricoeur

I come back to the one thing I know. There is my body, sitting here on the edge of the bed, trembling and sweating.

—John M. Hull

This chapter presents some new theories about the nature of self and self-experience that promise to enlarge our understanding of human identity formation, the lifelong process of making selves that we engage in daily and that informs all autobiographical writing. Because these theories share an anti-Cartesian posture as their point of departure, I need first to sketch out seventeenth-century philosopher René Descartes's notion of the *subject* as the disembodied linchpin of conscious experience. Then I describe new theories that, contrary to Descartes's formulation, ground our human identities in our experience of our bodies. In the last section of this chapter I examine a series of autobiographies by Oliver Sacks, John Hull, Robert Murphy, and Lucy Grealy that bring home the embodied nature of selfhood with a telling immediacy.

Subjects, Real Persons, Human Beings

Definitions of autobiography have never proved to be definitive, but they are instructive, reflecting characteristic assumptions about what may well be the slipperiest of literary genres—if indeed autobiography can be said to be a genre in the first place. Here's one of the best-known, formulated by Philippe Lejeune in the 1970s in a well-known essay, "The Autobiographical Pact":

> *Retrospective prose narrative written by a real person concerning his own existence, where the focus is his individual life, in particular the story of his personality.* (4)[1]

It isn't the "focus" on the "individual life" that I want to pick up on here, but rather the notion of "a real person." Lejeune defines "a real person" as "a person whose existence is certified by vital statistics and is verifiable." For Lejeune, the textual sign of the real person is the author's *proper name* on the title page—it is this name that is "certifiable," "verifiable," "the only mark in the text of an unquestionable world-beyond-the-text, referring to a real person" (11). Note, though, that verification confirms only the historicity of the referent—a particular human being identified by a discrete name; the nature of the "real person" remains unspecified.

While Lejeune sought to map the boundaries of autobiography as a distinct genre, anchoring it in a world of reference beyond the text, Michael Sprinker pictured such a task as hopeless. In "Fictions of the Self: The End of Autobiography" (1981), driving home his view that autobiography was fundamentally unstable and hence unclassifiable, a shifting, borderless locale where "concepts of subject, self, and author collapse into the act of producing a text" (342), Sprinker cited Nietzsche's corrosive analysis of the subject in *The Will to Power*.

> "The subject" is the fiction that many similar states in us are the effect of one substratum: but it is we who first created the "simi-

---

[1] Lejeune first presented this definition in *L'Autobiographie en France* in 1971. For Lejeune's later reflections on the definition, see "The Autobiographical Pact (bis)."

larity" of these states. . . . The fundamental false observation is
that I believe it is *I* who do something, suffer something, "have"
something, "have" a quality. (quoted in Sprinker 333–34)

Following the Nietzschean logic, Lejeunian autobiography could
hardly pass for a literature of fact despite its referential preten-
sions, for however historically "real" the name shared by the
text's protagonist, narrator, and author, the "I"-figure so named
remains no less a creature of fiction. Without an "I" to perform
actions, to possess feelings and qualities, the possibility of "having" a story of one's "own existence" to tell simply evaporates.
Having unmasked the subject as a fiction, Sprinker could proceed to pull the plug on life writing and announce "the end of
autobiography."

Lejeune's commitment to the referentiality of the autobiographical text and Sprinker's to the fictiveness of its subject, jux-
taposed, display the conceptual impasse that confronts theorists
of autobiography in the age of postmodernism: even if we were
to grant the referential claims of autobiography as Lejeune defines them, what would be the point of reporting the "individual
life" and "personality" of an "I" based on illusion? On the other
hand, why attempt, as Nietzsche does, to demystify "the fundamental false observation . . . that I believe it is *I* who do something" unless that belief is deeply rooted in human experience?
If we credit the testimony of most autobiographies, people do
found their conceptions of their lives on Nietzsche's "fundamental false observation." Why, we might go on to ask, has autobiography proved to be so resistant to the various deconstructions of
the subject proposed by Nietzsche, Jacques Lacan, and others?
Philosopher John Searle, refuting Daniel C. Dennett's denial of
the existence of consciousness, provides a memorable answer:

Couldn't we disprove the existence of these data [inner qualita-
tive mental states] by proving that they are only illusions? No, you
can't disprove the existence of conscious experiences by proving
that they are only an appearance disguising the underlying real-

ity, because *where consciousness is concerned the existence of the appearance is the reality.* (58)

Given the face-off between experiential accounts of the "I," on the one hand, and deconstructive analyses of the "I" as illusion on the other, my own instinct is to approach autobiography in the spirit of a cultural anthropologist, *asking what such texts can teach us about the ways in which individuals in a particular culture experience their sense of being "I"*—and, in some instructive cases that prove the rule, their sense of not being an "I."

Such an approach requires that we accept the gambit of autobiography's referential aesthetic, but what exactly are we accepting if we accept the notion that an autobiography is somehow rooted in biographical fact? When Lejeune certifies the existence of identically named protagonist-narrator-author figures as "real persons," he is only validating autobiographers' conventional posture of truth telling, leaving open the possibility that they may not be telling the truth. Moreover, even though I think there is a legitimate sense in which autobiographies testify to the individual's experience of selfhood, that testimony is necessarily mediated by available cultural models of identity and the discourses in which they are expressed. How much of what autobiographers say they experience is equivalent to what they really experience, and how much of it is merely what they know how to say? Is there, we should ask, a demonstrable difference between the psychological reality of selfhood and the linguistic articulation of that reality? Fieldwork devoted to the nature of subjectivity is obviously a tricky business, but I think it's worth the risks. Accordingly, in the later sections of this chapter and in the two chapters that follow, I pursue a quasi-anthropological, experientialist approach to the nature and sources of identity that autobiographers claim.

I want first, however, in the rest of this section, to consider briefly the notion of "the death of the subject," which, especially when coupled with "the death of the self," might seem to foreclose the possibility of such an inquiry. What exactly is the connection between autobiography and contemporary theorizing about the subject? Surveying the many different narratives of "the death of the subject," philosopher Agnes Heller cautions, "It would be the greatest blunder to identify the individual personality with the subject in any of the current interpretations of the latter" (280). Because this "blunder" is routinely made, because—in a parallel fashion—the death of the subject and the future of autobiography have been assumed by Sprinker and others to be intimately linked, I think it will help to clear the air for my discussion of models of the self in the rest of this chapter if I begin with the death of the subject.

For news of this notorious corpse, we must turn to philosophy, home base since Descartes to any such inquiry, although discussions of the self and the subject are prominent features in the landscape of many fields today, including psychology, psychoanalysis, anthropology, sociology, and feminist studies.[2] Eduardo Cadava's boldly titled anthology *Who Comes after the Subject?* (1991) seems to take the death of the subject for granted, but some of his contributors—I am thinking especially of Vincent Descombes, Gérard Granel and Michel Henry—refute the title's twin assumptions: that the subject is a "who," and that critique of the subject is complete. Granel, for instance, insists that Descartes's "*Cogito* was never a somebody"—"a René, for example, 'in his bed' "—but "an ontological puppet" (148). Again, Henry's "critique of the critique of the subject" (165) traces its collective failure to its "not knowing anything about the being of this subject that is to be cut into pieces" (158). The true "critique of the subject," he concludes, has yet to be transacted; his essay announces its "first coming" (165).

Descombes's essay "Apropos of the 'Critique of the Subject' and of the Critique of This Critique" clarifies the confusion that results when the subject of metaphysical speculation is conflated with the human person. According to Descombes, "critics of the

---

[2] See, e.g., Sampson (psychology); Loewenstein and Sass (psychoanalysis); Cohen and Harris (anthropology); Gubrium (sociology); Coward (semiology); and Benhabib and Butler (feminist studies—see also note 3).

subject"—Nietzsche, for example, in the passages cited by Sprinker—reject "the possibility that the human being can identify himself as the source of operations that he believes, insofar as he is naive (or mystified by the ideologies of subjectivity), to be his" (129).[3] Because some version of this "possibility" characteristically underwrites any form of life writing, should we apply this deconstruction of the subject to autobiography and write its obituary?[4] Interestingly, Descombes's analysis would seem to argue against making such a move, for it would blur the necessary distinction between "the ordinary use of the word *subject* and the properly philosophical use of this same word" (122), between "the *person* (understood here . . . in the sense of a human being, therefore of a body living a human life) and the *subject*" (124).

---

[3] For an instructive exchange on self and agency triggered by the notion of the death of the subject, see Judith Butler, "Contingent Foundations: Feminism and the Question of 'Postmodernism,' " and Seyla Benhabib, "Feminism and the Question of Postmodernism." In a characteristic passage, Butler writes: "What speaks when 'I' speak to you? What are the institutional histories of subjection and subjectivation that 'position' me here now? If there is something called 'Butler's position,' is this one that I devise, publish, and defend, that belongs to me as a kind of academic property? Or is there a grammar of the subject that merely encourages us to position me as the proprietor of those theories?" (160). In contrast, Benhabib asserts, "The view that the subject is not reducible to 'yet another position in language,' but that no matter how constituted by language the subject retains a certain autonomy and ability to rearrange the significations of language, is a regulative principle of all communication and social action" (216). Benhabib urges the importance of distinguishing between "the study of culturally diverse codes, which define individuality" and "the question as to *how* the human infant becomes the social self, regardless of the cultural and normative content which defines selfhood" (217). "To put it bluntly," Benhabib warns, "the thesis of the Death of the Subject presupposes a remarkably crude version of individuation and socialization processes when compared with currently available social-scientific reflections on the subject" (218). See also Fraser on the exchange between Benhabib and Butler.

[4] There are other deconstructions of the subject that pose a similar challenge to autobiography—Lacanian psychoanalysis would be a prominent one—but I have chosen to focus on the "quarrel" among philosophers over the Cartesian subject because it has played an important role in launching the debate about the subject in the West and because it poses the issue of the body—by excluding it—that I want to take up in the later sections of this chapter.

Continuing, Descombes attributes this distinction to Descartes: "The Cartesian argument requires that we do not understand the pronoun *I* (in the case when it is used by Descartes) and the name *Descartes* as mutually substitutable terms. For us, the word *Descartes* is the name of a particular person, born into a family from Poitiers, in 1596, in La Haye, etc. This name, like all human names, refers to an individual identifiable by his body" (124). (Like Lejeune, Descombes invokes the proper name as the identifying referential sign of the person but adds—significantly—the body as well. I will return, presently, to this crucial notion of "a body living a human life.")

Descombes's distinction between subject and person parallels Descartes's distinction between "I" and "this 'I' " in his account of his epochal thought experiment—the *Cogito*—in the fourth part of his *Discourse on Method* (1637):

> I thereby concluded that I was a substance, of which the whole essence or nature consists in thinking, and which, in order to exist, needs no place and depends on no material thing; so that *this "I," that is to say, the mind, by which I am what I am*, is entirely distinct from the body. (54, emphasis added)

In this passage the first person is split or doubled: the "I" that opens the passage, the autobiographical narrator of Descartes's intellectual autobiography, introduces a second "I," set off in quotation marks, the sign of Descartes's existence as "thinking substance" distinct from the body. Splitting the first person in this way, Descartes establishes "the philosophical notion of a subject distinct from the person" (Descombes 126).[5] Summarizing centuries of controversy concerning this crucial distinction, Descombes identifies two opposing camps: "the classical philosophers of the subject," who take "the word *subject* in a sense where it only applies to *that which thinks* in Descartes," and "the critics of the philosophical subject," who suspect the "classical philoso-

---

[5] For a parallel analysis of the "I" in Descartes, see Kerby 99–100.

phers" of transferring "certain attributes of the person to *that which thinks* in the person." These "critics" insist that "Descartes is a person: [whereas] the true subject will be impersonal. Descartes, like all persons, is identifiable thanks to the individuality of the body that constitutes him: the true subject escapes identification" (126). *The subject is not a person*; Descartes *is not* the Cartesian subject; protagonist-narrator-author figures endowed with proper names *are not* subjects—not in this strict philosophical sense. Thus the Cartesian subject can't be certified as real by any Lejeunian recourse to verification. Is there, then, any connection between the Cartesian subject and the "I" of autobiography—between "I" and "this 'I' "? As the doubling of the first person in the passage from Descartes indicates, the "I"-narrator can present a (Cartesian) subject ("this 'I' ") yet remain distinct from it. Moreover, to the extent that autobiography's "I" refers to a person, to "a body living a human life," it is by definition conceptually opposed to the *bodiless* "thinking substance" of the Cartesian subject.[6]

In this sense, the Cartesian subject—dead or alive—is not a suitable model for the self represented by the "I" of autobiographical discourse—it is not, for example, identical to the "I" who narrates the *Discourse on Method*. In the rest of this chapter I want to examine some alternative models. I have emphasized Descombes's account of the philosophers' "quarrel" over the Cartesian subject not only because it illustrates the controversies surrounding key terms commonly used by critics of autobiography but also because it highlights the dangers of an overly narrow approach to human subjectivity. To speak of such speculation as "dangerous" is to point to the underlying ethical concerns behind the reservations of Descombes, Heller, Paul Smith, and others—myself included—about poststructuralist theorizing of the subject. Thus Descombes opens by distinguishing a "*theory of the subject*" from an "*ethics of the subject*" (121), and

---

[6] Sprinker's thesis about the "end of autobiography" depends precisely on taking the metaphysical subject as identical to the "I" of autobiographical discourse, whereas Descombes—and Agnes Heller and Paul Smith (xxix)—demonstrate the importance of not confusing or conflating the two.

Heller, similarly, focuses her discussion on "the subject of men and women" as opposed to "the subject of the philosopher" (275). Calling for a new model of the subject, Smith indicts current conceptions for their tendency "to produce a purely *theoretical* 'subject,' removed almost entirely from the political and ethical realities in which human agents actually live" (xxix).

How, then, to close the gap between theory and experience when it comes to conceptualizing the "I," for autobiographies are committed without a doubt to representing how "human agents actually live"? The most promising initiatives—by Elizabeth Grosz, Oliver Sacks, Gerald Edelman, Anthony Kerby and others—are united in their repudiation of Cartesian dualism, which defines "this 'I' " as "entirely distinct from the body." Collectively, they agree that any attempt to remodel our concepts of the subject, self, or consciousness (as they variously term the subjectivity they study) requires a return to the body, undoing the original Cartesian exclusionary move.

Before turning, with them, to the body, I want to say a word about terminology. Even the most cursory survey of books on the self and the subject in a broad range of fields confirms not only that these concepts aren't "dead" but that they are essential terms required by, yet resisting, analysis.[7] I take it as a sign of the times that for every book like Cadava's *Who Comes after the Subject?* (1991), which seems to signal the subject's demise, there is another suggesting that the territory remains to be explored, such as the huge collection edited by Steve Pile and Nigel Thrift titled *Mapping the Subject: Geographies of Cultural Transformation* (1995). Like Smith, Heller, and Descombes, Pile and Thrift begin with definitions, devoting their preface to the terms that seem inevitably to spin in elliptical orbits around any attempt to conceptualize human beings: *body, self, person, identity,* and *subject.* Descombes's analysis of the slippage between *subject* and *person* in the philosophers' "quarrel" over the subject is a case in point. Despite continuing efforts to differentiate among these terms and

[7] For a suggestive overview of the contemporary debate over these terms, see Levine.

nail them down, they seem to be inherently unstable, with *subject* perhaps the most resistant to discipline of the lot.[8] *Subject*, for example, in the hands of Pile, Thrift, and their contributors, expands from the comparatively narrow Cartesian definition ("this 'I' ") to a much broader, socially and culturally inflected usage, as suggested by such essays as "Families and Domestic Routines," "The Sexed Self," "Bodies without Organs," and "Ethnic Entrepreneurs and Street Rebels."

In the sections that follow, I can only say that I will do my best to respect the usage of others when I cite their work. For reasons that will become clear, I am especially drawn to *self* when dealing with the representation of subjectivity in autobiography. Whereas some critics today seek to avoid *self* as variously compromised by bourgeois, transcendental, or androcentric assumptions and associations, I believe it to be indispensable to any treatment of autobiography.[9]

Bodies, Brains, Selves

In 1905 two French neurologists, G. Deny and P. Camus, reported the strange case of "Madame I," a young woman who lost "body awareness" and lost herself in the process:

> I'm no longer aware of myself as I used to be. I can no longer feel my arms, my legs, my head, and my hair. I have to touch myself constantly in order to know how I am. . . . I cannot find myself.
> (Rosenfield, *Strange* 39)

Madame I's pathetic touching of her limbs stages a startling inversion of Descartes's thought experiment: "I feel my body," she

---

[8] For characteristic attempts to settle on some distinctions among these terms, see Harris, Olshen, and Rorty.

[9] Sidonie Smith seeks to establish a distinction between *self* as signaling "an understanding of the human being as metaphysical, essential, and universal" and *subject* as implying "the culturally constructed nature of any notion of 'selfhood' " (*Subjectivity* 189 n. 9).

seems to say, "therefore I am." Her troubled condition reminds us that it is possession of a body image that anchors and sustains our sense of identity. In the light of such a case, and others like it in the literature of neuropathology, it is all the more striking that the argument is just now being marshaled, notably by the feminist scholar Elizabeth Grosz, for "the relevance of refocusing on bodies in accounts of subjectivity" (vii).[10]

Grosz's daring move in *Volatile Bodies* (1994), reversing Descartes's, is to start from the body, wagering "that all the effects of subjectivity, all the significant facets and complexities of subjects, can be as adequately explained using the subject's corporeality as a framework as it would be using consciousness or the unconscious" (vii). In making this move, however, Grosz is careful not to reinstitute the mind/body split that produced in the realm of theory precisely the loss of body awareness she seeks to rectify. Avoiding such dead-end dualism, she chooses the Möbius strip to illustrate the dynamic interrelation of body and mind, "the torsion of the one into the other." With its endless looping between dimensions of surface and depth, this model brilliantly captures her sense of the subject as process, as at once "psychical interior and . . . corporeal exterior" (xii).

As Grosz eloquently demonstrates, models of subjectivity and the body do make a difference; they have consequences, for they are not merely heuristic devices that exclude and include and formulate relation. Indeed, Grosz believes that such models have the potential to actually constitute the reality they purport to describe because nature itself is socially constituted—models of bodies "have tangible effects on the bodies studied" (xi): "Historical, social, and cultural exigencies . . . actively produce the body as a body of a determinate type" (x).[11] Despite her emphasis

---

[10] For parallel cases illustrating the connection between body image and identity, see my discussion of Oliver Sacks and John M. Hull later in this chapter. Israel Rosenfield's fascinating discussion of the case of Madame I (*Strange* 38–45) stimulated my own thinking about the relation between identity and the body.
[11] Drawing on findings in neuroscience and physical anthropology that "cultural requirements and opportunities played a critical role in selecting neural

on the body as a "product" of various forms of cultural "inscription," Grosz's thinking about the body is nuanced, escaping a narrow social determinism. Thus, while she speaks of the body's "organic or ontological 'incompleteness' or lack of finality, an amenability to social completion, social ordering and organization," she goes on—in what I think is the most original and radical aspect of her thinking about the body—to stress the "ability of bodies to always extend the frameworks which attempt to contain them, to seep beyond their domains of control" (xi).

Grosz's Möbius strip model of the mind-body relation is suggestively dynamic and interactive. It promotes in practice, however, a potentially restrictive notion of "corporeality" as "exterior surface," as when Grosz distinguishes between a "corporeal exterior" ("outside," "surface") and a "psychical interior" ("inside," "depth"). If, like Grosz, we approach subjectivity in "corporeal" terms, then, as contemporary neuroscientists recognize, we must deal as well with the "corporeality" of the "inside" or "psychical interior," the structure of the brain.

The neurobiologist and Nobel-laureate Gerald M. Edelman, author of what is surely the most ambitious attempt to date to construct a biological theory of mind, eagerly accepts, in effect, the terms of Grosz's wager to explain "all the effects of subjectivity . . . using the subject's corporeality as a framework." As Edelman puts it, recalling Descartes's "lonely music of the self," "we may profitably ask whether we can do better than postulate a thinking substance that is beyond the reach of a science of extended things" (Edelman 111).[12] Should anyone underestimate the magnitude of the challenge, Edelman reminds an interviewer of the brain's daunting complexity:

> If I unfolded [the cerebral] cortex and laid it out on the table, it
> would be the size of a large table napkin. And about as thick. It

---

characteristics in the evolution of man," Jerome Bruner argues "that it is culture, not biology, that shapes human life and the human mind" (*Acts* 34).

[12] Interestingly, Grosz's study omits any consideration of Edelman although it contains a fascinating chapter on neurology and the body image.

would have ten billion neurons, at least—and a million billion connections. If you counted the connections, one per second, you'd finish counting them all thirty-two million years later. (Levy 66)

"Completing Darwin's program" (Edelman 42), Edelman has "unfolded" the brain and "laid it out on the table" in an extraordinary series of studies—*Neural Darwinism: The Theory of Neuronal Group Selection* (1987), *Topobiology: An Introduction to Molecular Embryology* (1988), *The Remembered Present: A Biological Theory of Consciousness* (1989), and *Bright Air, Brilliant Fire: On the Matter of the Mind* (1992). Edelman's approach to the brain and to the emergence of consciousness in these volumes is resolutely Darwinian—"spirits and ghosts are out" (113). His Theory of Neural Group Selection (TNGS) or "neural Darwinism" articulates his sense of the way in which the brain's neural organization is constantly modified—both phylogenetically and ontogenetically—to adapt to the ever-changing demands of experience.

In Edelman's scheme, the actual configuration of the brain's circuitry in any individual is not fixed but evolves steadily from instructions coded in the genetic blueprint through a complex process of "reentrant-signaling" among the hundreds of "maps" or sheets of neurons layered in the cerebral cortex. Edelman's theory is intensely Darwinian in cast, deeply oriented to the impact of environment requiring changing behavior, and he is, accordingly, predictably dismissive of computational models of the brain as hard-wired, preprogrammed to respond; people who liken the brain to a computer are "not even wrong" as far as Edelman is concerned (Levy 66).[13] Because the brain's development is open-ended and adaptive, the neural configurations in any given individual that result from the process of "somatic selection" (Sacks, "Making" 43) are necessarily unique.[14]

[13] The cognitive scientist Daniel C. Dennett is a leading proponent of the computational model of brain function. See, e.g., *Consciousness Explained* (1991).
[14] Neurologist Antonio Damasio makes a similar case for the brain and its circuits as a continuously evolving organic system that changes to meet the demands of experience (112).

After quoting William James to the effect that consciousness is something the meaning of which "we know as long as no one asks us to define it" (Edelman 111), Edelman proceeds, un-daunted, to distinguish between "primary consciousness" and "higher-order consciousness." He defines primary consciousness as "the state of being mentally aware of things in the world—of having mental images in the present," and he believes that "some nonlinguistic and nonsemantic animals" (112) (including chim-panzees) may well possess it. Primary consciousness, however, "lacks an explicit *notion* or a concept of a personal self, and it does not afford the ability to model the past or the future as part of a correlated scene" (122).

Higher-order consciousness, by contrast, "is what we as hu-mans have in addition to primary consciousness" (112). It "in-volves the ability to construct a socially based selfhood, to model the world in terms of the past and the future, and to be directly aware" (125). John R. Searle, summarizing Edelman's prerequi-sites for the emergence of primary consciousness, stresses that the brain must have memory and also "the ability to discriminate the self from the nonself" (54).[15] With the movement from pri-mary to higher-order consciousness, however, facilitated by the acquisition of language, the human individual becomes " 'con-scious of being conscious,' " achieving "a conceptual model of selfhood" (Edelman 131). Edelman regards the capacity to for-mulate concepts of the self and of the past as conferring a dis-tinct evolutionary "value," freeing "the individual from the bondage of an immediate time frame or ongoing events occur-ring in real time" (133).

Edelman's neural Darwinism casts quite a new light on the re-lation between self and culture. Poststructuralist thought in the last twenty years, especially Foucault's analyses of a broad range of disciplinary institutions, has delineated the manifold ways in which cultures shape the individual subject. Inevitably, resisting

---

[15] In this context Edelman defines *self* as "a unique biological individual, not a socially constructed 'human' self" (120).

the more deterministic forms of social constructivism, others have sought to reaffirm the possibility of the individual's agency.[16] The issues in this debate look quite different when we shift from cultural theory to neurobiology. Whereas poststructuralism postulates a subjectivity that is "split" or "decentered," the point of departure for neurobiological accounts of subjectivity is the "binding problem," which "poses the question of how different stimulus inputs to different parts of the brain are bound together so as to produce a single, unified experience, for example, of seeing a cat" (Searle 54). The link between the neurobiologist's concern with seeing a cat and the cultural theorist's account of the individual's relation to the world is precisely the interface between the organism and the environment.

Edelman's neural Darwinism investigates the primary building blocks of this interface, what he terms perceptual categorizations—how we perceive colors, for example, in the visual world. And it is just here, at this elementary level of consciousness, that Edelman's TNGS makes the words characteristically employed to articulate our sense of the reception of sensory phenomena— and by extension, our sense of the relation between the individual and the world, between self and culture—seem inadequate. From the perspective of TNGS, the registering of the unitary events of consciousness, for example, is neither a "representation" nor an "inscription"; I draw here on the two key phases of Grosz's account of bodily subjectivity—how "the subject's corporeal exterior is psychically *represented* and lived by the subject" (xii, emphasis added) and how "social *inscriptions* of bodies produce the effects of depth" (xiii, emphasis added).[17]

Reflecting on "perceptual phenomena as the perhaps most

[16] The exchange between Benhabib and Butler, cited in note 3, is characteristic of the polarizing between agency and determinism in these discussions. Feminist scholars such as Nancy K. Miller and Elizabeth Grosz have sought to preserve the possibility of change without sacrificing the critique of institutionalized patriarchal power. For an incisive discussion of constructivism, agency, and the subject, see Butler's introduction to *Bodies That Matter*.

[17] Grosz herself is sensitive to precisely this issue of the inadequacy of so many of our familiar ways of speaking of the body: "[Bodies] require quite different

simple organizing, early function of the higher brain," Edelman observes, "Your brain *constructs*. . . . It doesn't mirror. . . . Even before language, your brain constructs and makes perceptual slices of the world" (Levy 62). And again, "Every perception is an act of creation" (Sacks, "Making" 44). In a favorite musical metaphor, Edelman evokes the complexity of the perceptual brain event structured by reentrant signaling:

> Think if you had a hundred thousand wires randomly connecting four string quartet players and that, even though they weren't speaking words, signals were going back and forth in all kinds of hidden ways [as you usually get them by the subtle nonverbal interactions between the players] that make the whole set of sounds a unified ensemble. That's how the maps of the brain work by rentry.

Quoting this comment, Sacks adds that in Edelman's conception of the brain there is "an orchestra, an ensemble—but without a conductor, an orchestra which makes its own music" ("Making" 44–45). "Without a conductor"—this is a portrait of primary consciousness in action; no locus of intentionality is involved. Only with the development of higher consciousness comes awareness of awareness together with the concept of a center of awareness and intentions, "a socially constructed self" (Edelman 124).[18]

In his review of Edelman's *Bright Air, Brilliant Fire*, John R. Searle cautions that Edelman's TNGS remains at present "a working hypothesis and not an established theory" (54). Searle carefully notes that the conditions Edelman posits as necessary for the presence of consciousness do not finally explain how con-

---

intellectual models than those that have been used thus far to represent and understand them" (xi). See also Butler, *Bodies* ix.

[18] Edelman does not explain how this sense of self emerges. Later in this chapter and in Chapter 2 I will present work by psychologists Ulric Neisser and Daniel Stern which suggests a possible solution to this problem. Sacks makes the link between Edelman's TNGS and Stern's work as follows: "Such a neuroevolutionary view is highly consistent with some of the conclusions of psychoanalysis and developmental psychology—in particular, the psychoanalyst Daniel Stern's description of 'an emergent self' " ("Making" 44).

sciousness is caused, and so "the mystery remains" (56). Nevertheless, commentary on Edelman's theories by Oliver Sacks and Israel Rosenfield suggests that, even as an unproved hypothesis, TNGS is generating new insights into the nature of self and memory that could revolutionize not only inquiry into the nature of subjectivity but study of autobiography as well.

Sacks's interpretation of Edelman, confirming Grosz's view of the body's agency, singles out the role of the body in the process of individuation. Working with patients suffering from post-encephalitic syndrome, Sacks became convinced that "movements and scenes from a person's experience could be embedded in his physiology," that "his physiology itself could evolve, could become 'personalized'" ("Neurology" 45).[19] This clinical experience led Sacks to seek a concept of individuation that would reflect his sense of the ways in which individuals' "growing and becoming are correlated with their physical bodies" (47). Edelman's neural Darwinism seemed to provide the answer, with its "picture of the evolution of the individual nervous system, as it reflects the life experience of each individual human being." Sacks comments, "The nervous system adapts, is tailored, evolves, so that experience, will, sensibility, moral sense, and all that one would call personality or soul becomes engraved in the nervous system. The result is that one's brain is one's own" (49). And not only is the brain unique but brain events as well, for "experience itself is not passive, a matter of 'impressions' or 'sense-data,' but active, and constructed by the organism from the start" ("Making" 44).

Under the spell of Edelman's TNGS, Sacks has exchanged the romantic or transcendental notion of the self in his earlier work, notably *A Leg to Stand On* (1984) and *The Man Who Mistook His Wife for a Hat* (1985), for a distinctly Darwinian, physiologically embedded conception. Thus, when he speaks of "one's brain" as being "one's own," he elaborates as follows: "One is not an immaterial soul, floating around in a machine. I do not feel alive, psychologically alive, except insofar as a stream of feeling—

---

[19] See Sacks, *Awakenings.*

perceiving, imagining, remembering, reflecting, revising, recategorizing runs through me. I am that stream—that stream is me" ("Neurology" 49). The life of the self is the life of the body—there is no other, no "spirits or ghosts," for Sacks. In this way, from a neuro-evolutionary perspective, the *bios* of autobiography and biography—"the course of life, a lifetime"—expands to include the life of the body and especially the nervous system.[20] The agency of the body that sustains, indeed constructs, Sacks's identity-conferring "stream" goes unwitnessed; it is the result of the seamless, "conductor"-less, cognitive "binding" effect that characterizes primary consciousness. As Edelman puts it, consciousness "just *is*—winking on with the light, multiple and simultaneous in its modes and objects, ineluctably ours" (111).

Biomedical technology provides, nevertheless, insight into what the *bios* of the body—could it ever be written—might include. Stressing the binding and centering of attention in the normal individual's primary consciousness, Sacks comments that patients suffering from Tourette's and post-encephalitic syndromes "had an exaggerated need to find ways of centering and organizing their so greatly disturbed physiology:

> There is good electroencephalographic evidence for this sort of unification—I often saw it in the striking effects of playing music, or imagining it, in the EEGs of my post-encephalitic patients, which would be suddenly transformed from gross irregularity of convulsiveness into a rhythmic state, and a state of synchronization. ("Neurology" 46)

The EEG here, we might say, is writing the discourse of the body.

Neural Darwinism has the potential to transform not only traditional conceptions of self but of memory as well, as the work of Israel Rosenfield, formerly Edelman's colleague and collaborator, suggests. Rosenfield believes, first of all, that memories are

---

[20] Olney cites this definition of the Greek meaning of *bios* in "Some Versions of Memory / Some Versions of *Bios*" (237).

perceptions newly occurring in the present rather than images fixed and stored in the past and somehow mysteriously recalled to present consciousness. As perceptions, memories share the constructed nature of all brain events that TNGS posits: "Recollection is a kind of perception, . . . *and every context will alter the nature of what is recalled*" (*Invention* 89, emphasis added). Rosenfield's second point about memory, a corollary of his view of memory as embedded in present consciousness, is that all memories are self-referential: "*Every recollection refers not only to the remembered event or person or object but to the person who is remembering*" (*Strange* 42). The bond between self and memory can be traced back to Locke, but Rosenfield puts a new spin on this linkage by factoring in the body as a necessary third term in the equation.

To illustrate how self, memory, and the body are intimately connected in this conception of consciousness, let me return to the strange case of Madame I and Rosenfield's analysis of the interrelationships among her troubling symptoms. The young woman had, quite literally, lost her awareness of her body: she had become insensitive to pain; in bed at night, she didn't know where her legs were; "when her mouth was closed she could not find her tongue because she thought it was in her throat" (*Strange* 39), and so forth. Accompanying, and related to, this bizarre disturbance in her body image were doubts of her own existence and doubts of the existence of others: she wasn't sure who she was, and she had difficulty remembering her parents, her house, her family. Rosenfield sees the body as the key to these losses, for he notes that while touching her body, Madame I was able momentarily not only to recover a sense of self but also to recognize in an attenuated fashion her husband and children. Underpinning the sense of self, underpinning memory, he believes, is the body image—"the body . . . is the brain's absolute frame of reference" (45). Rosenfield speculates, accordingly, that Madame I suffered a "breakdown" in the physiological mechanisms that normally establish awareness of the body's existence, triggering her disorientations. Ultimately, for Rosenfield, consciousness is "self-referential," and the baseline of consciousness, of memory, of identity, is the body image: "If the bodily structure is damaged, so is the sense of self, memory, and consciousness" (139).

What the case of Madame I confirms is that subjectivity and selfhood are deeply rooted in the body, that psychology and physiology are intimately linked.[21] In the age of Prozac this is hardly news, yet I suspect that, even though the mood-and-mind-altering potential of antidepressants has been widely featured in the media, most people continue to believe unreflectingly that human beings are born equipped with an invariant, timeless self, a kind of secular equivalent of the soul. The testimony of people on Prozac and similar medications, however, suggests that these drugs do more than cure depression, they literally alter personality: "I feel like a different person" is frequently the refrain.[22] Moreover, when we look at life history from the perspective of neural Darwinism, it is fair to say that we are all becoming different persons all the time, we are not what we were; self and memory are emergent, in process, constantly evolving, and both are grounded in the body and the body image. Responding to the flux of self-experience, we instinctively gravitate to identity-supporting structures: the notion of identity as continuous over time, and the use of autobiographical discourse to record its history.

For all its suggestiveness for rethinking the perennial problems of life writing, the nature of memory and self, however, Edelman's TNGS is focused on the physiology of the brain. Although Edelman argues that a "science of human beings" must include not only a biological explanation of consciousness but also of selfhood ("the personal individuality that emerges from developmental and social interactions"), he believes that "no scientific theory of an individual self can be given" (167).[23] Despite

[21] See, for example, Sacks's accounts of Korsakov's syndrome in *The Man Who Mistook His Wife for a Hat.*

[22] See Kramer, *Listening to Prozac.*

[23] Edelman's position here turns on his analysis of *qualia,* which he defines as "the collection of personal or subjective experiences, feelings, and sensations that accompany awareness" (114). See Edelman 114–16. In the index there is only one entry under *selfhood.*

Edelman's acknowledgment of the limits of a neurobiological approach to subjectivity, neural Darwinism and its elaborations by Sacks and Rosenfield make clear that any biologically informed model must be dynamic and open ended, conceiving of self and memory as interdependent dimensions of (higher) consciousness, anchored in the life of the body. I want now to consider the work of philosopher Anthony Paul Kerby and especially psychologist Ulric Neisser, whose theories of the self meet these criteria.

In *Narrative and the Self* (1991) Kerby stakes out a position on the self's ontology that is much like Edelman's—no "spirits" or "ethereal beings." Ruling out any notion of the self as some kind of transcendental (Cartesian or other) entity preexisting our lives as language speakers, Kerby defines the self as the product of "signifying practices," especially "narrative constructions or stories" (1). Much of Kerby's account of this "semiotic subject" retraces structuralist and poststructuralist ground reaching back to Saussurian linguistics. Emile Benveniste states the governing assumption of this tradition when he observes that "it is literally true that the basis of subjectivity is in the exercise of language" (226); in Benveniste's memorable phrase, " 'ego' is he who *says* 'ego' " (224). To this familiar language-centered view of the subject, Kerby adds a distinctive narrative emphasis, joining Jerome Bruner and other "narrative psychologists" in his belief that self-narration is the defining act of the human subject, an act which is not only "descriptive of the self" but "*fundamental to the emergence and reality of that subject*" (4). I want to note here Kerby's instinct to anchor in the body the "subject of speech floating in linguistic space" (107). In his narrative model of the subject, the body figures as "both the *site of narration* and the *site of ascription* for subjectivity": "In a face-to-face dialogue it is the other's 'body' that speaks to me. . . . This physical body, the site of narration, thereby becomes endowed with the status of selfhood" (71).

Although Kerby's model is, in this sense, an embodied subject, the body in question is not "the positivist material body of science" but "the speaking-feeling embodied subject (the person)" (107), the body of social experience encountered in speech acts.[24] For a more comprehensive model of the self, one that includes both the body of physiological process and the body of social, linguistic encounter, I turn now to the work of cognitive psychologist Ulric Neisser. In a remarkable paper titled "Five Kinds of Self-knowledge" (1988), Neisser attempts to distinguish "among several kinds of self-specifying information, each establishing a different aspect of the self." Although he speaks of "these aspects" as "so distinct that they are essentially different *selves*" with different "origins and developmental histories" (35), he argues that these selves "are not generally experienced as separate and distinct" (36). Self or selves? Although Neisser occasionally speaks of the self, he seems ultimately less interested in affirming the self as a single, unified entity than he is in stressing the variety of self-knowledge, the "self-specifying information" (35) that constitutes our experience.[25] His fivefold modeling counters the tendency toward an oversimplifying reification that is one of the principal drawbacks of *self* as a term, a reification that obscures the multiple registers of self-experience he seeks to display.

Neisser's selves include the following:

1. The *ecological self*: "the self as perceived with respect to the physical environment; 'I' am the person here in this place, engaged in this particular activity" (36). Present in infancy.

2. The *interpersonal self*: "the self as engaged in immediate unreflective social interaction with another person" (41); " 'I' am the person who is engaged, here, in this particular human interchange" (36). Present in infancy.

3. The *extended self*: the self of memory and anticipation, the

[24] In *Autobiographical Acts* (1976), Elizabeth Bruss presented a poetics of autobiography based on speech act theory.
[25] From a neurological perspective, the question is undecidable, for the brain constructs a single, unified perception from a vast array of sensory stimuli—the "binding" effect.

self existing outside the present moment; "I am the person who had certain specific experiences, who regularly engages in certain specific and familiar routines" (36). By the age of three, children are aware of themselves "as existing outside the present moment, and hence of the extended self" (47).

4. The *private self*: the self of "conscious experiences that are not available to anyone else" (50); "I am, in principle, the only person who can feel this unique and particular pain" (36). Although experts differ as to the emergence of this sense of privacy in developmental chronology, many studies show children as "aware of the privacy of mental life before the age of 5" (50).

5. The *conceptual self*: the extremely diverse forms of self-information—social roles, personal traits, theories of body and mind, of subject and person—that posit the self as a category, either explicitly or implicitly. (Neisser's discrimination of five primary kinds of self-information, of course, is one such conceptual model.)

Neisser's ecological and interpersonal selves precede the extended, private, and conceptual selves in the list because they precede them in the child's development. Countering the familiar view that the child's sense of self dates from the mirror phase (around two years old) (40 n. 7), Neisser holds that the "ecological self is present from the first"(40), and that "a very rich form of intersubjectivity is typically in place by the time the infant is 2 months old" (42). Unlike the extended, private, and conceptual selves, both the ecological and the interpersonal selves are characterized by direct perception unmediated by reflexive consciousness of any kind: "Very young infants have no internal self-representations to be conscious of or to think about" (41). These selves arise out of the immediacy of present experience, the encounter between the infant and the objects or persons of its physical environment.

Neisser's account of the ecological self is especially suggestive of the ways in which our possession of physical bodies of a particular design generates what we come to think of as a sense of self. Studies of the ecological self focus on how the reception of visual (and auditory and haptic) information from the environment specifies "the existence of a perceiving entity at a particular location in the environment" (39). This ecological dimension of experience accounts, in turn, for the child's tendency to locate the self "at the point of observation, as specified by the optical flow field": when "young children cover their eyes with their hands and say 'You can't see me!' . . . the child's 'me'—the entity to which the adult's question 'Can I see you?' refers—is evidently somewhere near the eyes" (38). As Eleanor Gibson explains in "Ontogenesis of the Perceived Self," ecological experience "provides a basis for perceiving the self as *this* object, moving around or stationed *here* in a persisting environmental layout" (31).

In contrast to the unmediated, direct perception of the ecological and interpersonal selves, the reflexiveness that distinguishes Neisser's extended, private, and conceptual selves is much like the "consciousness of consciousness" that distinguishes Edelman's higher consciousness from primary consciousness. Following the acquisition of language and the entry into symbol-making activity that accompanies it, the child now engages in the "self-representations" that these modes of selfhood predicate. Development of these selves is normally shaped and fostered in a concerted way at home and school by the adults of the child's immediate culture. These are the selves familiar to traditional autobiographers, who relate the story of the extended and private selves by drawing on their culture's store of conceptual selves.

If we accept Rosenfield's view that every memory, indeed all of consciousness, is self-referential, then any attempt to analyze "self-specifying information" proposes, in effect, to analyze our experience in its entirety. Is Neisser's five-part model adequate to perform so ambitious a task? Marjorie Grene, for one, argues that the ecological self, primary for her, includes the interpersonal self—the other person is part of one's environment.[26]

---

[26] See Grene 112–14.

Again, while Neisser appropriately identifies the body image as an aspect of the conceptual self (40 n. 8), neurological commentary on the body image, as we shall see, suggests that it also functions as an enabling endowment for the ecological self's agency. It is also true that the extended and private selves assume models or representations of the self of the sort that Neisser associates with the conceptual self. My point is, quite simply, that some will detect overlappings and slippage among Neisser's five selves, while others will doubtless be moved to expand the list.[27]

Despite these shortcomings—inevitable, I think, given the difficulties involved in conceptualizing the totality of subjectivity—I am drawn to Neisser's modeling for a number of reasons: (1) it avoids the venerable mind/body split that has hobbled so much theorizing of subjectivity, based instead on bodily perception experienced by the ecological self; (2) it does not posit a unified self, identifying instead prominent modes of self-information while privileging none of them;[28] (3) it acknowledges the formative role played by conceptual models in the development of the individual's self-concept; and (4) it enlarges the developmental history of selfhood, usually assumed to start with the acquisition of language, by annexing the prelinguistic, presymbolic registers of ecological and interpersonal experience deemed to operate from infancy. Neisser's model succeeds, more than any other, in highlighting the primary modes of experience that contribute to the individual's formation of a sense of self. The cognitive science of Edelman, Rosenfield, and Neisser suggests that it is time to discard restrictive notions of the self and the subject that make of them little more than metaphysical or narrative puppets, opening the way for a much broader, experientialist approach to the nature and origins of subjectivity.

---

[27] Neisser himself, moreover, is well aware of these interconnections among the modes of self-experience he posits: e.g., the remembered self is not independent of the conceptual self (49).

[28] Nonetheless, Neisser suggests several reasons for experiencing the self as unitary. Self-theories are culture-specific, some maintaining "that there is only one self, others that there are two or perhaps three," yet "the conceptual self still helps to hold all the others together" (55).

The Embodied Self

Contemporary medical technology, using computer imaging, fiberoptic photography, and a battery of "graphs" and "scans," permits us to witness an astonishing array of physiologic processes in the body's interior (we come close to watching our neurons fire), but it doesn't—yet—provide access to what Edelman calls primary consciousness. I want to look at two autobiographical texts that do, however, afford an indirect glimpse of this corporeal substratum of identity. Only when the link between sense of the body and sense of self is disrupted, as it was for Oliver Sacks and John Hull, do we grasp its decisive, normally invisible, functioning in our lives.

In the remarkable "Afterword (1993)" to the second edition of his memoir *A Leg to Stand On* (1984), Oliver Sacks reconstructs nearly twenty years of effort to understand what happened to him in the aftermath of a strangely traumatic leg injury he suffered during a solitary hike in Norway in 1974. Climbing a mountain above the Hardanger fjord, Sacks had encountered a huge, malevolent white bull; fleeing in a blind panic, he fell, violently twisting his left leg. After the accident, Sacks experienced two sets of symptoms, neurological and psychological: a loss or "extinction" of feeling *in* the leg (an anosognosia), and a sense of radical "alienation" *from* the leg. Two sets of symptoms and two stories, for the narrative recounts not only the doctor-turned-patient's struggle to learn to walk again but also his passage through an acute if peculiar identity crisis, "a total breakdown in his inner sense of identity, memory, 'space'; but one confined to the domain of a limb, the rest of consciousness being intact and complete" (199). Sacks was convinced that the neurological and psychological symptoms and stories were intimately linked, for he experienced the "*lesion in my muscle*" as "*a lesion in me*" (46).

How, though, to understand the injury to the leg as an injury to *identity*? Sacks got no help from the bluntly dismissive orthopedic surgeon who attended him in 1974, and by the time Sacks published his story ten years later he had concluded that the sense of alienation he regarded as the heart of the episode lay outside the boundaries of neurology and psychology as traditionally defined. Baffled, Sacks the patient called for a new disciplinary paradigm, "a neurology of identity" (199), that would address the link between body and self.

What *was* clear to Sacks the neurologist was that the locus of the link was the body image: the fall that had injured his leg had disrupted his body image as well: "I had lost the inner image, or representation, of the leg" (54). According to Sacks, three things—vision, balance organs (the vestibular system), and proprioception (position sense) (*Man* 46–47)—contribute to what we can loosely term the body image.[29] Elizabeth Grosz clarifies this concept when she summarizes Paul Schilder's pioneering work on it in the 1920s and 1930s:

> The body image unifies and coordinates postural, tactile, kinesthetic, and visual sensations so that these are experienced as the sensations of a subject coordinated into a single space; they are the experiences of a single identity. This image is the necessary precondition for undertaking voluntary action, the point at which the subject's intentions are translated into the beginning of movement, the point of transition in activating bones and muscles. (83)

For Grosz, the body image "attests . . . to the radical inseparability of biological from psychical elements" (85), while for Sacks it functions as "the fundamental, organic mooring of identity—at least of that corporeal identity, or 'body-ego,' which Freud sees as the basis of self" (*Man* 52).

In the account Sacks published in 1984, disturbance in the body image seemed to be the neurological key to his identity cri-

---

[29] Murphy's definition of proprioception, which he places in parallel with Sacks's, is admirably succinct: "the delicate, subliminal feedback mechanism that tells the brain about the position, tension, and general feeling of the body and its parts. It is this 'sixth sense' that allows for coordination of movement; without it, talking, walking, even standing, are virtually impossible" (*Body* 100).

sis. Yet, ten years later, in the "Afterword" of 1993, he bravely confessed that he had not understood the devastating alienation triggered by the injury to his leg: "I was never clear as to what had 'happened' in 1974, and none of the explanations I read, or which I was given, satisfied me" (*Leg* 188). By 1993, however, Sacks claims that two developments permitted him to reinterpret the injury and its identity-jolting aftermath: Michael Merzenich's use of electrodes to map neuronal activity in the cerebral cortex, and Edelman's neurobiological theories of primary and higher-order consciousness.

Merzenich's experiments demonstrate that the body image is "dynamic and plastic," that it "can reorganize itself radically with the contingencies of experience" (194). Sacks's case confirmed Merzenich's findings. Because the remodeled body image no longer included the injured leg, Sacks experienced his body, his very identity, in a new way: the body with the one good leg he accepted as "me"; the injured leg, however, now edited out of the body image, he regarded as a "thing." The loss of feeling in the injured leg ruptured the link between body and body image with the disconcerting result that the leg "had completely fallen out of consciousness" (196): "*I knew not my leg*" (51).

Edelman's two-tier model of consciousness—primary and higher-order—enabled Sacks to understand how a "local," "peripheral" neurological disorder could cause such a "massive disturbance" of "higher-order" consciousness (200–201), effecting a fundamental realignment in his sense of bodily identity. Again and again Sacks insists on his feeling of "the alienated part as being not-self" (199). What, though, does self have to do with the injured leg? As Sacks summarizes it, Edelman's conception of consciousness is "essentially personal," "essentially connected to the actual living body, its location and positing of a personal space" (199–200). "Personal" is used here in the sense of belonging to the organism, to the body—this is what Edelman means when he stresses the self/nonself discrimination that is a defining component of primary consciousness. It is this sense of self that Sacks draws on when, like Israel Rosenfield (whom he cites), he speaks of "all experience, all perception" as "*self-referential from the start*" (203, emphasis added). Edelman, Rosenfield, and Sacks argue that *this* self is the foundation for the more familiar self of our conscious lives, as Sacks suggests when he speaks of the lesion in his leg as a "*lesion in me.*" The logic of this model of embodied selfhood makes clear why Sacks's sense of alienation was so profound: the injured leg is experienced as "not-self" precisely because the realigned body image that supports the sense of self no longer includes it; body and body image are out of sync.

The body image—here specifically proprioception—emerges as the lifeline of identity, and Sacks invokes a metaphor of property and possession to conceptualize it:

> One may be said to "own" or "possess" one's body—at least its limbs and movable parts—by virtue of a constant flow of incoming information, arising ceaselessly, throughout life, from the muscles, joints and tendons. One has oneself, one *is* oneself, because the body knows itself, confirms itself, at all times, by this sixth sense [proprioception]. (*Leg* 50)

Are bodies and selves something we "have" or something we "are"? Interestingly, Sacks uses the two formulations interchangeably to express his sense that bodies and selves are intertwined and inseparable. Identity turns on the question of the organism acknowledging or "owning" what is proper to it; it is this sense of ownership that Sacks invokes when he speaks of the body "knowing" itself. This bodily knowledge is the basis of selfhood in organisms endowed with consciousness.[30]

[30] Edelman posits self/nonself discrimination as one of the defining features of primary consciousness. This fundamental sense of the organism "owning" or possessing its body opens up a new dimension to current discussions of the concept of possessive individualism. It is worth asking, again, are bodies—and selves—something we "have" or something we "are"? Even to write "bodies—and selves" is to pose the concept of embodied selfhood in a potentially misleading fashion. Developments in brain science pioneered by Edelman, Rosenfield, and others point to the "self-referential" nature of all bodily experience.

If Edelman's theory of consciousness seemed to Sacks to explain the link between the neurological and psychological dimensions of his puzzling injury, it is also true that the psychological experience seemed, reciprocally, to validate Edelman's two-tier model. Primary consciousness, the organism's unreflexive awareness of its bodily experience, crystallized in the body image, is normally "self-concealing" (*Leg* 202) and cannot be known directly; thus we do not *see* the body image, and so Sacks's anosognosia is "inaccessible to introspection, insight or report." By 1993, however, Sacks came to discern in the experience of alienation, which "*can* be perceived and reported" (198), "the basic structure of consciousness itself (for consciousness here is observing itself, is able to observe a particular form of breakdown in itself)" (199). Sacks suggests that his disturbing sense of alienation was the response of higher-order consciousness to "an abyss or hole" (200) in primary consciousness: when the identity-conferring sensory information normally transmitted through proprioception was interrupted, Sacks could no longer recognize or "own" the injured leg as part of his body's "self." Adopting Edelman's biological approach to consciousness, Sacks interprets not only the identity deficit—the alienation, the experience of the leg as "not-self"—but identity itself as "bottom-up" phenomena. His case confirmed Edelman's view that "alterations in primary receiving areas—disorders of local mapping—
. . . are a sufficient cause for alterations of consciousness" (201). Sacks even speculates that the body image "may be the first mental construct and self-construct there is, the one that acts as a model for all others" (192).

Whereas Sacks's "neurology of identity" is anchored in proprioception and the body image, the neurologist Antonio R. Damasio paints, in *Descartes' Error* (1994), a much more comprehensive picture of the body states that form the neural substrate of selfhood. As his title suggests, Damasio's posture is resolutely anti-Cartesian. Thus he specifies that "the self, that endows our experience with subjectivity, is not a central knower and inspector of everything that happens in our minds" (227). He holds, nevertheless, that "our experiences tend to have a consistent perspective, as if there were indeed an owner and knower for most, though not all, contents," and he attributes this centering of experience to the body: "I imagine this perspective to be rooted in a relatively stable, endlessly repeated biological state. The source of the stability is the predominantly invariant structure and operation of the organism, and the slowly evolving elements of autobiographical data" (238). "The neural basis" for the self, according to Damasio, "resides with the continuous reactivation of at least two sets of representations": "one set concerns representations of key events in an individual's autobiography," and the other set consists of representations of body states. Again and again, marshaling the neurological evidence, Damasio makes the case for the body as "a *content* that is part and parcel of the workings of the normal mind" (226): "The background body sense is continuous, although one may hardly notice it, since it represents not a specific part of anything in the body but rather an overall state of most everything in it" (152). It is the nexus of feelings and emotions that we consult, he suggests, when we respond directly to the question "How do you feel?" Damasio speculates, suggestively, on the adaptive value of his conception of "the neural self" (236): "If ensuring survival of the body proper is what the brain first evolved for, then, when minded brains appeared, they began by minding the body" (230).

Paralleling Sacks's account of embodied selfhood, John M. Hull's *Touching the Rock: An Experience of Blindness* (1990) shows how the vicissitudes of the body can radically redefine the experience of identity. More than any other autobiography I know, Hull's moving narrative brings home what psychologists mean when they refer to the *ecological* dimension of selfhood. As Eleanor Gibson explains, in her useful formulation cited earlier, ecological experience, the reception of visual (and auditory and haptic) information from objects in the environment, "provides a basis for perceiving the self as *this* object, moving around or stationed *here* in a persisting environmental layout" (31). For the sighted individual, visual stimuli provide the principal source of ecological information, and clinicians note that children tend to locate the self "at the point of observation, as specified by the optical flow field," "evidently somewhere near the eyes" (Neisser, "Five" 38). Moreover, confirming this connection between ecological experience and sense of identity, Ulric Neisser reports Selma Fraiberg's finding that "congenitally blind children are slow to develop an adequate sense of self"; blind children apparently "master the pronouns 'I' and 'you' much later than sighted children do" ("Five" 38 n. 5).

Ecological experience, like the body image, belongs to the unreflexive realm of primary consciousness and is, accordingly, normally inaccessible to conscious examination and representation. Hull's blindness, however, like Sacks's injury, seems to have created for him a window through which he was privileged to observe how his sense of self was shaped by the usually invisible sensory reception of data from the world.[31] In both cases a sensory deficit is experienced as a deficit of identity. Because Hull became blind only in midlife, in his forties, after a lifelong struggle with failing vision, his new condition sensitized him to probe the unexamined assumptions that the sighted take for granted in their conception of identity. Thus Hull queries, in one of the earliest entries in his diary-like narrative—"Does it matter what people look like?" (20). The face, "the appearance, the look of the person," he concludes, "is that around which all of the other items cluster" (96), and so, inevitably, he wonders whether he is destined to "become a blank on the wall of my own gallery?" "Loss of the image of the face," he speculates, may be "connected with loss of the image of the self" (25). As he "sinks"—a repeated figure—deeper and deeper into blindness, he is haunted, in fact, by a sense of the "dematerialization" (56) of body, body image, and self: "One can't glance down and see the reassuring continuity of one's own consciousness in the outlines

---

[31] I am grateful to Sacks for drawing my attention to Hull's memoir. In his foreword to the American paper edition of *Touching the Rock* (1992), Sacks links Hull's experience with his own in *A Leg to Stand On* (xv).

of one's own body. . . . I am no longer concentrated in a particular location" (64). Other people become for him similarly disembodied, "like voices suspended upon stilts" (97). Hull often finds himself feeling strangely evacuated and remote, numbed by a disturbing loss of affect. "Blindness," he observes, "is like a huge vacuum cleaner which comes down upon your life, sucking almost everything away" (178).

Countering Hull's sense of disembodiment and unreality are his remarkable evocations of pleasure in listening to rain, for at such moments his consciousness expands to become coterminous with the material world, his body and the rain become "one audio-tactile, three-dimensional universe, within which and throughout the whole of which lies my awareness" (133). In such passages as these, exploring the ecological foundations of our sense of time, space, and identity, Hull documents the gradual healing process of adaptation to his blindness through which his sense of his body is reconfigured and rematerialized: "Instead of having an image of my body, as being in what we call the 'human form,' I apprehend it now as these arrangements of sensitivities, *a conscious space* comparable to the patterns of the falling rain" (133, emphasis added). With the eclipse of the visual, hearing and touch are pressed into service to render a new model of the body as a space-occupying entity in the world. *Touching the Rock* records this process of sensory reconstruction over a period of about three years, culminating in Hull's new sense of himself not "so much as a blind person, which would define me with reference to sighted people and as lacking something, but simply as a whole-body-seer" (217). "Whole-body-seer"—in this memorable formulation body and consciousness are joined in a single, seamless model of identity.

The rain passage captures Hull's darkened identity at a rare moment of ecological poise, however, and even here the potential for the identity-threatening sensation of disembodiment persists. Figuring his thoughts as a "single-track line of consecutive speech," he writes:

This line of thought expressed in speech is not extended in space at all, but comes towards me like carriages in a goods train, one after the other, coming out of the darkness, passing under the floodlight of knowledge, and receding into memory. That line of consecutive thoughts is situated within the three-dimensional reality of the patterns of consciousness made up by the rain and my body, a bit like the axis of a spinning-top. It could be otherwise, however. If the rain were to stop and I remain motionless here, there would be silence. My awareness of the world would again shrink to the extremities of my skin. If I were paralysed from the neck down, the area would again be curtailed. How far could this process go? At what point do I become only a line of thought-speech, without an environment of sensation and perception? What happens to the tracks when there is no longer ground to support the line? What happens to the spinning-top when only the axis is left? (133–34)

By throwing into question the ecological foundation of selfhood—"the environment of sensation and perception"—on which the sighted unreflectingly rely, Hull's blindness paradoxically makes us see it. In a formula that recalls the Cartesian subject, Hull contemplates the disturbing alternative to embodied identity, a frightening reduction of self to a "line of thought . . . not extended in space at all." The idea of "thoughts" dissociated from "awareness" prompts chilling images of paralysis and dissolution: "How far could this process go?" For Madame I, for Sacks and Hull, the existence of the self and the existence of the body are inseparable.

Sacks's leg injury and Hull's descent into blindness profoundly alter their sense of body image, leading them to reflect on the ecological support system that sustains—literally positions in space—their sense of self. Only indirectly, through experiences of sensory deprivation like these, can we grasp the contribution of primary consciousness to identity formation. In presenting Sacks and Hull I have deliberately emphasized the body of physiologic process rather than the body of cultural construction that has been the focus of so much recent commentary, most strikingly by Michel Foucault in *Discipline and Punish: The Birth of the Prison* (1977) and by many feminists.[32] Such a distinction, I hasten to add, is largely heuristic. George Lakoff and Mark Johnson remind us that "all experience is cultural through and through": "What we call 'direct physical experience' is never merely a matter of having a body of a certain sort; rather, *every* experience takes place within a vast background of cultural presuppositions" (57). It is doubtless a similar conviction of the intimate bond between the physical and the cultural that leads Neisser, as I noted earlier, to identify "a representation of one's own body" ("Five" 40 n. 8) as an important component of what he terms the *conceptual self,* the theories, models, assumptions that comprise our self-concept. It is this self-conscious, reflexive notion of body image rather than the invisible functioning of proprioception that I want to consider now by way of conclusion to my examination of the embodied self.[33]

Much of the most interesting work in autobiography studies in the last ten years has, in fact, been devoted to the conceptual self, exploring the "vast background of cultural presuppositions" that informs it. Taken collectively, this body of criticism presents a comprehensive picture of some of the leading factors contributing to the production of conceptual selves: race and ethnicity (e.g., William Andrews, Arnold Krupat, Françoise Lionnet, Genaro M. Padilla), class (e.g., Regenia Gagnier), and gender (e.g., Felicity Nussbaum, Sidonie Smith). Until very recently, however, the body did not figure in these considerations or even,

---

[32] The evolution of feminist attitudes toward the body is quite complex. For a succinct summary, see Grosz 14–19. I am especially drawn to Grosz's work because she is equally interested in the body of physiological process and the body of cultural construction, and writes so suggestively on the interface between the physical and the cultural.

[33] While I have emphasized the ecological dimension of Sacks's and Hull's accounts, the conceptual, cultural content of their experience of disability is equally instructive. Both men stress the difficulty of communicating the sensory and psychological reality of their condition to individuals situated in the culture of the normal.

for that matter, in autobiography itself, according to Shirley Neuman, who speaks of the "near-effacement of bodies in autobiography" as a form of cultural "repression" ("Appearance" 1).[34] Similarly, Elizabeth Grosz's project to promote a "corporeal feminism" stems from her belief that "the body has remained a conceptual blindspot in both mainstream Western philosophical thought and contemporary feminist theory" (3). The work of Grosz, Sacks, Edelman, and Rosenfield that I described earlier, however, displays the new prominence of the body in our understanding of consciousness, memory, and self, while the current proliferation of narratives of illness and disability, together with commentaries on them by Arthur Kleinman, Anne Hunsaker Hawkins, Arthur W. Frank, and especially G. Thomas Couser, tells a similar story.

Why, then, the absence of the body in traditional autobiography? Neuman, for example, points to the mind/body dualism in several of the major traditions of Western thought (Platonism, Christianity, Cartesianism), a dualism discredited—as I suggested earlier—not only theoretically but also by its failure to square with the testimony of experience. In *Subjectivity, Identity, and the Body* (1993), Sidonie Smith supplies a more elaborate answer. In her capsule history of the conceptual self that has figured in Western culture since the Enlightenment, she argues that the mind/body dualism plays out along gender lines in traditional autobiography. In patriarchal culture men enjoy the privilege of conceiving of themselves as "the universal subject," rational, self-determining, transcendent, and *disembodied.* Smith quotes Judith Butler to articulate the logic of this ideology of gender that produces the female subject as the inverse of the male, as "the subject of embodiment":

> Masculine disembodiment is only possible on the condition that women occupy their bodies as their essential and enslaving identities. . . . By defining women as "Other," men are able through the shortcut of definition to dispose of their bodies, to make

---

[34] See also Roger J. Porter on this issue.

themselves other than their bodies. . . . From this belief that the body is Other, it is not a far leap to the conclusion that others *are* their bodies, while the masculine "I" is the noncorporeal soul. (quoted in Smith 11)

How this theoretical model of the subject—the disembodied male, the embodied female—translates into the experience of actual men and women is another story. Eve Kosofsky Sedgwick's theory of "homosexual panic" and Shere Hite's controversial survey of contemporary male attitudes toward sexuality, for example, suggest that men in Western culture in the nineteenth and twentieth centuries have not necessarily seen themselves as enjoying the transcendent and empowering freedom that their position as "universal" subjects would presumably confer, a freedom that according to the model delineated by Butler and others presumes a freedom from embodiment. Whatever the case may have been historically, there is widespread evidence in biography and autobiography today that living as bodies figures centrally *for both men and women* in their sense of themselves as selves. To illustrate the double impact of the body image—physical and conceptual—on the individual's sense of identity, I have chosen two narratives from the literature of illness and disability, Lucy Grealy's *Autobiography of a Face* (1994), and Robert F. Murphy's *The Body Silent* (1987). Grealy and Murphy present the case of the normal individual who undergoes a profound and transforming experience of illness in which cultural models of the body play a leading role. "Disablement," Murphy observes, "is preeminently a social state," "at one and the same time a condition of the body and an aspect of social identity" (195).

Grealy's striking title goes right to the heart of her story: it posits that faces have life stories. But in what sense is Grealy's story the story of her face? In what sense are our bodies our selves? Grealy is plunged into these identity dilemmas at age nine. Diagnosed with a potentially terminal cancer of the bone, the child undergoes an operation in which a large portion of her jaw is removed, leaving her face—and her identity—profoundly disfigured. The unrelenting cruelty of other children at school teaches her that "I *was* my face, I *was* ugliness" (7). Her mother reinforces the devastating truth of this equation in a brief, pointed exchange a few years later when teenage Lucy, recovering from chemotherapy, has lined up a summer job over the telephone:

> "Did you tell them about yourself?"
> I hesitated, and lied. "Yes, of course I did." (5)

Only after a seemingly endless series of reconstructive surgeries over the years does Grealy recognize that the truth that she was her face was itself a lie, a culturally sanctioned lie endowed with the power of identity-shattering fact.

As I noted earlier, Hull's blindness leads him to recognize the face as the site where identity is socially recognized and constituted. As long as he retains the assumptions about identity grounded in sighted experience, he feels himself becoming progressively unselved, ghostly, disembodied: "This means that I have a sense of cognitive dissonance when I think about myself" (144). Grealy's disfigurement creates an analogous dissonance. Looking at herself in the mirror generates both shame and alienation: she is, and she isn't, what she sees. Grealy suggests that her adolescent ego was remarkably resourceful in refusing the cancer's apparent legacy of a disfigured identity, in seeing "everything as fixable." Thus, returning to school after chemotherapy and encountering relentless teasing from the boys, she decides that "the problem" was her baldness, "this *thing* that wasn't really me but some digression from me" (106).

In a "turning point" (185) late in her narrative, however, she grasps definitively that her face is, inescapably, her "problem." The revelation occurs, appropriately, in a fitting room: trying on a shirt, she sees her reflection "in a mirror that was itself being reflected in a mirror opposite, reversing my face as I usually saw it" (184): "This reversed image of myself was the true image, the way other people saw me" (185). Trapped by the insidious logic that she *is* as others see her, Grealy comes to accept a body plot as the story of her life: "fix my face, fix my life, my soul" (215).[35] In this sense Grealy's autobiography truly is the autobiography of her face, for she long believed in the plastic surgery reconstructing her face as a surgery of identity. Grealy's search for "the face I was 'supposed' to have" (179), moreover, is only an extreme illustration of the place of the body image in the cultural construction of identity. In the age of silicone, Americans' conceptual selves are heavily invested in their bodies: the identity wishes transacted daily over cosmetic counters and in fitness classes are only milder versions of the more urgent quests for beauty, success, and even a new gender that drive both men and women to plastic surgery to get the identity work done.

The autobiography of Grealy's face comes to an end when she finally abandons the old body plot that structures the narrative, "the framework of *when my face gets fixed, then I'll start living*" (221): "As a child I had expected my liberation to come from getting a new face to put on, but now I saw it came from shedding something, shedding my image." Grealy recognizes that she had allowed herself to be more deeply scarred by culturally imposed shame than she ever had been by the original cancer. Surgery can never make her look like herself, while society urges that "we can most be ourselves by acting and looking like someone else, only to leave our original faces behind to turn into ghosts" (222). Grealy's face is no longer her "original face," and it certainly isn't the face she had long dreamed of having—after the final operation she writes, "I didn't look like me" (219).

In the last line, as Grealy steps confidently into an unnarrated future, she pauses to test out her new resolve to shed her image by looking at herself once more: "I looked with curiosity at the window . . . , its night-silvered glass reflecting the entire café, to see if I could, now, recognize myself" (223). The answer to this challenge to herself is implied, I think, in the fact of the finished narrative and the act of writing that produced it. The possibility of resolving her identity problems, Grealy affirms, can come fi-

---

[35] For other passages featuring this sense of body plot, see 179, 187, 204, and 221.

nally only from herself: it is she who will *recognize* herself—*recognize* in the sense of "identify" and also in the sense of "acknowledge the worth of"—but she will do so against the reflecting social surface of the café glass. Identity, as I will argue in the next chapter, is always negotiated interpersonally, relationally, and I don't see Grealy here as taking refuge in a posture of romantic self-determination. She, if anyone, is the realist; she knows that we are bodies and selves in a social world.

In his mid-fifties, at the peak of his career, the anthropologist Robert F. Murphy becomes progressively paralyzed as an inoperable spinal tumor grows steadily upward inside his spinal column. This bodily event is also an identity event; physical circumstances trigger cultural and psychological consequences. Like Sacks, Hull, and Grealy, Murphy experiences a sense of estrangement from his body, a dissociation of identity that is, paradoxically, predicated on the fact of embodied selfhood in the first place, for Murphy opens his narrative by reminding us that the organs of sense and "the body itself" "are among the foundations upon which we build our sense of who and what we are" (12).

Initially, Murphy's identity troubles, like Sacks's, are caused by a loss of proprioception; in losing full use of his legs, he writes, "I had also lost a part of my self. It was not just that people acted differently toward me, which they did, but rather that I felt differently toward myself" (85). But people *did* act differently toward Murphy once he became confined to a wheelchair, and in the remarkable middle section of the book, "Body, Self, and Society," the anthropologist delineates the "liminal," devalued status of the disabled in contemporary American culture.[36] Like Grealy, he joins the company of "damaged" selves for whom there is no conceptual place in the culture of the normal. Citing the anthropologists Mary Douglas, Claude Lévi-Strauss, and Victor Turner, who have developed theories about the "deviant" individual, Murphy argues that the disabled, who " 'gross out' ordinary

---

[36] For Murphy's application of Victor Turner's notion of *liminality* to the status of the disabled, see 131–36.

folks" (132), are compromised in their status not only as gendered individuals but even as human beings. They belong to the category of the category-less.

Much of the power and many of the insights in Murphy's narrative derive from the narrator's alignment with both the normal (he is an anthropologist observing) and the disabled (he is his own informant). This dual perspective creates a cognitive dissonance, a sense of his identity as being out of sync with his body, that parallels Hull's and Grealy's; he is, and he isn't, his body—"I began to think of myself as if a part of me were perched over the headboard, watching the rest" (5). In an early stage of denial, for example, Murphy accelerates his professional activity at Columbia University as if to shout to his students and colleagues, " 'Hey, it's the same old me inside this body!' " (81). But his paralysis, in fact, works "a revolution of consciousness," "a metamorphosis" (87). Again, on the plane of theory, citing Freud and Merleau-Ponty, Murphy affirms the grounding of mind in the body, and yet, experientially, his paralysis "shatters" Merleau-Ponty's "mind-body system" (102).

Although disability sensitizes Murphy to the somatic foundation of his identity, he cultivates nonetheless a "radical dissociation from the body" (101) as a strategy for psychological survival: "I have also become rather emotionally detached from my body, often referring to one of my limbs as *the* leg or *the* arm" (100). Does Murphy embrace here the very dehumanization of the disabled that he condemns in the culture of the normal? How could it be otherwise, though, if the "I" is both damaged and intact, belonging to both cultures and neither? As the tumor pushes Murphy inexorably down the road to entropy, as his body becomes increasingly silent, he observes, "My thoughts and sense of being alive have been driven back into my brain, where I now reside" (102). His reduced condition conjures up memories of a science-fiction movie "in which a quite nefarious brain is kept alive in a jar with mysterious wires and tubes attached to it" (101). "Murphy's brain," he suggests, the final refuge of his embattled self, is analogously outlandish and thinglike, confined, dependent, and vulnerable. What Murphy contemplates here, and lives, is precisely the dissolution of embodiment that Hull finds so threatening to his sense of identity—"What happens to the spinning-top when only the axis is left?"

Although Murphy does not propose *The Body Silent* as his autobiography, but rather as an anthropological study of the culture of disability, it is both. The book is an autobiography of a rather special kind, which succeeds in displaying the somatic deep structure of all identity narrative: a story of embodiment and disembodiment. "The disabled," Murphy persuades, "represent humanity reduced to its bare essentials" (5). In the early stages of his debilitation, as Murphy slowly joins the ranks of the disabled, the body functions as the site of alienation, where he learns the culture's identity-altering lessons in defamiliarization and difference. Murphy eventually accepts his disability, however, as a metaphor for what Henry James speaks of memorably in *The Beast in the Jungle* as "the common doom." Life, Murphy affirms, is "the only transcendent value," "a process, a drama with an inevitable denouement, for quiescence and dissolution are the fate of everything" (230). If Murphy's self is damaged by the tumor, as it is, it is also true that every self is damaged, in a larger and deeper sense, by living in *and as* a mortal body: thus the body teaches as its final lesson, "there's no cure for life" (229). Murphy speaks, I believe, for everyone, when he writes in the last sentence, "the paralytic—and all of us" (231).[37]

---

[37] Robert F. Murphy died in 1990, surviving *The Body Silent* by only three years.

CHAPTER TWO

Relational Selves, Relational Lives: Autobiography and the Myth of Autonomy

One must start from the structure of the relations *between* individuals in order to understand the "psyche" of the individual person.

—Norbert Elias

We tend to think of autobiography as a literature of the first person, but the subject of autobiography to which the pronoun "I" refers is neither singular nor first, and we do well to demystify its claims. Why do we so easily forget that the first person of autobiography is truly plural in its origins and subsequent formation? Because autobiography promotes an illusion of self-determination: *I* write my story; *I* say who I am; *I* create my self. The myth of autonomy dies hard, and autobiography criticism has not yet fully addressed the extent to which the self is defined by—and lives in terms of—its relations with others. I want to begin this chapter on the relational self and the relational life by reflecting on two narratives that radically changed my thinking about autobiography and about the nature of the self that is its subject: the story of a young man's strange death in Alaska, and the story of a British historian's troubled relationship with her working-class mother. These two stories, and others that I will discuss presently, crystallized my belief that *all* identity is relational, and that the definition of autobiography, and its history as well, must be stretched to reflect the kinds of self-writing in which relational identity is characteristically displayed. In later sections of this chapter, I will review some theories about the relational self and present some characteristic examples of the relational life.

Recognitions: New Views of Self and Autobiography

A Death in Alaska

In September, 1992, in the Alaskan wilderness, the body of a young man was discovered lying in his sleeping bag in an abandoned bus where he had sought shelter. Dental records and a series of self-portraits found in the dead man's camera eventually identified him as twenty-three-year-old Christopher McCandless of Chesapeake Beach, Maryland. He had apparently died of starvation. When I read about McCandless in the *New Yorker* a few months later, two things in Chip Brown's profile story captured my attention. The first was Brown's description of McCandless's last self-portrait: in it the young man is seated, with one hand raised and holding in the other a block-letter note on which he has written, "I have had a happy life and Thank the Lord. Goodbye and may God Bless All!" (47). The picture and its message—the very idea of this photographic testament and the circumstances that prompted it—were overwhelming. I was moved by the existential fortitude the photograph displays—this was my initial reaction.

The second thing in the story that hooked me—and complicated my response—was the fact that a coverless, annotated copy of *Walden* was one of the books found in the bus near McCandless's body. I was teaching *Walden* at the time in a course on Emersonian individualism, and I read Chip Brown's narrative to my class the next day, for McCandless had carried the Thoreauvian injunction "simplify, simplify!" to a radical reduction. "In the end," Chip Brown observes, "he pared away himself" (38). Already a loner at Emory University, McCandless isolated himself from family and friends after his graduation, embarking on a series of transcontinental adventures and wanderings during which he discarded his social security number, burned up his money, and shed his old name, calling himself "Alex" and sometimes "Alex Supertramp" in his life on the road. Poised to enter his final wilderness, McCandless rejected map, compass, and watch, telling the man who had driven him to the edge of Denali National Park, "I won't run into anything I can't deal with on my own" (Krakauer, "Death" 39). What McCandless's fate seemed to suggest, I told my students, was the dangerous underside of transcendentalist self-reliance.

Besides the photographs, McCandless left two other autobiographical accounts of his last adventure, which record between them a decidedly darker version of romantic individualism than anything to be found in *Walden*, the picture of a radically autonomous identity gone wrong. The first is a mini-biography of about a hundred words, scratched in capital letters on a plywood-covered window of the bus that became his last refuge: "Two Years He Walks The Earth. . . . Ultimate Freedom. An Extremist. An Aesthetic Voyager Whose Home *is The Road*. . . . No Longer to Be Poisoned By Civilization He Flees, and Walks Alone Upon the Land To Become *Lost* in the *Wild*" (Brown 44). In stark contrast to this larger-than-life neo-Byronic posturing—which McCandless may well have intended as a parody of the romantic hero's stance—the other record is a fragmentary journal he kept on two blank pages at the back of a book on edible plants. Most of the entries apparently center on food—what he did and didn't manage to find to eat. As the days slipped by and he believed his escape route cut off by a raging glacial river ("Rained in, river look impossible. Lonely, Scared" [45]), he knew he was starving, and doubtless the haunting farewell photograph dates from this time. After the "beautiful blueberries" noted on the one hundred and seventh day of his ordeal, the final entries are unspeakable: no words, only a circle around the number of each day he survived and a dash. The record ends on Day 113.

McCandless's Alaskan adventure left me with conflicting feelings: was it an edifying and heroic story, as I might once have thought, or was it, as I now seemed to see, a cautionary tale about a victim of fatally misguided beliefs, about someone who thought he could do without other people? The distance between these two readings registers an important shift in my thinking about self and self-experience, a shift that led me to write this book. I began to think about autobiography in a new way.

Conflicted Categories

Models of identity are centrally implicated in the way we live and write about our lives. As Paul Smith puts it, "None of us lives without reference to an imaginative singularity which we call our 'self' " (6). I take this sense of self to be an existential necessity, and we need only consider the plight of individuals suffering from Korsakov's syndrome, movingly described by Oliver Sacks, or from Alzheimer's disease, for a grim picture of the death of the self.[1] It is always possible, moreover, for the human individual not to become a self at all if the process of individuation is interfered with, as it was in the case of "Genie," a girl who was strapped to a potty chair in a darkened room during most of her childhood. Russ Rymer, her biographer, writes: "She never figured out who she was and who was somebody else" (124). In forming our sustaining sense of self, we draw on models of identity provided by the cultures we inhabit. Some of these models are life enhancing, some not. In the case of McCandless, it isn't easy to pass judgment, for if we have his word that he lived a happy life, we also have the grim testimony of the fragmentary journal.[2]

---

[1] See Sacks, *Man* 23–42, 108–15.

[2] My interpretation of Chris McCandless's life story changed significantly after reading Krakauer's book-length treatment, *Into the Wild* (1996). Krakauer's study is meticulous and probing, and he believes that McCandless reached a turning point in his solitary experiment after two months in the wilderness: "He seemed to have moved beyond his need to assert so adamantly his autonomy, his need to separate himself from his parents" (168). For further evidence of this shift, see 188–89. Krakauer makes a good case that McCandless's undoing stemmed from his otherwise astonishingly successful survival by foraging: he mistook the wild sweet pea for the wild potato, and ate some toxic seeds which incapacitated him and precipitated his ensuing starvation (190–95).

Models of identity may be central to lives and life writing, but the attention they have received from students of autobiography leaves a good deal to be desired. I will review the relevant discussion quickly, for the terrain has been surveyed several times in the last few years, notably by Sidonie Smith ("[Female]"), Joy Hooton, and Nancy K. Miller ("Representing"). The contemporary debate about the nature of the self portrayed in autobiography was launched forty years ago in a remarkably influential essay written by the French critic Georges Gusdorf, "Conditions and Limits of Autobiography" (1956). The model Gusdorf posited for the identity that autobiographies presuppose—let us call it the Gusdorf model—was emphatically individualistic, featuring a "separate and unique selfhood" (Friedman 34).[3] In a similar vein, writing in the 1970s, Philippe Lejeune (*L'Autobiographie*) and Karl J. Weintraub traced the rise of modern autobiography to Rousseau and Enlightenment individualism. Then, in 1980, Mary Mason became the first of a long line of feminist critics to repudiate the universalizing claims of this model and question its place in the history of the genre. The model might suitably describe the experience of Augustine and Rousseau, she conceded, but it did not fit the contours of women's lives. Correcting this gender bias, she proposed an alternative model for women: "identity through relation to the chosen other" (210).

A few years later, Domna Stanton asked, "Is the [female] subject different?" and by implication, "Is women's autobiography different from men's?" Answering yes to these questions, subsequent scholars—and I am thinking especially of Susan Stanford Friedman, Bella Brodzki, and Celeste Schenck—have returned most often to Mason's notion of relational identity as the distin-

[3] Gusdorf's famous essay, "Conditions et limites de l'autobiographie," originally published in 1956, was reprinted by Philippe Lejeune in 1971 (*L'Autobiographie*) and translated into English by James Olney in 1980. Acknowledging Gusdorf as the founding figure of twentieth-century autobiography studies, Olney writes, "In the beginning . . . was Georges Gusdorf" ("Autobiography" 8). I should emphasize that in the present discussion I am concerned with the way in which his views have been construed by feminist critics.

guishing mark of women's lives. Thus, in her essay "Individuation and Autobiography," an indictment of "the conflation of autobiography with male life-writing" and "the conflation of male experience with critical ideologies" (60), Joy Hooton observes, "The presentation of the self as related rather than single and isolate is . . . the most distinctive and consistent difference between male and female life-writing" (70).[4] Following Friedman, Hooton cites research in developmental psychology and sociology, by Carol Gilligan and especially Nancy Chodorow, to support this view that individuation is decisively inflected by gender. The female subject, then, *is* different, and so is her life story.

The critique of the Gusdorf model of selfhood and the positing of a female alternative paved the way for the serious and sustained study of women's autobiography—the single most important achievement of autobiography studies in the last decade. One of the consequences, however, and perhaps an inevitable one given the project to distinguish female from male autobiography, has been an unfortunate polarization by gender of the categories we use to define self and self-experience. The three most prominent of these male-female binaries are the individual as opposed to the collective, the autonomous as opposed to the relational, and, in a different register, narrative as opposed to nonlinear, discontinuous, nonteleological forms.[5] For some critics, the very terms of the discussion—*self, autobiography, narrative, individual*—become suspect, contaminated by patriarchal usage.[6]

---

[4] For similar formulations, see, e.g., Friedman 41, and Brodzki and Schenck 8.
[5] For the individual as opposed to the collective binary, see Friedman; for the autonomous as opposed to the relational binary, see Mason; for narrative as opposed to discontinuous, nonlinear forms, see Jelinek, Juhasz, and Hogan. Friedman's essay illustrates the problems that result in an argument that relies on narrowly conceived gender binaries. Despite her attack on individualism, once she launches into a discussion of Anaïs Nin, she begins to draw on terms such as "self" and "uniqueness," and she is obliged to recuperate individualism, constructing a special "relational" variety of "uniqueness" to work out her argument. Friedman is attacking individualism itself as the basis for autobiography, whereas I would suggest that it is the masculinist bias in our understanding of individualism that needs correction.
[6] See, e.g., Watson's critique of "the metaphysical self of canonical autobiography" (57).

In addition to this polarization of categories, a second, related consequence of the attempt to define women's autobiography has been the widespread acceptance of a concomitantly narrow definition of male selfhood and autobiography. Gusdorf's stress on the separate, autonomous individual, Rousseau's celebration of his uniqueness and singularity—these formulations have been accepted at face value. Do they, we need to ask, accurately describe Rousseau's self-representation in *The Confessions*? The understandable pressure to settle on reliable criteria for identifying difference in autobiography, together with the rarity of comparative analysis, has promoted the myth of autonomy that governs our vision of male lives.[7] I hasten to add that men are hardly the victims alone of critical misdescription; like women, men also are constructed by patriarchal ideology.[8] Consolidating the gains of feminist scholarship, and emulating what Sidonie Smith and others have achieved for women's autobiography, we need to liberate men's autobiography from the inadequate model that has guided our reading to date. As Chris McCandless's story demonstrates, the Gusdorf model is potentially a killer.[9]

Why, it is fair to ask, didn't critics pick up on the implications for male identity of Mary Mason's early critique of the Gusdorf model? Part of the answer, I believe, is that Mason, Friedman, and other feminist critics helped to keep the old Gusdorf model in place—paradoxically—by attacking it: it didn't apply to women, they argued, but it did to men, leaving men stuck with a model of identity that seems in retrospect rather like a two-dimensional caricature: so-called traditional autobiography became the province of the Marlboro Man. Inevitably, the discrepancy between the model and the lives it was presumed to represent triggered its present rejection. Nancy K. Miller identifies its inadequacy precisely when she writes, "In the narrative of

[7] Françoise Lionnet's *Autobiographical Voices* and Felicity A. Nussbaum's *The Autobiographical Subject* represent important exceptions here.
[8] See Claridge and Langland, especially 4–5.
[9] Neither gender has a monopoly on killer models of identity. See, e.g., Patricia Hampl's account of "the beauty disease" and the anorexic ideal of the mannequin in contemporary culture (85–133).

autobiography theory, the model of an imperial masculinity—providential or secular—*reads out* the self's passionate, vulnerable attachment to the other" ("Representing" 14).

How can we acknowledge the decisive importance of gender in the process of individuation without veering to either Gusdorfian or anti-Gusdorfian extremes? Can we escape the sterile binary logic of categories aligned strictly by gender? If female, then relational, collectivist, and, for some reason, nonnarrative; if male, then autonomous, individualistic, and narrative. I keep encountering women's autobiographies that strike me as individualistic and narrative in character; I keep finding important evidence of relationality in men's autobiographies.[10]

Here there are no easy answers. Linda Peterson notes—and apparently dissents from—the recent tendency to read women's autobiographies as if gender were some all-purpose "hermeneutic key" (81), while Sidonie Smith warns in a general way against the dangers of essentializing and totalizing ("[Female]" 116).[11] Nevertheless, reading books by the psychoanalyst Jessica Benjamin and the historian Carolyn Kay Steedman has helped me work through the impasse of these conflicted categories.[12] It is not my intent in the discussion that follows to destabilize the criteria for defining women's lives—"autogynography"[13]—but rather to suggest that the criterion of relationality applies equally *if not identically* to male experience. All selfhood, I argue, is relational despite differences that fall out along gender lines. Here I should acknowledge that such a proposition may well strike observers from other fields—from developmental psychology, say, or sociology, or cognitive studies—as self-evident and even commonplace.[14] The fact that a case for it should need to be made in

---

[10] Nancy K. Miller reports a similar experience ("Representing" 4).

[11] See also Brodzki and Schenck 11.

[12] I am grateful to Nancy K. Miller for prompting me to read Benjamin. Claridge and Langland make a strong case for moving beyond narrowly conceived gender typologies and the binary thinking that supports them. See also Brée 175.

[13] I believe that Domna Stanton coined the term (5).

[14] See my review in Chapter 3 of contemporary research by developmental psychologists on the child's initiation into the practice of self-narration.

autobiography studies shows just how profoundly the myth of autonomous individualism has marked the thinking of autobiographers and their critics, including resisting feminists, including myself.

Françoise Lionnet's *Autobiographical Voices: Race, Gender, Selfortraiture* (1989) is instructive in this regard. Lionnet, like the five woman writers she features in part 2 of her study "Creating a Tradition," is "engaged in an attempt to excavate those elements of the female self which have been buried under the cultural and patriarchal myths of selfhood" (91). While commendably repudiating "the whole Western tradition of binary thinking, which contributes to the naturalization of such distinctions as male/female" (68), she continues nonetheless to align relationality along an axis of gender. It is refreshing that Lionnet should include Augustine and Nietzsche in a project on women's autobiography and that she should expressly—and successfully—avoid treating them (in part 1) as "male paradigms or antimodels to be criticized and refuted"—contrast the demonization of Gusdorf that has become a standard move in a good deal of feminist commentary. "I want to examine how dimensions of their work that might be called feminine," she writes, "tend to be either ignored or coded in reference to a more 'masculine' and hierarchical framework" (19). Continuing, she formulates her approach to them as "a feminist reappropriation of the covertly maternal elements of both the *Confessions* and *Ecce Homo*" (19). Lionnet's editors, Shari Benstock and Celeste Schenck, follow suit, stressing that Lionnet invokes Augustine and Nietzsche for "the feminine in them" (viii). Doesn't Lionnet's insistence on reading relational identity through the lens of gender, with the relational coded as feminine and the autonomous as masculine, expose her to the risk that Peterson and Smith seek to avoid, putting her treatment of relationality in sync with the very patriarchal binaries she otherwise seeks to resist? Lionnet acknowledges the relational dimension of both men's and women's lives, but must we continue to think of the relational in male cases as "feminine," as "*covertly* maternal"? What I am getting at is the persistence of gender binaries in the articulation of an otherwise exemplary project.

How, then, to recognize both the autonomous and the relational dimensions of men's and women's lives without placing them in opposition? In *The Bonds of Love* (1988), Jessica Benjamin presents an attractively balanced approach to the relation between gender and identity formation, one that resists ascribing, moreover, an intrinsic value to either the autonomous or the relational per se. "Relational" selves and lives are neither better—nor worse—than "autonomous" ones. In Benjamin's view, these terms identify developmental tendencies that are inextricably intertwined in a complex process of individuation. According to Benjamin, "most theories of [infant] development have emphasized the goal of autonomy more than relatedness to others." They accept Margaret Mahler's "unilinear trajectory that leads from oneness [with the mother] to separateness," "leaving unexplored the territory in which subjects meet" (25). As a corrective to Mahler's model, Benjamin stresses accordingly the "intersubjective dimension" (49) of individuation and its central paradox: "at the very moment of realizing our own independence, we are dependent upon another to recognize it" (33). Thus, because the assertion of autonomy is dependent on this dynamic of recognition, identity is *necessarily* relational. Avoiding a "polarized structure of gender difference," which posits "irrational oneness and rational autonomy" (183–84) as the only alternatives, Benjamin argues that "along with a conviction of gender identity, individuals ideally should integrate and express both male and female aspects of selfhood (as culturally defined)" (113).[15] Benjamin persuades me that as long as we accept the notion of the individual as "a closed system" (49), we remain diminished by our categories. For students of autobiography's history, there is no little irony in the thought that the very Enlightenment model of the autonomous, rational individual that fostered the rise of

---

[15] Because Carol Gilligan's work is so frequently cited in support of the notion that relational identity is peculiarly female, it is useful to recall that she aligns all selfhood as developing along a continuum between the poles of attachment and separation. See, e.g., Gilligan 151.

the genre may also be responsible—now more than ever—for restricting its possibilities.

A Working-Class Childhood

Carolyn Kay Steedman's *Landscape for a Good Woman: A Story of Two Lives* (1986) may serve as a lively reminder of the possibilities we risk foreclosing when we subscribe to overly narrow categories of gender and genre in reading lives. If any text deserves to be identified as an "autogynography," surely this one does, yet, instructively, it defies narrowly conceived expectations of the gendered text, transgressing the familiar polarities: *Landscape* is female and relational, yet also individualist and narrative in conception. The book, in fact, is a strikingly original piece of life writing that breaks generic conventions: it is mixed in mode—expository and narrative by turns—and hybrid in form, neither an autobiography nor a biography but an amalgam of both and of history as well.

Like Benjamin, Steedman conceives of identity as relational, and the autobiography she writes is also relational, for she believes that her mother's self and story provide the key to her own. "Children are always episodes in someone else's narrative," she affirms, "not their own people, but rather brought into being for particular purposes" (122). In this way the familiar and perfunctory beginning of so many autobiographies—"I was born . . . " — acquires a new and signal importance, for Steedman argues that her dawning recognition of the circumstances of her conception—her realization that she was neither a wanted nor a legitimate child—determined the very structure of her personality.

"My mother's longing shaped my own childhood" (6). This is the opening, founding proposition of the relational life that Steedman develops in *Landscape for a Good Woman*. Central to her understanding of the psychological individuality of her mother's character is this sense of a lifelong desire—never satisfactorily fulfilled—for material things: with proper clothes a determined woman could escape the prison of class and take her rightful place in a comfortable world of privilege. Steedman believes that her working-class mother attempted to realize her dreams of rising in the world through the conception of children. Steedman's father had abandoned the wife and children of his first marriage, but he never married Steedman's mother. Steedman surmises that her mother hoped the birth of her children would pressure the father to marry her, and she sees this hope as coloring the first four years of her life, from her own birth to that of her sister. At this point, however, the mother seems to have realized that her strategy had failed, and Steedman relates that, from that time on, her mother made her feel that her very existence—and her sister's—was to blame for the failure of the mother's life: " 'If it wasn't for you two,' my mother told us, 'I could be off somewhere else' " (39). The reason for Steedman's decision to cast her autobiography in the form of the relational life becomes increasingly clear: she is making a case that the key events of her mother's life and personality shaped the design of her own in the most direct and lasting fashion.

Steedman's quest for her own origins, then, focuses on the figure of her mother, yet as she attempts to tell her mother's story she discovers that "the stories that people tell themselves in order to explain how they got to the place they currently inhabit . . . are often in deep and ambiguous conflict with the official interpretative devices of a culture" (6). Much of Steedman's book is devoted accordingly to a sustained critique of such "devices," patterns of contemporary cultural and psychological analysis that, as she puts it, make her mother hard to see (16). Accounts of white middle-class mothering such as Nancy Chodorow's, for example, have nothing useful to say to Steedman about the "not-mothering" (88) that characterized her own working-class upbringing. As in the case of "people's history" (13) and working-class autobiography, Steedman faults the "interpretative devices" of feminist psychology because they are rigidly totalizing, not sufficiently supple to register the difference of the individual case.[16]

---

[16] For Steedman's critique of "people's history," see 5–16, 100, 107–8; for her

The Gusdorf model, I might add, and the kind of autobiography it predicates have proved to be similarly limiting "interpretative devices" in autobiography studies. Susanna Egan draws the moral: "Instead . . . of adhering to the procrustean beds of traditional autobiography, we need as theorists to relax our comfort zones, recognize what autobiographers are writing, and respond to that" ("Encounters" 598).

In writing *Landscape for a Good Woman*, Steedman affirms the possibility of self-determination, of appropriating her working-class story from the dominant culture's controlling designs by interpreting it herself. Thus, she can announce her revisionist project as a rehabilitation of self and narrative in order to give voice to silent stories like her own, "so that the people in exile, the inhabitants of the long streets, may start to use the autobiographical 'I,' and tell the stories of their life" (16). Nevertheless, Steedman's wariness of narrative as an "interpretative device" has the last word: concluding her autobiography, she expresses her willingness to erase the story she has written of her mother and herself, to "consign it to the dark" (144).

"Memoirs" Reconsidered: Autobiography as the Other's Story

If Jessica Benjamin and Carolyn Steedman are right, if we are indeed relational selves living relational lives, the reign of the Gusdorf model will surely end, and in its place we will see more narratives of the kind I am about to describe in the rest of this chapter. When I say "we will see more narratives," I mean not only that more will be written, for shifts in conception of self will entail shifts in the kinds of lives we write, but also that we will increasingly recognize the extensive body of relational autobiography that already exists. So far such recognition has been limited to particular varieties of autobiography, to women's autobiography, to Native American autobiography. Once we begin to enter-

---

critique of working-class autobiography, see 9–10, 72–73, 74; and for her critique of feminist psychology, see 16–18, 82–97.

tain a notion of autobiography in which the focus is, paradoxically, on someone else's story, the hitherto neglected class of narratives we often call memoirs will emerge in quite a new and revealing light, as I want to show in the rest of this section. We will
also begin to acknowledge the relational dimension of narratives
that ostensibly reflect the Gusdorf paradigm.

The time is ripe for a much more broadly based initiative of reconstruction, which will involve redefining autobiography, re-
casting its canon, and rewriting its history. I share with Nancy K.
Miller, Susanna Egan, and Shirley Neuman a desire to track relational identity across gender boundaries. In "Representing Others: Gender and the Subjects of Autobiography," Miller calls for
"a way of thinking flexible enough to accommodate styles of self-
production that cross the lines of the models we have established." "This would have to include," she continues, "a rethinking of gender *like identity* as an intrinsically relational process"
(17). Miller has taken a bold first step toward such a "rethinking"
in *Bequest and Betrayal: Memoirs of a Parent's Death* (1996), which focuses on "narratives of the dying other" ("Facts" 13)—"au-
tothanatography"—a category of memoir "generally familial, in
which the other provides the map of the self" (14).

Susanna Egan joins Miller in indicting contemporary theory
for its failure to address autobiography as "an interactive genre
even at the very simple level of what one might call 'interpersonal relations.' " In *Mirror-Talk: Genres of Crisis in Contemporary
Autobiography* (1999) she examines an unusually heterogeneous
sample of contemporary life writing by both men and women to
show how autobiography "adjusts self-definition in order to accommodate unexpected or original relations with others" ("Encounters" 597). While Miller and Egan direct our attention to
the presence of the relational in autobiography, Shirley Neuman
has studied one of its surprising and revealing absences, the sup-
pression of the maternal body. The mother may well be the primary source of relational identity, she argues, but her invisibility
in stories of "self-individuation" has contributed to our difficulty

in recognizing identity precisely *as relational.*[17] As Neuman wisely concludes, "what goes unrepresented in culture is difficult to recognize as one's own experience" (" 'Your' " 76). This is Steedman's situation exactly—the "interpretative devices" of the culture made her mother hard to see.[18]

Like Miller and Egan, I too feel increasingly uncomfortable about the mismatch between contemporary life writing on the one hand and received categories of gender and genre on the other. The discussion of identity and genre that follows is an outgrowth of my reading not only of Steedman's *Landscape for a Good Woman* but also of a large class of memoirs which brought home to me the importance of what I have been calling *the relational life,* a term I use to describe the story of a relational model of identity, developed collaboratively with others, often family members. I will mention only a few characteristic examples of this literature that began to draw me—there are many others: *Father and Son* (1907) by Edmund Gosse; "A Sketch of the Past" (1939–40) by Virginia Woolf; *Because I Was Flesh* (1965) by Edward Dahlberg; *Pentimento* (1973) and *Maybe* (1980) by Lillian Hellman; *The Woman Warrior* (1976) and *China Men* (1980) by Maxine Hong Kingston; and *Patrimony* (1991) by Philip Roth.

From this large and various class of narratives I want now to discuss a rather special but peculiarly interesting corpus of texts which, because of their collaborative nature, highlight the relational dimension that is fundamental to all human experience of identity. Let me return to Philippe Lejeune's memorable early attempt to define autobiography as a *"retrospective prose narrative written by a real person concerning his own existence, where the focus is his individual life, in particular the story of his personality"* ("Autobiographical Pact" 4). Even though the lives I am about to present

---

[17] Neuman's research confirms Benjamin's view that current theories of individuation have overvalued separation and autonomy.
[18] Nancy K. Miller has noted a similar phenomenon, the virtual "erasure" of Augustine's mother Monica in the commentaries on the *Confessions* ("Representing" 9–14).

certainly don't focus on the "individual life" of the self, I instinctively read them as autobiographies. Lejeune, of course, sought usefully to distinguish autobiography from memoir, biography, and other related autobiographical forms, but the individualistic assumptions that underwrite his system of generic classification make no place for relational identity and the hybrid forms in which it characteristically finds expression. In the memoir as traditionally defined, for example, the story of the self, the "I," is subordinated to the story of some other for whom the self serves as privileged witness—I think of William Dean Howells's *My Mark Twain* (1910).

By contrast, in the relational lives in my corpus, the story of the self is not ancillary to the story of the other, although its primacy may be partly concealed by the fact that it is constructed through the story told *of* and *by* someone else. Because identity is conceived as relational in these cases, these narratives defy the boundaries we try to establish between genres, for they are autobiographies that offer not only the autobiography of the self but the biography *and* the autobiography of the other. In addition, and equally important, what I call the story of the story plays a determining role in these texts. I shall have more to say about these narratives of narrative making in Chapters 3 and 4.

In order to give a clearer idea of the material I am working with and what I mean by "the story of the story," I want to present capsule summaries of four characteristic examples, emphasizing the collaborative nature of these narratives:

1. *In My Mother's House: A Daughter's Story* (1983) by Kim Chernin. In 1974 Rose Chernin, a feisty Russian immigrant and tireless organizer for the Communist Party, asks her daughter Kim to write the story of her tumultuous career. Their work together on this project off and on over the next seven years produces a complex memoir that traces the conflicted mother-daughter relation across four generations of Chernin women.

2. *Brothers and Keepers* (1984) by John Edgar Wideman. As the paperback cover of this account of the author and his brother tells us, "One became a college professor and a prize-winning

novelist—the other was sentenced to life imprisonment." Wideman seeks the answer to this conundrum by creating a collaborative narrative in which the two brothers excavate the past, uncovering within the walls of the prison that paradoxically brings them together the walls that kept them apart when they were growing up in a black ghetto of Pittsburgh.

3. *My Place* (1987) by Sally Morgan. Determined to break the family conspiracy of silence and shame that clouded her childhood in western Australia, Morgan succeeds in eliciting the truth about her Aboriginal origins from her great-uncle, her mother, and finally her grandmother. She tapes, transcribes, and presents their stories of miscegenation, incest, and servitude as the climax of her family narrative.

4. *Maus: A Survivor's Tale* in two volumes (1986 and 1991) by Art Spiegelman. The cartoonist Spiegelman records, transcribes, and translates into comic strip form his father's astonishing tale of his survival at Auschwitz. In retelling his father's story, Spiegelman confronts the Holocaust and its consequences for his parents, his older brother, and himself.

This corpus of texts differs in important ways from the large class of collaborative or "as-told-to" autobiographies to which it belongs. To begin with, in these instances the autobiographical act is doubled, for the story of the other, of the informant (Art Spiegelman's father, Vladek, for example), is accompanied by the story of the individual gathering this oral history (Art Spiegelman himself). This second narrative I term the story of the story. In the case of *Maus*, the story of the story (Art Spiegelman's work of recovery) relates the genesis and execution of the collaborative enterprise that produces the first story (Vladek's experience of the Holocaust). Far from being relegated to an introduction or an epilogue, as was the case for the classic Native American autobiographies gathered by journalists and anthropologists, in my corpus the story of the story structures the narrative we read; the stress is on the performance of the collaboration and therefore on the relation between the two individuals involved.

Surprising as it may seem, given the very great intrinsic interest of the story of the other—the informant—in these cases, I argue that the two narratives—Art's and Vladek's—are not offered to us on an equal footing. If my reading is correct, it is the story of the story that has the upper hand. That is to say, for example, that *Maus* is in the last analysis Art Spiegelman's autobiography. Spiegelman himself supported this view in an interview with Robert Siegel on National Public Radio, taped in 1991, when the second and concluding volume of *Maus* appeared:

> SIEGEL: One of the things that makes this story so realistic is that throughout the story of "Maus" you're trying to elicit this information from your father, and the process of getting him to sit down and talk to you is part of the story. . . . *how important to you is that dimension of the entire story?*
> A. SPIEGELMAN: *Oh, I think it's the actual story.* This book grew out of me wanting to have some kind of relationship with my father, and the only relationship I found possible was that of journalist. And it allowed me to get near my father and listen to him without arguing with him. . . . when we finished taping over a couple of years, I'd say, "OK, let's start again." . . . And that went on till he died in '82. (28, emphasis added)

If I say, with Art Spiegelman's support, that *Maus* is in the last analysis his own autobiography, however, I risk oversimplifying a very complex situation, for the power relations between Art and his father—between Kim and Rose Chernin, between John and Robby Wideman, between Sally Morgan and her mother and grandmother—are very intricate indeed.

Narrative structure in these cases is telling us something fundamental about the relational structure of the autobiographer's identity, about its roots and involvement in another's life and story. Thus, the focus of the autobiography is on someone else's story, and the primary activity of the autobiographer is the telling of this story. This display of the story of the other in what is nevertheless an autobiography illustrates Steedman's assertion that "children are always episodes in someone else's narrative." The implicit determinism of this view of relational identity is inescapable, and it informs the act of self-representation accordingly: the space of autobiography, the space of the self, is literally occupied by the autobiography and self of the other. Yet, at the same time, the telling of the story of the other offers these oral historians a measure of self-determination, for the other's story, the other's life, is possessed—indeed created—by the recording self. I will return to these narratives in Chapter 4, where I will examine the ethical problems generated by the tension between self and other in relational lives, where narrative lines and lifelines are inextricably intertwined.

From "I" to "You": Modeling the Social Self

After reading the lives of Chris McCandless, Carolyn Steedman, Kim Chernin, Art Spiegelman, and many others, I find myself approaching life writing in the 1990s in a way that is quite different from my approach when I first began work on it in the 1970s. For example, a book such as Michael Ondaatje's *Running in the Family* (1982), which I once thought peripheral to my concerns—a "memoir" rather than an autobiography proper—now seems to me central to the genre. Moreover, I see relational paradigms prominently displayed in texts that I have read otherwise in other days—I am thinking of *The Autobiography of Malcolm X* (1965) and Alfred Kazin's *Walker in the City* (1951). Why, though, I keep asking, did it take me so long to respond to the relational dimension of identity experience if it is indeed as fundamental as I now claim?

I began this chapter by invoking the myth of autonomy, suggesting that the very act of writing a life story promotes a sense of self-determination not only in autobiographers but also in their readers: *I* write my story; *I* say who I am. But the forms of self-representation, ultimately of a piece with the nature of the selves that they display, can hardly be adduced to account for such selves. The psychologist John Shotter has worked out a much more searching answer to the enduring vitality of the myth of autonomy. In order to correct psychology's—and his own—one-sided preoccupation with inner states, Shotter proposes "to repudiate the traditional 'Cartesian' starting-point for psychological research located in the 'I' of the individual, . . . and to replace it by taking as basic not the inner subjectivity of the individual, but the practical social processes going on 'between' people" (137).

"In my earlier views," Shotter writes, "I was clearly still in the thrall of the classic 'text' of identity, possessive individualism" (147).[19] Possessive individualism is C. B. Macpherson's term for the proto-capitalist model of identity proposed by Hobbes and Locke, which posits the individual as "essentially the proprietor of his own person or capacities, owing nothing to society for them" (quoted in Shotter 136). Stepping back, Shotter asks why he—why we all—continue to account "for our experience of ourselves . . . in such an individualistic way [as Macpherson describes]: as if we all existed from birth as separate, isolated individuals *already* containing 'minds' or 'mentalities' wholly within ourselves, set over against a material world itself devoid of any mental processes" (136). We talk in this way, he answers, because we are disciplined to do so by "social accountability": "what we talk of *as* our experience of our reality is constituted for us very largely by the *already established* ways in which we *must* talk in our attempts to *account* for ourselves—and for it—to the others around us. . . . And only certain ways of talking are deemed legitimate." So pervasive is this discursive discipline that not only our talking but "our understanding, and apparently our experience of ourselves, *will be constrained also*" (141).

---

[19] Certainly autobiography as traditionally conceived could be said to be such a text. Interestingly, the most sustained account we have of the rise of Western autobiography, Kark J. Weintraub's *The Value of the Individual: Self and Circumstance in Autobiography* (1978), views the history of the genre in terms of the gradual emergence of the ideal of individuality since the Renaissance.

The premise of Shotter's concept of social accountability is that "one *ontologically* learns how *to be* this or that kind of person" in conversation with others (138). Identity formation, then, is socially and (more specifically) discursively transacted: thus "the capacity to be addressed as a 'you' by others is a preliminary to the ultimate capacity of being able to say 'I' of oneself" (143).[20] In contrast to the comparatively abstract analyses of Michel Foucault and Louis Althusser, which unfold at the level of social institutions and the state, Shotter's focus on the structure of interpersonal communication models the interface between the individual and culture with a telling immediacy: Shotter invites us to witness the "I" at the moment it is "interpellated" by the "you." An important corollary of the child's intersubjective instruction in personhood, which I will examine in some detail in my discussion of "memory talk" in Chapter 3, is learning that "people not only have a *life history*: they are expected to be knowledgeable about it in some way" (146). If Shotter's theory of social accountability is correct, and I think it is, the longevity of the myth of autonomy is hardly surprising: in this view, we are conditioned precisely *not* to recognize the relational dimension of selfhood; possessive individualism, functioning as the dominant social "text" to which we are held "accountable," masks the contribution of the "practical social processes going on 'between' people" (137) toward making us what we are: "we fail to register the fact of our involvement with others" (142).[21]

Shotter is only one of the most recent in a long line of commentators seeking to undo the conceptual legacy of a culture of individualism that has blinded us to the relational dimension of

---

[20] Similarly, Norbert Elias observes: "The interpersonal functions and relations that we express by grammatical particles such as 'I,' 'you,' 'he,' 'she,' 'we' and 'they' are interdependent. . . . each 'I' is irrevocably embedded in a 'we' " (61–62).

[21] Shotter's point is not novel, but his sense of the need to reiterate it testifies to the tenaciousness of possessive individualism. Norbert Elias, writing in 1939, presents a similar formulation in *The Society of Individuals* (published eventually in 1991), 37.

identity formation. Ian Burkitt's *Social Selves: Theories of the Social Formation of Personality* (1991) draws together a broad and diverse tradition of twentieth-century thought that challenges the notion of the individual as a closed system or "monad." If Shotter argues that the individual's sense of self is generated in conversation with others, several theorists in Burkitt's survey—including George Herbert Mead and Rom Harré—propose that our subjectivity is itself structured as a conversation. Harré writes: "The fundamental human reality is a conversation, effectively without beginning or end, to which, from time to time, individuals may make contributions. All that is personal in our mental and emotional lives is individually appropriated from the conversation going on around us and perhaps idiosyncratically transformed" (quoted in Burkitt 67). In the same vein, Daniel C. Dennett observes that "conscious thinking seems—much of it—to be a variety of particularly efficient and private talking to oneself" ("Self" 113).[22]

Despite Burkitt's stress on the discursive structure of self and subjectivity, he criticizes the social constructivism of Foucault and Derrida for its emphasis on discourse "at the expense of understanding humans as embodied social beings" ("Shifting" 8).[23] Drawing on the work of Mikhail Bakhtin, Mead, L. S. Vygotsky, and Norbert Elias, Burkitt seeks to expand what he regards as an overly narrow interpretation of "the human activity of *communication*" as "enclosure in a world of self-referring signs" ("Shifting" 14). In a move that expands Shotter's notion of social accountability, Burkitt points to Elias's understanding of "the association

---

[22] In developing this view, Dennett draws on Julian Jaynes's theory of the discursive origins of consciousness ("Self" 112–13).

[23] Foucault's views of the subject evolved considerably from the stark determinism of his early and best-known work, where the notion of the subject is invariably linked to subjection. Thomas McCarthy notes "a major shift from his earlier emphasis on networks or fields of power, in which individuals were only nodal points, and his methodological injunction to do without the subject and modes of analysis that rely on it": "Both the ethical subject and the strategic subject are now represented as acting intentionally and voluntarily—within, to be sure, cultural and institutional systems that organize their ways of doing things" (70).

between the development of the self and the *embodiment* of human beings, who, in the course of their upbringing, learn to discipline and control their own bodies in ways that are socially prescribed." Elias and Pierre Bourdieu call this usually "nonreflective" process of bodily self-regulation the *social habitus,* "the dispositions of a social class or group due to their common codes of conduct and the similar patterns of their upbringing" ("Shifting" 20–21). The upshot of Burkitt's commentary is to stress "a level of the self and its understanding of the world that is not just textual or cognitive, but is grounded in the experience of the body" ("Shifting" 26).

Reviewing theories of the social formation of personality inevitably prompts questions about power and agency, for lurking in such notions as "accountability" and "habitus" is a potentially deterministic vision of the individual's social construction. Given the primary importance attached to discourse in many of these theories, does it make sense to say that we are "spoken" by the language we speak? Burkitt's account of the work of the psychologists and linguists of the Soviet "cultural-historical school"—including L. S. Vygotsky and A. N. Leontyev—offers an attractively balanced answer. Consider their analysis of the child's relation to the adults who serve as "the conductors of the social-historical world through which the child forms its own self" (*Social* 136). Vygotsky may well state that the nature of mental processes is "quasi-social" (quoted in Burkitt, *Social* 143), but Burkitt stresses the *dialogic* nature of identity formation as conceived by these Soviet theorists. For Vygotsky and his colleagues, "the self is a dialogue which reflects and refracts concrete social interactions in which it plays a part. . . . The personality is not a product of social discourse, but is a self-created aspect of concrete social dialogue" (*Social* 143). Similarly, Norbert Elias captures the necessary interdependency of self and other that characterizes the matrix of social relations in which identity formation unfolds:

What are often conceptually separated as two different substances or two different strata within the human being, his "individuality" and his "social conditioning," are in fact nothing other than two different functions of people in their relations to each other, one of which cannot exist without the other. They are terms for the specific activity of the individual in relation to his fellows, and for his capacity to be influenced and shaped by their activity; for the dependence of others on him and his dependence on others; expressions for his function as both *die* and *coin*. (60)

In an earlier inquiry into the origins of selfhood, I presented self and language as mutually implicated in an interdependent system of symbolic behavior. To illustrate the dawn of the self-consciousness that is the stuff of autobiographical discourse, I focused on the celebrated well-house episode in Helen Keller's *Story of My Life* (1902), arguing that it offers "a rare, possibly unique, account . . . of the emergence of selfhood that occurs . . . at the moment when language is acquired" (*Fictions* 209–10). Although Keller had previously mastered a small vocabulary of finger-words spelled into her hand by her teacher, Anne Sullivan, it was only when Sullivan placed one of her hands under the spout and spelled into the other the word *water* that Keller achieved simultaneously a sense of language and self. It was truly a kind of intellectual and spiritual baptism: "I knew then that 'w-a-t-e-r' meant the wonderful cool something that was flowing over my hand. That living word awakened my soul" (*Story* 23). I summarized the upshot of the well-house episode schematically as follows: "the self ('my soul') emerges in the presence of language ('w-a-t-e-r') and the other ('Teacher')" (*Fictions* 212).

In its basic outline, this analysis of the Keller episode squares with the social constructivist perspective on identity formation. My schematic, freeze-frame account (self/language/other) reflects the fact that an entire passage of developmental history, normally requiring many months to transact, is compressed in Keller's case into the space of a revelatory moment. Now, however, rereading the well-house passage, I am struck by the extraordinary dynamism Keller attributes to her life-altering experience: the flowing of the water over one of her hands, the motion of Sullivan's finger on the surface of the other, the ensuing movement of mind generated in bodily sensation. Keller stresses both the relational dimension of the episode (the decisive role of "Teacher") and the grounding of the entire experience in her body. The Keller-Sullivan encounter dramatizes, moreover, the dialogic nature of the exchange between self and other that Vygotsky and Elias seek to capture: Keller is clearly both "die" and "coin."

I spoke in Chapter 1 of the "corporeal substratum of identity," the domain of Ulric Neisser's "ecological self." There I argued that the narratives of Sacks and Hull offer a precious glimpse of this register of experience that is, as Sacks puts it, normally "self-oncealing" and hence "inaccessible to introspection, insight or report." What Keller describes is, in effect, the passage from the organism's unreflexive awareness of its bodily experience (Edelman's primary consciousness) to a new, reflexive consciousness of being conscious (Edelman's higher-order consciousness). Notably, the somatic foundations of identity that precede the child's achievement of self-consciousness remain inaccessible to *conscious* retrospect: Keller can speak only in approximations and negatives—"no-world" (*World* 113) and "non-personality" (*Teacher* 121)—for she is convinced that the content of her mind in the shadowy period of her existence before the well-house "cannot be made a part of discourse" (*World* 160).

Chapter 3 returns to this issue of the self's origins by taking up the child's acquisition of narrative competence; there I will argue that, developmentally speaking, the rise of the self that is the subject of autobiographical discourse dates from the child's initiation into a lifelong practice of self-narration. Before I conclude this brief discussion of the social self, however, I want to acknowledge the importance of Daniel N. Stern's inquiry into the earliest phases of the self's emergence. In *The Interpersonal World of the Infant: A View from Psychoanalysis and Developmental Psychology* (1985), Stern argues—as Neisser does—that some senses of self exist "long prior to self-awareness and language" (6). (I should add that while Keller may characterize her life before the well-house as "an unconscious yet conscious interval of non-personality," she does claim a sense of self nonetheless, which she calls "Phantom" [*Teacher* 37].) Indeed, Stern assumes that preverbal senses of self start to form at birth, "if not before" (6). During the first six months the infant develops what Stern terms a sense of core self, and he stresses that this sense is not a "concept of" or "knowledge of" or "awareness of" but rather "an experiential integration" (71).[24] Like Jessica Benjamin, Stern repudiates the traditional view of individuation as a progressive movement away from a state of undifferentiated union with the mother: "There is no confusion between self and other in the beginning or at any point during infancy" (10). At the same time, Stern holds that "the subjective world of infants is deeply social" (123). If Stern and Neisser are correct, the early life of the relational self, however inaccessible to autobiographical recall, begins on day one.

From "You" to "I": Relational Environments

What does identity formation, theorized by social constructivists such as John Shotter as a process of social accountability, look like? As I proceed to answer this question in the next two sections, I want at the same time to propose the beginnings of a typology of the relational life, which I defined earlier as the story of a relational model of identity, developed collaboratively with

---

[24] When Stern comments that he finds it reasonable to believe "that many higher nonhuman animals form such a sense of a core self" (71 n. 2), I am reminded of Gerald Edelman's characterization of primary consciousness, of Ulric Neisser's characterization of the ecological and interpersonal selves. Stern's definition of the "sense of self" in the following passage illustrates the parallel: "By 'sense' I mean simple (non-self-reflexive) awareness. We are speaking at the level of direct experience, not concept. By 'of self' I mean an invariant pattern of awarenesses that arise only on the occasion of the infant's actions or mental processes. An invariant pattern of awareness is a form of organization. It is the organizing subjective experience of whatever it is that will later be verbally referenced as the 'self.' This organizing subjective experience is the preverbal, existential counterpart of the objectifiable, self-reflective verbalizable self" (7).

others, often family members. If we accept the weekly *New York Times Book Review* as a reliable indicator of trends in contemporary publishing, it is clear that relational lives represent the most prominent form of life writing in the United States today. What, though, counts as a relational life? If, as I contended earlier, all selfhood is relational despite differences that fall out along gender lines, isn't every autobiography going to reflect this aspect of identity formation? While acknowledging the relational dimension that makes its presence known in any life, I want to preserve the usefulness of the label by applying it to those autobiographies that feature the decisive impact on the autobiographer of either (1) an entire social environment (a particular kind of family, or a community and its social institutions—schools, churches, and so forth) or (2) key other individuals, usually family members, especially parents.

Testing the limits, I want to begin with an example in which the relational dimension of experience looms so large that one may well ask whether, in fact, it can properly be said to be an autobiography at all: Leslie Marmon Silko's *Storyteller* (1981). Silko, I should point out, does not propose such an identification herself. There is nothing in the book's packaging, moreover, that explicitly confirms an identification of the work as an autobiography.[25] Even the book's unusual physical dimensions—a broad, low rectangle—proclaim its difference from familiar categories and classifications; it literally stands out on the shelf. I suspect that it was the emphatic horizontality of the spreading mesa-rimmed landscapes in the photographs accompanying the text that prompted the book's shape. In this sense *Storyteller* reflects the environment of the Laguna Pueblo reservation in New Mexico where Silko grew up. When you open this handsome volume,

---

[25] If we were to apply Lejeune's notion of an "autobiographical pact," in which protagonist, narrator, and author share the same name, we would have to conclude that *Storyteller* does not qualify as an autobiography in any traditional definition of the genre. See Lejeune, "Autobiographical Pact." There are, I infer, four photographs of Silko included in the book (the paperback cover, and photographs 2, 9, and 24), but in none of these cases does she explicitly make this identification.

you discover that everything in it, from the title to the dedication to the text to the photographs ("which are themselves part of the stories") turns on story; you discover that Silko's concern, first and last, is with the narrative practices of her Laguna Pueblo culture.

In addition to the twenty-six photographs drawn from the Marmon family collection for which Silko provides identifying documentary captions, the book comprises sixty-seven pieces that are presented variously as short stories in double columns of prose, as poems whose lines are displayed in distinctly formal patterns, and as free-verse-like narratives, usually explicitly autobiographical in nature. These proto-generic distinctions, however, are no sooner made than they dissolve in this shifting, fluid text in which the deep lesson is that everything is a part of everything else: everything and everyone in *Storyteller* is story.[26] Underlying the different registers of experience—whether it is a question specifically of Silko's own life story and Marmon family history or, more generally, of Laguna and Native American history in the nineteenth and twentieth centuries—is a common body of myths, featuring such traditional figures as Yellow Woman (Kochininako), Spider Woman, Arrowboy (Estoy-eh-muut), Coyote, and the Twin Brothers.

In one of the contemporary stories, for example, about a woman who leaves her family for a brief affair with a cattle rustler named Silva, Silko shows us how the protagonist's consciousness is informed by the stories her "old grandpa liked to tell," "the old stories about the ka'tsina spirit and Yellow Woman" (55). The playful lover of the piece draws his line from myth, claiming to be the mountain spirit who compels Yellow Woman to do his bidding. However, in an age when "Jell-O" (62) is part of supper and "fading vapor trails left by jets" (61) mark the sky, the woman reflects: "I don't have to go. What they tell in stories was real only

---

[26] In an essay that dates from roughly the same period as *Storyteller*, Silko stresses the evolutionary significance of this interpenetration of parts in Pueblo culture: "Only through interdependence could the human beings survive" ("Landscape" 92).

then, back in time immemorial, like they say." She knows full well that she lives not then but now: "I've been to school and there are highways and pickup trucks that Yellow Woman never saw" (56). Yet hers is a storied consciousness, first and last, in which then and now coalesce in a narrative continuum; the time stretching before and after the present is a time of stories. Thus, when she imagines not returning home, she muses, "There will be a story about the day I disappeared while I was walking along the river" (59); later, having decided to return home after all, she thinks, "I was sorry that old Grandpa wasn't alive to hear my story because it was the Yellow Woman stories he liked to tell best" (62). In this world, experience is understood in terms of story and the telling of stories, and the appearance of a traditional figure like Yellow Woman in this contemporary tale of infidelity suggests the remarkable continuity of Laguna symbolic resources: traditional material coexists with, informs, is part of, present reality.

Laguna narrative culture is sustained by its storytellers, and Silko pays special attention to those members of her family who played this role in her childhood, modeling for her the artist and writer she has become: Grandma A'mooh, Grandma Lillie, and her great-aunts Alice and Susie—all members of "the last generation here at Laguna, / that passed down an entire culture / by word of mouth." Especially notable is Aunt Susie, whom Silko presents as a transitional figure who sought to preserve in writing "the oral tradition" which "had been irrevocably altered by the European intrusion" (5–6). Silko, writing now what Aunt Susie heard, told, and wrote, proceeds to align her own telling with Aunt Susie's, one more link in the narrative chain: "This is the way Aunt Susie told the story. / . . . I write when I still hear / her voice as she tells the story." Silko recalls that as Aunt Susie related the story "about the little girl who ran away" (7), she provided explanatory commentary about Laguna language and customs, illustrating what Silko means when she states that "the tellers . . . told the children / an entire culture" (6). In this story, for example, Aunt Susie glosses the word *upstairs* as follows: "*The pueblo people always called 'upstairs' / because long ago their homes were two, three stories high / and that was their entrance / from the top"* (9).

In the course of reading *Storyteller,* we learn a great deal about Laguna narrative practices—the kinds of stories they tell and how they tell them, on what occasions and why—but what justification is there for understanding *Storyteller* as an autobiography?[27] Certainly "I"-narrative is at a minimum in these pages, and the portion of it that is directly identified with Silko herself is even smaller—excerpts from two or three letters, commentary on family members, and the attribution of certain memories as her own. Significantly, when we consider Silko's autobiographical memories, we realize that most of them concern storytelling—when she heard a story, from whom, under what circumstances—which takes us full circle back to Laguna narrative practices.

What do we learn of Leslie Marmon Silko? That she is a Native American writer in various forms, and above all that she is a storyteller. That she grew up on the Laguna Pueblo reservation in a community in which an oral tradition of storytelling was still alive and central to the lives of her people. And what we learn of Marmon family history also features storytelling and storytellers. We can only conclude that *Silko's* story is in fact *stories,* as Arnold Krupat observes, "Silko's relation to every kind of story becomes the story of her life" (*Voice* 164). It is Silko herself, in a remarkable essay on the Pueblo imagination, who best captures the link between narrative and identity in Laguna culture: "through the stories we hear who we are" ("Landscape" 86).

Deferring to Chapter 3 a full-scale exploration of the link between narrative and identity, I want nonetheless to anticipate my discussion of the child's introduction into his or her culture's narrative practices by considering research that sheds light on the Pueblo version of this process. Silko herself, of course, de-

---

[27] Several of the stories contain instructive information about Laguna narrative practices. One story begins as follows: "*The Laguna people / always begin their stories / with 'humma-hah': / that means 'long ago.' / And the ones who are listening / say 'aaaa-eh' "* (38).

scribes her narrative socialization extensively, but the work of developmental psychologists provides additional support for her account. Peggy J. Miller, studying the narrative practice "in which a child appropriates another's story as his or her own," reports the following interesting finding in her work with a group of Zuni first graders. When asked a question by the teacher, each of the Zuni children replied by appropriating all of the other classmates' personal narratives he or she had already heard, incorporating this material into his or her own "I"-narrative. "This jointly constructed narrative," Miller observes, "ended up being a repository of the group's experience although it was told not as a we-experience but as an I-experience." Miller concludes: "This observation alerted us to the possibility of a socially expansive notion of personal experience" (302).[28] The Zunis, I should point out, are a Pueblo people dwelling in New Mexico immediately adjacent to Silko's Lagunas, and I suspect that observation of a group of Laguna first graders would produce a comparable result. If my hunch is right, then Silko's transmission of other people's stories, stories that are in turn versions of a shared body of myths and legends, is properly understood as an act of self-definition. In *Storyteller* there is a radical equivalence between self and other at the level of narrative: Silko's own story and the stories of others are one and the same. Storyteller: this is what she does and who she is.

I want to linger over Peggy Miller's observation that the Zuni children incorporated "we"-experience into "I"-narrative, suggesting "a socially expansive notion of personal experience." It is an instructive moment of defamiliarization in which we—and not the children—are obliged to confront the unspoken assumptions that guide our use of identity narrative. For the children, of course, there is no point to be made, whereas for the re-

---

[28] For further discussion of Native American models of identity and identity narrative, see Krupat, "Native American Autobiography and the Synecdochic Self." I am indebted to Krupat for sensitizing me to the richness of Native American autobiographical expression, and in particular to his suggestive reading of Silko (see *Voice* 161–70).

searcher, there is indeed a point that turns precisely on *the re-searcher's* assumptions about the way in which boundaries between "I" and "we," between self and other, are customarily drawn in her own culture. These normative assumptions play into our understanding of what autobiography is.[29] When I teach courses on autobiography, my students never fail to make clear that they expect an autobiography to deliver an "I"-narrative with a certain kind of content. This issue invariably arises when they confront a text that does not reflect the identity narrative practices they have been socialized to accept. In a graduate seminar on twentieth-century American autobiography, for example, *Storyteller* elicited responses like these: "Very little of this work is addressed to Silko's life per se, which gives me little of the autobiographical information I have come to expect"; "We do not get the traditional development of an individual, the personal story of individuation as a subject's development and movement out into the world."[30] Armed with our own notions of what a "life per se" is, what a "story of individuation is," we may not necessarily recognize another culture's practice of identity narrative as such when we encounter it. I think, for example, of Lisa McNee's work on the autobiographical import of *taasu,* a form of praise poetry performed by Senegalese women. As Elizabeth Bruss observes, "There is no intrinsically autobiographical form" (10).

Storyteller may well challenge conventional notions of what an identity narrative ought to look like, but the growing acceptance

---

[29] Cross-cultural situations such as Miller's encounter with the Zuni children are particularly fertile sites for the investigation of a culture's identity narrative practices. Nelson summarizes two cross-cultural studies that suggest that the development of autobiographical memory and of individual self-concept seems to unfold differently from culture to culture as a function of the kinds of discourse that parents engage in with their children (*Language* 171–72). Collaborative autobiographies produced by a professional ethnographic observer working with a (usually unlettered) informant provide an equally revealing, if problematic, area for an investigation of this kind.

[30] I quote from response papers written by Rocco Versaci and Audrey Levasseur from the fall of 1992.

of a relational model of identity is conditioning us to accept an increasingly large component of "we"-experience in the "I"-narratives we associate with autobiography. Take, for example, *Colored People: A Memoir* (1994) by Henry Louis Gates, Jr. The packaging of the paperback edition (Vintage, 1995) signals that the book is Gates's autobiography: a photograph of the author dominates the cover, the blurbs and jacket copy describe his narrative as a "memoir" and "coming-of-age story," and the shelving indicator on the back cover classifies the text as "Autobiography/African American Studies." At the same time, the title targets the African-American culture of his childhood, and the blurbs and jacket copy confirm this cue, celebrating the book's portrait of family and community that conjures up "a now-vanished 'colored' world," "the exuberant society blacks created for themselves under the veil of segregation."

In the preface that frames *Colored People*, Gates himself identifies the narrative as the story of a community, "a story of a village, a family, and its friends" (xvi). Casting the preface in the form of a letter to his daughters Maggie and Liza, products of a different time and place, he adopts an ethnographic posture toward the world of his childhood, for he fears that this "world that nurtured and sustained me" is threatened with extinction (xi). Specifically, he traces the impulse behind his autobiographical project to a desire to explain to his children why one "colored" man greets another in public, repeating his father's explanation to him when he was a boy: "It's just something that you do" (xii). Learning to be this "you" marks a decisive stage in the child's identity formation. Gates's sensitive—and also startlingly funny—account of the permutations of racial identity, of "being colored" (xiv), demonstrates how "we"-experience shapes the trajectory of "I"-narrative, not only his own but the one he projects for his children: "In your lifetimes, I suspect, you will go from being African Americans, to 'people of color,' to being, once again, 'colored people.' . . . But I have to confess that I like 'colored' best, maybe because when I hear the word, I hear it in my mother's voice and in the sepia tones of my childhood." The lessons learned about the community's identity conventions run deep, for he concludes, "And I hope you'll understand why I continue to speak to colored people I pass on the streets" (xvi).

The preface and its emphasis on the experience of the group prepare the reader for the fact that Skip, the Gates-as-child character, doesn't really emerge and occupy the center of the narrative stage until more than a third of the way through the book (in chapter 7). At this point Skip's story comes into sharp focus; the boy is ten or so, bright, plump, different, and painfully self-conscious about his father's disappointment in his lack of athletic ability. The narrative about Skip in the following chapters becomes increasingly personal, detailed, and circumstantial, especially when Gates relates his fears about "what was happening to my mother" (137). Her depression sets in when the boy is twelve, and difficulties begin to cluster for him; joining a fundamentalist church provides a temporary escape, but then a problem with his knee develops that requires a series of operations. Then Skip's story picks up speed, taking us through the transformative experience of reading James Baldwin's *Notes of a Native Son*, through his sexual awakening, through the rebellion of his high school years when he "stopped being a Negro, turned black, and grew the first Afro in Piedmont" (184), and eventually to college at Yale. All of this material belongs to the "coming-of-age story" highlighted in the back-cover blurb, standard "I"-story fare for an autobiography. This, surely, is Gates's "life per se," "the personal story of individuation as a subject's development and movement out into the world," but such formulations don't adequately embrace the content of the narrative, especially some of its richest and most rewarding sections. We need to heed Gates's auto-ethnographic observations in the preface about the mores of his social group.[31]

---

[31] The auto-ethnographic cast of *Colored People* is not, of course, a novelty, for one of the perennially stated motives for writing one's life is the conviction that one's own experience is somehow representative of the experience of one's social community or group. See, e.g., Lucy Larcom, *A New England Girlhood* (1889), or Susan Allen Toth, *Blooming: A Small-Town Girlhood* (1981). In a manner similar to Gates, Toth addresses her autobiography to her daughter; her

If we do, we can more easily recognize that *Colored People* presents a distinctly different, relational form of "I"-narrative, despite the resemblances I have noted to a more traditional coming-of-age conception of autobiography, a conception that Philippe Lejeune invoked when he defined autobiography as a *"retrospective prose narrative written by a real person concerning his own existence, where the focus is his individual life, in particular the story of his personality"* ("Autobiographical Pact" 4). If we apply Lejeune's definition to Gates's story, we would have to say that the focus is on Gates's individual life only part of the time. As for the story of his personality, I think we're left largely to our own devices to infer it, especially from Gates's discussion of his relation to his mother; the book's dominant mode is reporting and observation rather than introspective investigation of Gates's inner life. I would add, moreover, that it is precisely those ways in which *Colored People* differs from the Lejeunian model that make it a distinctly relational life. In saying this, I need to acknowledge that in one sense the text is, of course, an "I"-narrative first and last, for an "I" is always speaking, the "I" of Gates the ubiquitous cultural commentator on the contemporary scene, whose shrewd voice is well known to television audiences and to the readers of the *New Yorker*, the *Village Voice*, and other magazines. In this instance, the "I" functions as auto-ethnographer, the insider who explains to the uninitiated the customs, the way of life, of the African-American community of his childhood.

In order to sort out the relation between "we"-experience and "I"-narrative in *Colored People*, a comparison between Gates's autobiography and Zora Neale Hurston's *Dust Tracks on a Road* (1942) is instructive, a comparison Gates prompts us to make by quoting Hurston in an opening epigraph: "I remember the very day when I became colored."[32] Despite apparent similarities, the two narratives approach this proposition of "becoming colored"

---

narrative attempts to recover a vanished world, to recapture what it meant to "grow up in a small Midwestern college town in the 1950s" (3).

[32] Gates provides an "Afterword" to the HarperPerennial 1991 edition of *Dust Tracks*.

very differently. The chapter titles in Hurston's table of contents rehearse the familiar developmental course of so much traditional autobiography ("I Get Born," "Wandering," "School Again," and so forth), modulating eventually to a topical organization ("Love," "Religion") once the story of maturation and choice of career is complete. Accompanying this "I"-narrative, especially in the early chapters, is a good deal of information about the black community of Eatonville, Florida, where Hurston spent her childhood. Like Gates addressing his children in his preface, Hurston sounds a similarly ethnographic note on the opening page when she instructs the reader to look to her Eatonville beginnings for the sources of her life story: "So you will have to know something about the time and place where I came from, in order that you may interpret the incidents and directions of my life" (1). As if to prove this explanatory link between self and environment, the autobiographer conjures up a childhood self who was all ears when the community talked about itself. "Joe Clarke's store was the heart and spring of the town" (45), she writes, and the child was hungry for the gossip, "the adult double talk" she overheard as she crossed its porch ("I could and did drag my feet going in and out" [46]). Hurston the adult, the ethnographer trained by Franz Boas at Columbia, cherishes "the menfolks holding a 'lying' session . . . telling folks tales"—"how and why Sis Snail quit her husband" (47). Joe Clarke's porch serves as the stage where the community's narrative sense of itself is performed: here is where the commerce in self and life story is daily transacted; here is where Eatonville's narrative practices and identity narratives are on display. These pages are among the most memorable in *Dust Tracks*, and the reader intuits that the fresh images and arresting rhythms of Hurston's prose stem in no small part from the lively folk speech of this black oral culture.[33] The narrative testifies that, early and late, both Hurston

---

[33] Gates makes a similar point about the black "speech community" as a key source of inspiration for Hurston (see "Afterword" 264–65). See Carlson, who drew my attention to the interest of this section of *Dust Tracks*.

the child and Hurston the writer were shaped decisively by the Eatonville world of her youth.

As an individual and artist acutely conscious of her distinctiveness and difference, however, Hurston qualifies her initial assertion of the formative influence of her Eatonville childhood. Thus, at other points in her narrative, notably in the chapter "My People! My People!" she makes clear that she refuses race as an interpretative category that could provide the key to her self and story.[34] "Don't fence me in" seems to be the subtext of Hurston's identity narrative, and Maya Angelou, in her preface to the most recent edition of *Dust Tracks* (HarperPerennial, 1991), is only one of many critics who note that Hurston keeps her distance in this book. Like other readers before her, Angelou faults the autobiography both for its evasiveness about Hurston's private life and for its silence on racial issues.

Hurston herself, I think, helps to explain why the relation between "I" and "we" is so problematic in this text, why the ethnographer could find "Negro" culture to be a coherent object for fieldwork observation while the autobiographer could resolutely disavow any simple connection between that environment and her own identity: "I maintain that I have been a Negro three times—a Negro baby, a Negro girl and a Negro woman. Still, if you have received no clear cut impression of what the Negro in America is like, then you are in the same place with me. There is no *The Negro* here" (172). Angelou's strictures do not really address Hurston's point about the inadequacy of racial models of identity, while Gates's preface and narrative confirm that fifty years after *Dust Tracks* first appeared, the issue persists unresolved, with Gates going so far as to predict that the search for satisfactory identity categories—"African American," "people of color," "colored people"—will continue into his children's generation.

---

[34] See Fox-Genovese, who argues that Hurston aspired "to transcend the constraints of group identification" (82).

Colored People, in contrast to *Dust Tracks,* makes the link between self and environment directly and decisively: Gates presents Piedmont, West Virginia, as "the place where I learned how to be a colored boy" (4). This process of identity formation motivates Gates's loving description of the mill town's folkways, of the kitchen where his Mama did her neighbors' hair, of the buzz of gossip and racy stories in Mr. Comby Carroll's barbershop, of the churchgoing, the annual colored mill picnic, and much more. Gates's charming portrait of his Uncle Nemo (chapter 14, "Just Talking to the Lord"), who taught him to hunt and fish, represents the climax of his nostalgic treatment of his home town, the "world that nurtured and sustained me" (xi). Gates's obvious pleasure in these reminiscences, the gusto with which he savors the past, is infectious, and it is almost as though Gates himself were writing a blurb for his book when he evokes the sentimental burden of the word *colored,* his Proustian *madeleine:* "when I hear the word, I hear it in my mother's voice and in the sepia tones of my childhood."

There is more to life in Piedmont, however, than *sepia* can possibly convey, and his mother is indeed the key to the truth about the world of his past. Gates opens his portrait of his mother by recalling his anger when his daughter Maggie thoughtlessly cut him short. He had been "going on about Mama, . . . about how elegant, graceful, and beautiful she was when I was growing up": " 'Too bad she was never like that when *I* knew her,' Maggie called from the back seat" (29). Maggie has, unwittingly, touched a nerve by calling attention to the change that had overtaken her grandmother. We do not learn about the last phase of Mama's darkened life until the very end of the narrative, but the autobiographer offers the beginning of an explanation presently, when he singles out his mother's courage as her most important quality: "She did not seem to fear white people. She simply hated them, hated them with a passion she seldom disclosed" (34). But she did disclose this hatred to Skip in 1959, when she listened with passionate approval ("Amen") to Malcolm X's excoriation of whites as devils; again, looking at the Martin Luther King riots on television, Mama "watched the flames with dancing eyes" (35). Young Skip finds this fiery side of Mama "terrifying and thrilling," and also a surprising "revelation": "It was like watching the Wicked Witch of the West emerge out of the transforming features of Dorothy" (34).

Gates lived to witness a different and darker revelation about Mama's hatred. In the penultimate chapter of the autobiography, "Walk the Last Mile," he relates that, returning home from college one summer, he saw Mama "as if for the first time: so old and tired and despondent" (205). He and his father and brother contrive to fulfill what they believe to be her lifelong dream of owning a house by buying the home of her former employer. When Gates, baffled by his mother's refusal to move in, presses her for a reason, Mama finally tells him the truth:

> Skippy, you'll never know, she said.
>
> Then, haltingly, she began to talk.
>
> Mrs. Thomas used to make me sit out in the kitchen, at a little wooden table, and eat the scraps. She was a mean woman. She used to leave money around, to see if I would steal it. She made me work on Thanksgiving and Christmas. She treated me bad. . . . The thought of moving into this house . . . I wanted to burn this house down.
>
> Her eyes were glassy; she lowered her head, placing two fingers on the bridge of her nose. It was a gesture of resignation; she was angry that the memories still had that power. (206–7, ellipses in the original)

Shaken by her hurt and humiliation, Gates writes, "I'll never know if we did the right thing by buying her that house" (207).

The thesis of Gates's affectionate reconstruction of his childhood world is that, strangely enough, segregation had had beneficent consequences for Piedmont: blacks responded to their exclusion by creating a close-knit community of their own that did, as he says, sustain and nurture him as a child. Mama's devastating disclosure, however, reveals a different product of segregation, a corrosive hatred with the power to blight the dreams of a lifetime. Inheriting Mama's courage, Gates made it out of the closed circle of Piedmont; Mama didn't. In this sense, *sepia* shows as the autobiographer's luxury; there is nothing *sepia* about Mama. It is the fierce energy of his mother in her youth that drives the autobiography's most powerful prose, culminating in the son's magnificent elegy on the occasion of her death in 1987 (209–10). I am not sure that the autobiographer is prepared to pursue the darker phase of the Piedmont experience that the pages on Mama represent—hence what I think of as the double ending of *Colored People*, for after the chapter on Mama's last years, Gates returns—seeks refuge?—in the last chapter to the comfortable, celebratory *sepia* mode of the opening sections of the book. And so he turns back the narrative clock from 1987 to the last mill picnic in 1970, when "hundreds of Negroes gathered to say goodbye to themselves, their heritage, and their sole link to each other, wiped out of existence by the newly enforced anti–Jim Crow laws" (216). Gates's treatment here is snappy, indulgent, and as sentimental as anything in Harriet Beecher Stowe, and there is no question but that the picnic, the community's "most beloved, and cementing, ritual" (213), supplies a nice ending to the Piedmont story, reassembling for one final bow all the colorful characters of Gates's childhood—Mr. Comby Curl, Roebuck Johnson, Uncle Earkie, Uncle Nemo, and the rest.

While I believe that Gates's picture of his mother in her final years casts a longer and deeper shadow than he may have intended over his otherwise largely upbeat evocation of Piedmont, the autobiographical narrator is confident and authoritative in his knowledge of the place where he "learned how to be a colored boy." While all autobiographies, of course, report an analogous identity lesson, some, like Gates's, do so more explicitly and self-consciously than others, heightening their profile as relational lives. Whether or not the community's identity lesson is presented as well learned is another matter. Barbara J. Scot's *Prairie Reunion* (1995) is the story of one such lesson learned too well, and she seeks to teach a new one in its place. The narrators of *Dust Tracks* and *Colored People* impress me as already in possession of the knowledge they relate to us about their childhood worlds. By contrast, Scot sets out, belatedly, to discover the truth about her Iowa heritage. "For a long time I did not look back" (3), she writes in the opening line of her prologue, but now, past fifty, she feels ready to revisit the past in hopes of resolving her "confused resentment" (4) toward her mother and her own childhood.

Scot defines her project, which takes the form of a journey back to Iowa in June 1993, in distinctly relational terms: "The quest began as an attempt to understand my mother. It developed into a quest to understand myself and my own connections with the people and place of my childhood. Finally, it became a search to connect to the past of the land itself" (4). The motive for Scot's resentment and quest, we learn, lies in her fear of the disturbing parallel between her mother's life and her own: like her mother, she, too, "had married a profligate spender, . . . had been left alone with two babies and no money." "The thought of becoming my mother completely terrified me," she confesses (59). Her father's life had ended in suicide, and she, too, had flirted with suicide. The psychology of this autobiographical search is strangely paradoxical: she will repeat the past in an effort to exorcise the threat of repeating the past. Complicating the success of Scot's undertaking is the fact that her potentially dangerous identification with her mother is offset by her feminist repudiation of "the farm, the church, and the traditional woman's role—with its deference to men—which had been her [mother's] existence" (29).

I have suggested the ethnographic dimension in *Dust Tracks* and *Colored People*; in *Prairie Reunion* it is pervasive. Scot manages to orchestrate the delivery of a huge amount of social, cultural, and historical material in the most natural way, using the conventional framework of her actual journey to the country of the past as a loose structure for her inquiry. Scot delivers her own story in bits and pieces along the way, whereas her investigation of its environmental contexts is systematic and focused. This is the kind of narrative where you need maps and genealogical charts, and they are provided in an extensive appendix which also includes a series of documentary photographs. Specific chapters feature particular topics or themes: "The Holy Farm," "The Scots," "Faith of Our Fathers," "Women's Work," and so forth. Scot is by instinct a historian, and she sets her own history and that of her parents in a series of ever widening historical frames. She interprets the lives of her ne'er-do-well father and dutiful mother and herself as products of a repressive patriarchal Scottish Presbyterian culture; the four lines in her family genealogy—Hughes, Rickels, Clark, and Norris—seem to bind Scot like links in a chain to a deadly past.[35] In the later sections of the book, however, as she explores the collections of the local historical society, nearby Effigy Mounds National Monument, and prehistoric Hadfields Cave, Scot becomes increasingly aware not only of the much earlier, pre-Columbian history of the Woodland peoples, but also of vast expanses of geologic time stretching back 450 million years to a period when the Iowa settlement of her ancestors had been the site of "shallow warm-water seas" (185). Against this evolutionary backdrop, the legalistic Calvinist righteousness of the Scotch Grove Presbyterian Church seems diminished and ephemeral.

Scot's imagination, educated to a new resilience in the course of her research, manages at last to understand the rigidity of her mother's life with healing compassion. Appropriately, she draws on the artifacts of the early Woodland peoples of the area to fashion a metaphor for her mother's socially constructed identity:

> As surely as a vessel of Hadfields Cave, my mother reflected the intertwined strands that had molded her. The religion of the Scots, the mythology of the farm, the dignity of the women's ser-

---

[35] At several points in the narrative, Scot's identification with various women from the past—a nineteenth-century woman who bore an illegitimate child (138–39ff.), a precontact Indian woman (189)—suggest her desire to locate an alternative matrilineal tradition to the repressive Calvinist patriarchy of her youth.

vice had impressed on the vessel a tight, complicated pattern. For my mother, as for the Madison Ware, the walls were fine and thin. When the blow came, it spread throughout the vase in fractured lines. *To move would have meant to shatter into jagged shards. And so my mother remained still.* (209).

Although the mother had accepted, as the daughter could not, her place in the world that had formed her, Scot now recognizes that the shape of her mother's life, for all its personal tragedy, possessed nonetheless an austere beauty. Scot's own story, however, demonstrates the possibility of change, now that her deterministic fears of repeating her mother's life are safely behind her. She concludes by voicing aloud—as in a vow—her intention to restore the family farm to tallgrass prairie, a symbolic erasure of the painful human history she has labored to reconstruct.

Dealing with the Proximate Other

I have presented Silko's, Gates's, and Scot's narratives in considerable detail because they provide unusually comprehensive accounts of the social communities in which their earlier selves were formed. Theirs are situated selves, products of a particular time and place; the identity-shaping environments in these autobiographies are nested one within the other—self, family, community set in a physical and cultural geography, in an unfolding history (reaching back in Silko and Scot to the beginnings of the world). If this breadth of vision sets these narratives apart from most relational lives, however, they share with all the rest the conviction that the key environment in the individual's formation is the family, which serves as the community's primary conduit for the transmission of its cultural values. Not surprisingly, one important variety of relational autobiography takes the form of the family memoir, in which the lives of other family members are rendered as either equal in importance to or more important than the life of the reporting self. The following titles suggest something of the range of this form: Henry James, *A Small Boy and Others* (1913) and *Notes of a Son and Brother* (1914); Virginia Woolf, "A Sketch of the Past" (written in 1939–40); William Maxwell, *Ancestors: A Family History* (1971); Maureen Howard, *Facts of Life* (1978); Michael Ondaatje, *Running in the Family* (1982); Eudora Welty, *One Writer's Beginnings* (1984); Shirlee Taylor Haizlip, *The Sweeter the Juice: A Family Memoir in Black and White* (1994); and Mikal Gilmore, *Shot in the Heart* (1994).

In this section, however, I want to consider the most common form of the relational life, the self's story viewed through the lens of its relation with some key other person, sometimes a sibling, friend, or lover, but most often a parent—we might call such an individual the *proximate other* to signify the intimate tie to the relational autobiographer. Earlier, commenting on Carolyn Steedman's *Landscape for a Good Woman*, I presented the case she makes that she could approach her own life only by investigating its relation to her mother's. Mutatis mutandis, Steedman's argument articulates the rationale of these relational lives. Sometimes the relational autobiographer will go so far as to present the autobiography of the proximate other, as in the group of texts I discussed earlier—Kim Chernin's *In My Mother's House: A Daughter's Story* (1983), John Edgar Wideman's *Brothers and Keepers* (1984), Sally Morgan's *My Place* (1987), and Art Spiegelman's *Maus* volumes (1986, 1991). More often, however, the relational autobiographer settles for presenting an extended portrait—sometimes tantamount to a biography—of the proximate other. To give a sampling of characteristic recent titles that have impressed me in this large and growing literature, let me cite the following:

- *The father-son relation*: Philip Roth, *Patrimony: A True Story* (1991); Blake Morrison, *And When Did You Last See Your Father? A Son's Memoir of Love and Loss* (1993); and John Edgar Wideman, *Fatheralong: A Meditation on Fathers and Sons, Race and Society* (1994);

- *The mother-daughter relation*: Vivian Gornick, *Fierce Attachments: A Memoir* (1987); Drusilla Modjeska, *Poppy* (1990); and Janet Campbell Hale, *Bloodlines: Odyssey of a Native Daughter* (1993);

- *The father-daughter relation:* Mary Gordon, *The Shadow Man* (1996);

- *The mother-son relation:* Robert Dessaix, *A Mother's Disgrace* (1994), and James McBride, *The Color of Water: A Black Man's Tribute to His White Mother* (1996).

Complementing this extensive literature of children writing about their parents is a smaller but notable group of texts in which parents write about their children, most frequently because of a child's disability (for example, Michael Bérubé's *Life as We Know It: A Father, a Family, and an Exceptional Child* [1996]) or early death (for example, John Gunther's *Death Be Not Proud: A Memoir* [1949]).

When children write about their parents, the memoirs are as varied as the bonds they record. When the bond is untroubled, we are likely to get a memoir of a traditional sort, in which filial piety produces a memorial to a beloved parent—Calvin Trillin's *Messages from My Father* (1996) offers a characteristic and charming example. When the bond is conflicted, however, the motive for memoir is likely to be more intense, and a great number of relational lives could be classed under the heading of "unfinished business." These lives are set in motion by the existence of tensions and secrets; there is a disruption, distortion, or omission in the family narrative that must be repaired. Sometimes the secret takes the form of suppressing some shameful fact (Carolyn Steedman's illegitimacy) or identity (Sally Morgan's Aboriginal heritage); sometimes it is a question of repressing a death or loss and the guilts deriving from it (the death of Kim Chernin's older sister, the suicide of Art Spiegelman's mother). The autobiographical act in these cases affords the opportunity to speak the previously unspoken, to reveal what has been hidden or repressed. Week in, week out, relational lives are published that chronicle the damage done by the graver family troubles—alcoholism, mental illness, incest, and all the rest.

Children suffer when family bonds are abused; they also suffer from neglect and loss, and one of the most striking varieties of

the relational life concerns the parent who is—literally or figura-
tively—absent. I want to return to Steedman's assertion that
"children are always episodes in someone else's narrative." This
is a hard truth for children to accept, for we naturally assume
that we are not only the central but the exclusive figures in our
parents' lives. Part of the pain of growing up is learning otherwise. Sometimes, however, circumstances conspire to throw this
identity-altering shift in perspective into high relief. I want to
look at two narratives—Paul Auster's *The Invention of Solitude*
(1982) and Mary Gordon's *The Shadow Man* (1996)—that depict
the autobiographer's struggle to come to terms with Steedman's
insight. Auster and Gordon are doubly displaced, for the
parental narratives in which they figure as only episodes were
largely unknown to them. They make good this narrative deficit
by doubling the dose of narrative: their response to identity
handicap is not only to search out the elusive facts of their fathers' stories but to feature the story of this search. This story of
their stories structures the relational lives they write.

Paul Auster's two-part narrative, *The Invention of Solitude*, is triggered by his father's death, which the son recognizes as only the
latest installment in a lifelong history of "absence." Haunted by
his father's lack of substance—"my father had left no traces"—
Auster's immediate impulse is to write about him: "If I do not act
quickly, his entire life will vanish along with him" (6). Proceed-
ing to reconstruct the meager facts of his father's life in the
memoir's first part, "Portrait of an Invisible Man," he performs a
tour de force, for the father seems to be the most unpromising
biographical subject imaginable. "It was as though his inner life
eluded even him" (20), Auster comments. "Often, he seemed . . .
to forget where he was, as if he had lost the sense of his own continuity" (29). Digging deeper, however, into his father's boyhood
past in Kenosha, Wisconsin, Auster learns that on January 23,
1919, his grandmother had shot and killed his grandfather, with
his father, age nine, looking on. This family trauma seems to
Auster to "explain a great deal" (36) about his father: the psychic

wound inflicted, Auster surmises, taught his father "never to trust anyone. Not even himself" (50).

In the memoir's second, and longer, part, "The Book of Memory," Auster writes about himself in the third person, continuing the theme of distanced identity that he pursued in his father's story: "A. realizes, as he sits in his room writing The Book of Memory, he speaks of himself as another in order to tell the story of himself" (154). In contrast to the absent father in "Portrait of an Invisible Man," however, "The Book of Memory" presents alternative, and more satisfying stories of fathers and sons: Auster experiences with an older man (a Russian named "S.") what it felt like to have a father, and he relates his own passionate love for his son Daniel—"the boy's life meant more to him than his own" (109–10). Yet if in some ways Auster seems so different from his ghostly father, whom he defines in terms of absence of affect, in other ways the son seems curiously fated to repeat the father's life. "The Book of Memory" stresses Auster's isolation, portraying him as "a man sitting alone in a room" (76). Uncannily, disturbingly, Auster describes himself in terms that echo his earlier description of his father: "He feels himself sliding through events, hovering like a ghost around his own presence, as if he were living somewhere to the side of himself—not really here, but not anywhere else either" (78).

On the face of it, Mary Gordon's situation is radically different from Auster's. She was the daughter of a doting father who treated her to lavish displays of affection. So central is the father's love to the child's sense of her own identity that his early death when she is seven creates a profound sense of lack, of want, that Gordon in her forties—successful novelist, happily married, with a child of her own—is still trying to fill. Auster could be speaking for Gordon when he observes, wisely, "You do not stop hungering for your father's love, even after you are grown up" (19). Now, in midlife, however, when Gordon sets out to recover her father and his story, she discovers that she wasn't the central figure in his life. Archival research in Washington, in

Providence, and in Lorain, Ohio, turns into a painful process of disconfirmation in which everything she thought she knew about her father turns out to have been a lie: reinventing himself (like Fitzgerald's Jay Gatsby), David Gordon had edited his siblings, his working-class childhood, and an earlier marriage out of his story, passing himself off as a Harvard graduate, who had converted later on to Catholicism. The records disclose an unattractive stranger, a disreputable man-on-the-make, an Eastern European Jew who wrote for pornographic magazines in which he indulged in anti-Semitic jokes. Struggling to reconcile the idealized image of childhood memory with the stubborn truth of the biographical record, Gordon even attempts briefly to assume her father's identity in order to understand it, conjuring up the immigrant Jewish child's oppressive sense of being burdened with the "wrong" identity to succeed in the American culture of his day.

The turning point in her quest comes when she concludes that "David Gordon is a man I cannot know." Refusing to be merely an episode in his story, she appropriates him for her own: "The man I know is a man I gave birth to. His name is not David. . . . It is My Father" (194). Her act of possession is as total as she can make it. Not only does she "give birth to" her father in this narrative, but she literally revises his death as well: in the final section of *The Shadow Man* Gordon has her father's body exhumed from its place in her mother's family's plot and reburied in Calvary, a cemetery of her own choosing. This is certainly extravagant stuff, as Gordon is certainly aware. On the day of the reburial, she writes: "I thank my father and my mother for the gift of their extreme, excessive, passionate, exclusive love" (273). Gordon and Auster conclude that the story of the proximate other is ultimately unknowable. For Gordon, moreover, it proves to be a story she would prefer not to know, for it can't be integrated into her own identity narrative. Because this story can't be told, it is overlaid in these cases with the story of the story to give it structure, body, and substance. I suspect that this need accounts for the considerable amount of overwriting that mars these otherwise powerful narratives.

I want to round out this account of the relational life by mentioning a couple of interesting variations. In *The Enigma of Arrival* (1987), V. S. Naipaul works a daring extension of the form by transacting his own story in terms of the lives of others who are neither family nor intimates—merely accidental acquaintances whom Naipaul meets in his isolated life in the English countryside. The stunning, genre-breaking originality of this autobiographical work is overwhelming, and I am not sure that the book has been well served by Naipaul's decision to call it a novel. The mood of the narrative is cool, detached, brooding; the writer's vision is profoundly historical. Here, truly, the relational life is seen *sub specie aeternitatis*—Naipaul's, anyone's. Change—social and cultural—is the great theme in these pages, and Naipaul argues that his "I"-narrative is properly understood as a tiny part of the great diaspora of our time: "In 1950 in London I was at the beginning of that movement of peoples that was to take place in the second half of the twentieth century—a movement and a cultural mixing greater than the peopling of the United States, . . . a movement between all the continents" (141). "Men need history," Naipaul observes; "it helps them to have an idea of who they are" (353).

Naipaul's philosophic acceptance of the relational nature of all lives isn't easily achieved, however, and there are those, such as Brent Staples and Mikal Gilmore, who seek to escape the bonds of relational identity as an act of self-preservation. In the dramatic opening to *Parallel Time: Growing Up in Black and White* (1994), journalist Brent Staples recalls the sight of his brother Blake's bullet-ridden body on the coroner's table. In the antirelational life that follows, Staples narrates the story of his flight from family, from a world that had left his brother, a drug dealer, dead at twenty-two. Even as he stresses his distance from his family—"as a child I was never where I was" (9)—Staples asserts its central place in his life: Blake, the murdered brother, emerges as a kind of alter ego for Brent, the self who didn't manage to escape the dangerous environment of his youth. Staples the University of Chicago Ph.D., Staples the nationally syndicated columnist, continues to wrestle with his dangerous family legacy; the stark fact of Blake's death calls him back to the past and to this narrative. He closes his story with a description of a family photograph: "I stand apart from this portrait, studying my family from a distance. This is the way it has always been" (274).

Can we, though, really keep our distance from our families? In *Shot in the Heart* (1994), Mikal Gilmore struggles to convince himself that he has done so. And he has every reason to hope that he has, for he is the brother of Gary Gilmore, one of the nation's most notorious murderers, executed by firing squad in Utah in January, 1978. Gilmore understandably resents the deterministic thesis lurking in his inevitable identification as Gary Gilmore's brother, the notion that anyone who emerges from a family that produced a murderer "must also be formed by the same causes, the same evil, must in some way also be responsible for the violence that resulted" (358). Yet the premise of the book, displayed in its title, is that Mikal Gilmore, like Gary, was in some profound way shot in the heart by his raw and brutal formation in the crucible of Gilmore family violence. As the Gilmore and Staples narratives testify, the relational autobiographer in the act of writing does indeed stand apart, studying family from a distance, and the sense of detachment, of separation, that this posture affords is doubtless one of its primary attractions. Photographs of family, however, of the individual as part of the group, remain stubbornly intact, setting up a kind of tension between the reality of the collectively assembled bodies and the individual's story of the journey away from them told in the accompanying life story. Many relational lives include a substantial number of family photographs—Gilmore prints forty, strategically displayed throughout the book—and it would be hard to say, finally, whether the photographs *accompany* the text in such cases, or vice versa, especially since the photographs almost invariably precede the text in the unfolding chronology of identity documents. As the Gilmore photographs suggest, Mikal's text is one long struggle to interpret the meaning of his place in the family circle.

The Self as Other

John Updike has identified autobiographical writing as a way of coping with the otherwise "unbearable" knowledge "that we age and leave behind this litter of dead, unrecoverable selves" (226). In this sense, the selves we have been may seem to us as discrete and separate as the other persons with whom we live our relational lives. This experiential truth points to the fact that our sense of continuous identity is a fiction, the primary fiction of all self-narration. Occasionally, autobiographers remind us of this fact by casting their identity narratives in the form of an *intra*subjective dialogue—between "you" and "I" in Nathalie Sarraute's *Childhood* (1983), and between "you" and "she" in Christa Wolf's *Patterns of Childhood* (1976). Most autobiographers, however, proclaim the continuous identity of selves early and late, and they do so through the use of the first person, autobiography's most distinctive—if problematic—generic marker: the "I" speaking in the present—the utterer—is somehow continuous with the "I" acting in the past—the subject of the utterance. This simultaneous double reference of first-person autobiographical discourse to the present and the past masks the disruptions of identity produced by passing time and memory's limitations.

I have chosen Christa Wolf's *Patterns of Childhood* to illustrate the problems involved in autobiographers' use of the memory-based concept of continuous identity precisely because this text rejects any easy acceptance of this fiction as fact. Wolf's narrative deconstructs the notion that who we were and who we are now can be said in any simple sense to be the same person: as David Malouf reminds us in his brilliant memoir of childhood, "12 Edmondstone Street," the body changes, consciousness changes, memories change, and identity changes too, whether we like it or not. Thus Wolf's text does not employ the first person, signaling to the reader that the genre's conventional assumption of continuous identity is not operating in her self-narration in the familiar way. Here the narrator speaks not as "I" but as "you," and she addresses her earlier self not as "I" or Christa but as "she"— her earlier self even has a different name: Nelly.[36] Yet *Patterns of Childhood* is indeed Wolf's self-narration, an *intra*relational life which works steadily, as we shall see, to reforge the link between selves past and present. Wolf recognizes continuous identity not only as a fiction of memory but also as an existential fact, necessary for our psychological survival amid the flux of experience.

Looking back some twenty-five years after the end of World War II, the German novelist seeks to understand her own participation in the pernicious ideology of the Third Reich: as a teenager, she had been an ardent member of a Hitler youth group. But how, the narrator asks, can she connect with an earlier self she has repudiated and repressed? How to begin, when at least three distinct stories claim her attention? In this intricately layered narrative, Wolf tracks all three chronologies of her inquiry into the past simultaneously: Nelly's childhood in the 1930s through World War II up to 1946, the narrator's trip to Poland to revisit Nelly's childhood home in July 1971, and the narrator's writing of Nelly's story from November 1972 to 1975. What, Wolf would have us ask, can possibly bind these periods of personal history together? Memory? Narrative? Identity? The use of the first person? "We would suffer continuous estrangement from ourselves," she observes, "if it weren't for our memory of the things we have done, of the things that have happened to us. If it weren't for the memory of ourselves" (4).

Does memory indeed provide a basis for continuous identity,

---

[36] Like Silko's *Storyteller*, Wolf's autobiography violates Philippe Lejeune's notion of the autobiographical pact and the related convention that author, narrator, and protagonist of an autobiographical text share the same name and identity (see "Autobiographical Pact"). Contributing to this scrambling of autobiography's conventional generic signals, the back cover of the paperback edition identifies *Patterns of Childhood* as "a novel."

uniting us to our acts, our experiences, our earlier selves? For Wolf's narrator, who cannot say "I" to herself, to remember is to fall into "a time shaft, at the bottom of which the child sits on a stone step, in all her innocence, saying 'I' to herself for the first time in her life" (5). This initial probe into the past, into her earliest childhood memory, however, only deepens the narrator's sense of self-estrangement; time and the narrator's "unreliable memory" make Nelly, her earlier self, "inaccessible" to her. This sense of rupture, moreover, is compounded when she interprets the child's discovery of the first person as a rupture in its turn: the child who says "I" "severs himself from the third person in which he has thought of himself up to that point" (7). The use of the first person, then, provides no shield against self-estrangement, early and late. No wonder, then, that the narrator proceeds warily, speaking of herself as an "intruding stranger" (119) who approaches Nelly sometimes with diffidence, more often with aggression. She reminds us endlessly of the limits of her knowledge of Nelly, for Nelly, in turn, is another stranger.

The narrator's refusal of the first person, her "strange" (3) choice of the second and third persons to portray her relation to her earlier self—these rhetorical moves mirror Nelly's psychological situation, the fissure in the fiction of continuous identity wrought by the trauma of the war. One of Wolf's great achievements in *Patterns* is her reconstruction of Nelly's progressive sense of dissociation, giving us the etiology of the narrator's view of her earlier self as a "third person." The early stages show us a child splitting in two, acting and observing at the same time and learning to fib (131–32). Sensitively attuned to how others see her, Nelly learns "to cheat herself out of her true feelings" (160). By the time she embraces the heroic fantasies of her Hitler youth group, she has waded so far into denial, she has become so practiced in dissimulation and self-deception, that it takes the screams of a refugee mother at the death of her frozen baby to shock Nelly into the collapse of her illusions in the last days of the war; her brain shuts down, leaving a "memory gap" (281).

Nelly becomes a refugee herself, fleeing with her family across a ravaged landscape, putting Germany's recent past and her own behind her, or so it would seem. The flight becomes a metaphor for the movement of Nelly's consciousness from manifold fears and "inner alienation" (231) into a general "emotional numbness" (297) and disintegration. Wolf interprets Nelly's subsequent recovery during the Occupation as a kind of "emergency maturity" whose premise is "being quite unfamiliar with herself" (350); Nelly, she believes, had become a new person (368, 379).

As the narrator reconstructs it, then, Nelly's story opens and closes with discontinuities of identity: the child sitting on the stone step saying "I" and the teenager at the end of the war are both dissociated from the selves they had been. The curious result, however, is that the narrator's dissociation from Nelly becomes one more link in a lengthening chain of dissociations. Thus the rhetorical premise (the refusal of "I") designed to represent the autobiographer's disidentification with her early self is steadily controverted by parallel behaviors that reveal the underlying continuities between identities early and late.[37] What Nelly feared then, the narrator fears now: their participation in the enormities of the Third Reich—Kristallnacht, the final solution, the camps. Amnesia, fueled by fear, binds them together. When the narrator revisits the site where Nelly's Jungmädel unit held its rallies, she finds that she cannot recall a single face:

> Where Nelly's participation was deepest, where she showed devotion, where she gave of herself, all relevant details have been obliterated. Gradually, one might assume. And it isn't difficult to guess the reason: the forgetting must have gratified a deeply insecure awareness which, as we all know, can instruct our memory behind our own backs, such as: Stop thinking about it. Instruc-

---

[37] We need to recognize an inevitable circularity in the evidence here, keeping in mind that everything that we know about Nelly is supplied by the autobiographical narrator performing an act of retrospect twenty-five years after the fact. Wolf's narrator projects a lively sense of the extent to which she may be manipulating the character Nelly for purposes of her own: "Aren't you fooling yourself by thinking that this child is moving on her own, according to her own inner laws? . . . The child is your vehicle" (210).

tions that are faithfully followed through the years. Avoid certain memories. Don't speak about them. Suppress words, sentences, whole chains of thought, that might give rise to remembering. Don't ask your contemporaries certain questions. Because it is unbearable to think the tiny word "I" in connection with the word "Auschwitz." "I" in the past conditional: I would have. I might have. I could have. Done it. Obeyed orders. (229–30)

To speak in the first person, then, is to assume the burden of history in the face of the collective repression of an entire generation determined not to wake up, to remember (149, 154). From this perspective, Wolf's seemingly unusual choice to write about her earlier self in the second and third persons seems if anything overdetermined. No wonder, too, that the act of composition was halting and protracted.[38]

The narrator's perseverance in the process of anamnesis and identity reconstruction despite her manifold ambivalences and fears recalls Nelly's courage at the end of the war in willing her battered identity into a form of "emergency maturity." In returning to the past, she confronts the identity costs of Nelly's premature, accelerated maturation, deferred and repressed; whether the costs can ever be repaid is another story. Wolf's narrator, however, doesn't claim therapeutic power to heal the wounds that experience and history visited upon her identity. She wisely concludes:

> The child who was hidden in me—has she come forth? Or has she been scared into looking for a deeper, more inaccessible hiding place? . . . And the past, which can still split the first person into the second and the third—has its hegemony been broken? . . . I don't know. (406)

In the light of the existential imperative driving our claims to continuous identity, it is hardly surprising that an autobiogra-

[38] For characteristic passages on the difficulties encountered in writing this narrative, see, e.g., 164, 357–58.

pher should have such doubts. As makers themselves, autobiographers are primed to recognize the constructed nature of the past, yet they need at the same time to believe that in writing about the past they are performing an act of recovery: narrative teleology models the trajectory of continuous identity, reporting the supreme fiction of memory as fact. "You" and "I" and "she" and "he" and "we"—the dialogic play of pronouns in these texts tracks the unfolding of relational identity in many registers, in discourse with others and within ourselves. The lesson these identity narratives are teaching, again and again, is that the self is dynamic, changing, and plural.

CHAPTER THREE

Storied Selves:
Identity through Self-Narration

> . . . a model of the human subject that takes acts of *self-narration* not only as descriptive of the self but, more importantly, as *fundamental to the emergence and reality of that subject.*
>
> —Anthony Paul Kerby

Although we often speak of "life stories" and (frequently now) of "life writing," the relation such phrases pose between the individual's experience and its representation deserves more scrutiny than we usually give it. Is it, in fact, anything more than literary convention that prompts most autobiographers to write their lives as narrative? We know perfectly well that life certainly isn't a story, at least not in any simple, literary sense, and we also know that a person isn't a book, even though Walt Whitman, for one, urges the reader of *Leaves of Grass* to think so when he emotes extravagantly, "Camerado, this is no book, / Who touches this touches a man." Some version of this linked notion of self and story, nevertheless, is lurking whenever autobiographical practices are engaged, for life writing—whatever else it is or may be—certainly involves the assumption that the self and its experiences may somehow be represented in a text.[1]

---

[1] In speaking of *life writing* I mean to be as expansive and inclusive as possible. Even though print is the medium with which I am chiefly concerned, I hasten to add that other media also lend themselves to self-representation, notably photography and film. I maintain nonetheless that the success with which vari-

To speak of self-representation in this way, however, involves familiar but potentially misleading distinctions between experience and expression, content and form, distinctions that need to be set aside if we are to achieve a useful understanding of what I call *narrative identity* in the pages that follow. When it comes to autobiography, *narrative* and *identity* are so intimately linked that each constantly and properly gravitates into the conceptual field of the other.[2] Thus, narrative is not merely a literary form but a mode of phenomenological and cognitive self-experience, while self—the self of autobiographical discourse—does not necessarily precede its constitution in narrative. I have always been convinced that narrative occupies a central and determining place in the autobiographical enterprise, but I now make a much bolder claim for its function in self-representation. Initially, following Paul Ricoeur and others who argue that narrative is the supremely temporal form, I regarded narrative as peculiarly suited on the grounds of verisimilitude to the task of representing our lives in time. Later on, inspired by Jerome Bruner and the "narrative psychologists," I asked whether the self could be said to be narratively structured. I concluded that self and story were "complementary, mutually constituting aspects of a single process of identity formation" (*Touching* 198). In this view, narrative is not merely an appropriate form for the expression of identity; it is an identity content.

Oliver Sacks nicely captures this intimate linkage of narrative and identity in a provocative observation he makes in one of his case studies in *The Man Who Mistook His Wife for a Hat* (1985). In the case in question, concerning a patient with Korsakov's syndrome, Sacks highlights the role of memory in sustaining the individual's sense of continuous identity. "Mr. Thompson," who "remembered nothing for more than a few seconds" (109), was obliged to "*literally make himself (and his world) up every moment.*"

---

ous media manage the task of self-representation will be directly proportional to the presence of a sustaining *narrative* structure.

[2] See Bruner's illuminating discussion in "Life as Narrative" for an analogous and related treatment of the way in which *life* and *narrative* feed into each other, interpenetrating and overlapping.

Sacks concludes, memorably, "It might be said that each of us constructs and lives a 'narrative,' and that this narrative *is* us, our identities" (110). I have quoted this passage frequently in recent years, but what exactly does it mean to claim that such a self-narrative "*is* us, our identities"? In what sense can a narrative about identity be said to be equivalent to that same identity? Or is it rather that identity can be said to be a narrative of some kind? Readers of autobiography can easily concede the literal truth of this equivalence of identity and narrative in the lives they read, for the selves they encounter in such texts are obviously constituted through narrative. Moreover, in acknowledging that these textual selves are narratively produced, readers might distance themselves from any notion of the self as a preexisting endowment of some kind that the individual would proceed to express in autobiography.[3]

Sacks, however, is not talking here about writing autobiography, which most of us never get around to doing anyway, but rather about *living* autobiography, performing it in our daily lives. Narrative and identity are performed simultaneously—frantically in the case of "Mr. Thompson"—in a single act of self-narration; the self in question is a self defined by and transacted in narrative process. What is arresting about this radical equation between narrative and identity is the notion that narrative here is not merely *about* the self but rather in some profound way a constituent part *of* self—of the self, I should be careful to specify, that is expressed in self-narrations, for narrative is not (and cannot be) coextensive with all of selfhood, given the multiple registers of selfhood, about which I will say more in a moment. It follows that the writing of autobiography is properly understood as an integral part of a lifelong process of identity formation in which acts of self-narration play a major part. In the first section

[3] Kerby offers a strong version of this view: "On a narrative account, the self is to be construed not as a prelinguistic given that merely employs language, much as we might employ a tool, but rather as a product of language—what might be called the *implied subject* of self-referring utterances. The self, or subject, then becomes a result of discursive praxis rather than either a substantial entity having ontological priority over praxis or a self with epistemological priority, an originator of meaning" (4).

of this chapter I will examine the role of narrative practices in the emergence of what Ulric Neisser terms *the extended self* in early childhood; in the second section I investigate the consequences for identity when those practices are interrupted, function irregularly, or are never engaged in the first place.

One last word at the outset: I have suggested that Sacks's radical claim for an equivalence between narrative and identity—"this narrative *is* us, our identities"—may seem unlikely and indeed extravagant: how could a story be presumed to stand for all that we believe we are? Of course, it couldn't, not if we accept the expanded notion of selfhood presented in Chapter 1, with its manifold registers of neural, psychological, social, and cultural experience. There I presented Ulric Neisser's fivefold model of self-experience as a plausibly comprehensive account of our current knowledge of human subjectivity, and it is important to recall that Neisser's first two "selves," the ecological and interpersonal, are characterized by direct perception unmediated by reflexive consciousness of any kind. Because these registers of self are normally inaccessible to conscious awareness, they are unavailable for self-representation.[4] Of Neisser's three reflexive selves, the extended, the private, and the conceptual, the extended self—the self of memory and anticipation, the self in time—is the earliest to emerge, normally by the age of three, and I shall argue in the rest of this chapter that this self constitutes the foundation of the self represented in autobiography, providing a proto-narrative, temporal armature that supports and sustains our operative sense of who we are.

The Narrative Culture of Memory in Early Childhood

"Jacaranda, oleander . . . oleander, jacaranda"

What does it mean to be "an extended self"? What does the child's experience of extended selfhood look like? The British

---

[4] But see the section titled "The Embodied Self" in Chapter 1 for commentary on the rare cases (Sacks and Hull) that afford glimpses of the ecological self.

novelist Penelope Lively gives a memorable answer in the first scene of her crisp, shrewd memoir of her early years in Egypt, *Oleander, Jacaranda: A Childhood Perceived* (1994). She concedes in the preface that "the experience of childhood is irretrievable," and that even "the headful of brilliant frozen moments" that survive is "already dangerously distorted by the wisdoms of maturity." She proposes nonetheless to translate this haunting residue of images into language in search of clues to "the way in which the child sees" (vii). Boldly setting aside her prefatory reservations, Lively inaugurates her project with a plunge back into the consciousness of herself as a six- or seven-year-old girl riding in a car from Cairo to Heliopolis. We enter the child's mind precisely at the moment when she herself becomes aware that she can revisit the past, when she realizes that passing time through which she travels, carrying her inexorably forward into the future, will create—paradoxically—the possibility of repeating the present now past, fostering continuities of self and experience:

> We are going by car from Bulaq Dakhrur to Heliopolis. I am in the back. The leather of the seat sticks to my bare legs. We travel along a road lined at either side with oleander and jacaranda trees, alternate splashes of white and blue. I chant, quietly: "Jacaranda, oleander . . . Jacaranda, oleander . . . " And as I do so there comes to me the revelation that in a few hours' time we shall return by the same route and that I shall pass the same trees, in reverse order—oleander, jacaranda, oleander, jacaranda—and that, by the same token, I can look back upon myself of now, of this moment. I shall be able to think about myself now, thinking this—but it will be then, not now.
>
> And in due course I did so, and perceived with excitement the chasm between past and future, the perpetual slide of the present. As, writing this, I think with equal wonder of the irretrievable child, and of the eerie relationship between her mind and mine. She is myself, but a self which is unreachable except by means of such miraculously surviving moments of being: the alien within. (1)

It is language that triggers the child's "revelation" of the extension of experience and self across time, and with it the proto-autobiographical possibility of repetition of the past with the experiencing self at its center—"I shall be able to think about myself now, thinking this." The power of the passage, its immediacy, lies not so much with the conventional signaling of a child's perception conveyed by the present tense and the simplicity of the opening sentences but rather in the rhythmic chanting that expresses the child's processing of experience: we almost see the seeing, the passage from an unreflecting marking of the trajectory through space to a reflexive and then self-reflexive grasp that a memory and a remembering self are in the making. According to Lively, even as the child realizes that she can repeat the present, that she will be able to pass by "the same route," observing "the same trees" and "by the same token" the same self, she also has an inkling that she cannot quite do so: "I can look back upon myself of now . . . but it will be then, not now." If language promotes the idea of the extension of self across time, it also points to its undoing: "jacaranda, oleander" gives way to "oleander, jacaranda" as "now" becomes "not now." (Adopting the child's chant as the title of her memoir, Lively underscores the narrative implications of the child's realization of retrospect's "reverse order.") The child intuits and the autobiographer confirms that repetition of past and self is always repetition with a difference: "she is myself"; she is "the alien within."

There is much in the passage that seems to confirm the findings of developmental psychology (as Lively points out)—the dialectical interplay between experience and emergent selfhood, the passage from unmediated to reflexive self-awareness, the enabling role of language. But how reliable is this account of childhood perception? How much can the autobiographer's memory recover after a lapse of fifty years? Lively herself is at once skeptical and believing, and she adds an additional long paragraph of commentary in which she replays this early memory as if to disarm her doubts—and the reader's. In the vein of Wordsworth's "Intimations" ode, she speaks of "the rainbow experience we have all lost but of which we occasionally retrieve a brilliant glimpse," affirming that "something of the reality of the moment survives this destructive weight of wisdom and rationality." The ground of her appeal to truth is memory. Note in the following sequence of sentences how the voice of retrospective commentary slides into the voice of childhood perception as the passage blends selves early and late ("my mind," "my knees," "I see still," "I roll") in a charged moment of reenactment and recovery:

> In my mind, there is still the tacky sensation of the leather car seat which sticks to the back of my knees. I see still the bright flower-laden trees. I roll the lavish names around on the tongue: "Jacaranda, oleander . . . "

And so she concludes that the child's "private" perception—"the significance of it and the excitement"—can be "shared" with the adult autobiographer, "myself" (2). Somehow, she claims, the re-iterated impossibility of her project notwithstanding, her reconstruction of childhood perception works.[5]

I have chosen the episode from *Oleander, Jacaranda* precisely for the paradigmatic clarity with which it displays a child's self-conscious awareness of extended selfhood. Experience, self, time—each is bound up with the other in the little girl's mind. She grasps the foundation of autobiographical retrospect ("in reverse order"), anticipating that her memory of the trip will also be a memory of herself experiencing the trip. Interestingly, these recognitions are generated by her intuition of the spatial/temporal structure of her movement through the flowering trees; "jacaranda, oleander . . . oleander, jacaranda"—it is this embryonic narrative form that will preserve the present episode for recall later on, "in a few hours' time" and fifty years later as well, as the memoir's title suggests.[6] But the child in question, riding through the Egyptian heat and dust, is already six or seven,

---

[5] Nathalie Sarraute's *Childhood* records an analogous struggle to recover the experience of childhood consciousness.

[6] Barsalou speculates that "children's ability to extend the metaphor of space may ultimately determine when they begin to view events [in terms of extended time lines]" (235).

whereas developmental psychologists agree in dating the emergence of extended selfhood to a considerably earlier period, from age 2½ to about 4. That is to say that children may possess an operative sense of their place in time well before achieving the remarkable reflexive "revelation" of it described by Lively. In turning to recorded self-narrations of children themselves, their "memory talk," moreover, we can deal with testimony unclouded by the limitations of adult retrospect.

Memory and Autobiography; Autobiographical Memory

In *Fictions in Autobiography* I argued that from a developmental perspective, self emerges at the moment when language is acquired. "Self and language," I suggested, "are mutually implicated in a single, interdependent system of symbolic behavior" (192). The discussion of "memory talk" that follows seeks to sharpen this general proposition about the origins of self in three key respects. First, given the registers of self-experience presented in Chapter 1, I have identified the self in question as the extended self. Second, I will specify the phase of language acquisition involved as the achievement of narrative competence. Finally, following Katherine Nelson, I will argue that "memory talk" inaugurates what she terms "the personal memory system" (*Language* 179): these early conversations between children and their caregivers lay the foundation for adult life writing much later on. In order to examine "memory talk" productively, however, I need first to make some preliminary observations about the relation between memory and autobiography.

The latest developments in brain science today confirm the extent to which memory, the would-be anchor of selves and lives, constructs the materials from the past that an earlier, more innocent view would have us believe it merely stored. As we saw in Chapter 1, Israel Rosenfield argues that memories share the constructed nature of all brain events: "recollection is a kind of perception, . . . *and every context will alter the nature of what is recalled*" (*Invention* 89, emphasis added). The discussion of memory that follows, then, unfolds against a constructivist backdrop, a sense that our representations of reality—literary, psychological, neurological—are dynamic and constructed rather than static and mimetic in nature.[7]

Brain research is one thing, however, and writing memoirs another. The overwhelming majority of autobiographers continue to place their trust in the concept of an invariant memory that preserves the past intact, allowing the original experience to be repeated in present consciousness. In the celebrated episode of the *petite madeleine* dipped in tea, Marcel Proust gives the dream version of invariant memory: "eat, drink, and the past shall be yours," the passage seems to say. And who can resist the appeal of the Proustian sacrament of memory? The eating of the cake and the drinking of the tea trigger an ecstasy of recall in which the very "souls" of past things, all the "residue of Combray," "overcome death and return to share our life."[8] From Wordsworth right up to Lively, epiphanies of recall like Proust's abound in autobiography: "I see still the bright flower-laden trees." Such ecstasies notwithstanding, students of memory today hold that past experience is necessarily—both psychologically and neurologically—*constructed* anew in each memory event or act of recall. Memories, then, are constructed, and memory itself, moreover, is plural. Despite the traditional notion of memory as a single mental faculty varying only in strength and accessibility, memory is not, Larry R. Squire reminds us, "a single faculty but consists of different systems that depend on different brain structures and connections" (198).

First, some definitions. In his survey of memory research by Endel Tulving and many others, cognitive psychologist Daniel L. Schacter identifies three major memory systems: "*semantic memory*, which contains conceptual and factual knowledge," "*proce-*

---

[7] Surveying memory research in the twentieth century, Schacter emphasizes the "constructivist" tendency of recent findings ("Memory" 12–13).

[8] For the *petite madeleine* episode, see Proust 1:33–36. Sheringham wisely cautions, "Memory in Proust is by no means a purely joyous affair," for it displays "a power to disrupt and problematize identity" (292).

dural memory, which allows us to learn skills and acquire habits," and "*episodic memory,* which allows us explicitly to recall the personal incidents that uniquely define our lives" (*Searching* 17).[9] Of special interest to students of autobiography is the emergence of a particular variety of episodic memory that these researchers refer to as *autobiographical memory,* "enduring chronologically sequenced memory for significant events from one's own life" (Nelson, *Language* 162). Noting the delayed onset of autobiographical memory, which emerges "only during the later preschool years, 3½ to 4 years on average," the developmental psychologist Katherine Nelson tackles the perplexing phenomenon of infantile amnesia, "a total blocking of memories, usually prior to about 3 years, and . . . a significant lack of many accessible memories relative to later memories between 3 and 6 years" (157).[10] She plunges to the heart of the matter when she notes that "the important question to ask is not 'Why does forgetting occur?' but 'What is the function of memory for a one-time experience?' " (158).

Since it has been established that very young children do in fact have episodic memories (162), it becomes reasonable to ask why they don't retain them. Rejecting any Freudian notion of repression, Nelson embraces instead an evolutionary perspective which prompts her to focus on the *function* of event-memories: "As an adaptive system, the general function of memory is to predict and prepare for future encounters, actions, and experiences. That is, memory as such has no value in and of itself, but takes on value only as it contributes to the individual's ability to behave adaptively" ("Ontogeny" 265). In early childhood, accordingly, memory work is dedicated to the generation of general event-memories or scripts that help to organize the child's knowledge of daily routines—bathing, eating, going to bed, and so forth. In this early developmental context, Nelson reasons,

---

[9] Tulving's distinction between *semantic* and *episodic* memory (1972) marks a turning point in the modern classification of memory systems.
[10] Nelson draws here on Pillemer and White's 1989 summary of the relevant research.

memory for novel experience (the one-time event that at a later stage will be valued and stored as autobiographical memory) "does not have the same functional value, *unless it is repeated*" (*Language* 158), and so, if it is not incorporated into a general event-memory, it is not retained.

With the acquisition of language, however, and the beginnings of "memory talk," the child discovers new uses for memory, passing from "memories of the future" to memories of the past.[11] "The distinctive thing about the autobiographical memory system," Nelson observes, "is that the memories it contains do appear to be valued for themselves."[12] The interpersonal, relational dimension of identity formation that I presented in Chapter 2 comes into play here, for Nelson stresses that "the autobiographical memory system is a product of social and cultural construction":

> Sharing memories with others is in fact a prime social activity . . . learned in early childhood, and the result of this learning is the establishment of a store of memories that are shareable and ultimately reviewable by the individual, forming a personal history that has its own value independent of the general memory function of prediction and preparation for future events.
> ("Ontogeny" 266–67)

If we accept this account of the comparatively late emergence of autobiographical memory in early childhood, it does much to explain the fragmentary quality of the earliest memories claimed by most adults. Joyce got it right in the opening lines of *A Portrait of the Artist as a Young Man* when he conjured up those bits of the past that seem devoid of any of the large-scale temporal narrative

---

[11] I borrow this suggestive phrase from Damasio (262).

[12] Commenting on this view, Fivush notes that the same event memory may have a dual function, both predictive and autobiographical. If she is correct, this would link autobiographical memory to event memories with a more obviously identifiable adaptive purpose. As a student of self-narration, I would like to think of its having an adaptive value of some kind in the perspective of human evolution. See Fivush, "Functions."

framing that later memories tend to carry with them; the shape of a nursery rhyme is about as much in the way of narrative as these fragments warrant:

> Once upon a time and a very good time it was there was a moocow coming down along the road and this moocow that was coming down along the road met a nicens little boy named baby tuckoo . . . His father told him that story: his father looked at him through a glass: he had a hairy face.

"Memory Talk" and the Emergence of the Extended Self

The notion that autobiographical memory is socially and culturally constructed may at first seem counterintuitive. From Rousseau's *Confessions* on down, readers have been conditioned by the ideology of individualism to think of autobiography as a theater in which the self's uniqueness, privacy, and interiority are on display. Instead, Kenneth J. Gergen argues aggressively for "social constructivism" as the most appropriate perspective through which to approach the phenomena of autobiographical memory: "To report on one's memories is not so much a matter of consulting mental images as it is engaging in a sanctioned form of telling" (90). Other developmental psychologists working on autobiographical memory in the last decade—I am thinking not only of Katherine Nelson but of Robyn Fivush, Peggy J. Miller, Catherine E. Snow, and Dennie Palmer Wolf—support Gergen's social constructivist assumptions. Analyzing parent-child conversations about the past, they stress the interpersonal context in which the extended self emerges, they highlight the role of rules and conventions in the formation of autobiographical memories, and they show how the young child gradually assimilates these narrative practices.[13] A study by Robyn Fivush and Elaine Reese, "The Social Construction of Autobiographical

[13] In these adult-child exchanges about the past the child learns what is "reportable": "such discussions mark for the child the incidents that should qualify as memorable and thus as narratable" (Snow 225).

Memory," is characteristic of the drift of this research. Tracing the process through which the child "internalizes" "the culturally available narrative forms for recounting and for representing past experiences" (115), they conclude: "In this way, children begin forming a more overarching, narratively organized life story" (117). The child's "memory talk" training, I might add, confirms John Shotter's concept of "social accountability" presented in Chapter 2: the child learns that she is expected to be able to display to others autobiographical memories arranged in narrative form.

At the outset of this discussion of "memory talk," I pause to note the special place in this research of the presleep dialogues and monologues of a child named Emily. This bright child's crib speech was captured on tape—122 sessions in all—over a period of a little more than a year, from the age of twenty-one months to thirty-six months.[14] This body of data provides the basis for a remarkable series of studies on child language collected by Katherine Nelson in *Narratives from the Crib* (1989), and it marks a turning point in the investigation of the child's acquisition of language and narrative competence that has followed.

Robyn Fivush identifies the primary function of autobiographical memory as that of "organizing our knowledge about ourselves, a self-defining function." Indeed, she argues "it is the sense of self that is crucial for *autobiographical memory*" ("Functions" 277), a sense of self that is lacking in very young children. "As children begin to represent events that extend over longer time periods, from daily routines, to weekly routines, and so on, they also begin to develop a sense of self that continues to exist through time" (280). Fivush articulates, moreover, the complex interrelationship between the extended self (the self in time) and its store of autobiographical memories, and the difficulty of sorting out the ways in which language and narrative, interpersonal exchange and cultural formations, contribute to its unfolding:

[14] For more on the Emily tapes, see Nelson, "Introduction."

The self-concept and memories of past experiences develop di-
alectically and begin to form a life history. The life history, in
turn, helps organize both memories of past experiences and the
self-concept. The life history is essentially what Barsalou calls the
extended time lines, or the person's "story line." It is only with the
construction of the life history that we have true autobiographical
memory. (280–81).

As the dialectical cast of this formulation suggests, Fivush and
Reese, like Nelson and the other developmental psychologists to
whom I refer, avoid any notion of determinism in their account
of the parent-child conversations in which "children learn the
conventionalized narrative forms that eventually provide a structure for internally represented memories" ("Social" 115): they
view "both the child and the adult as playing active roles in the
construction of autobiography" (118).[15] Thus Fivush and Reese
take pains to characterize the "memory talk" exchange as "social
construction" rather than "socialization," rejecting any notion of
"linear causality from adult to child" (118) associated with the
latter term.

It is surely no accident that the narrative practices of "memory
talk" promote the child's sense of extended selfhood, for awareness of time is central to both. Indeed, Nelson notes in her study
of Emily's presleep monologues that the system of temporal reference emerges at precisely the same moment (beginning at
twenty-four months) that the child's system of self-reference undergoes a major reorganization ("Monologue" 305). Lawrence
W. Barsalou's work on extended event time lines, to which Fivush
alludes, suggests the critical importance of generating a system
of temporal reference, for he proposes that these time lines pro-

---

[15] Similarly, Nelson speaks of "a dialectical process of collaborative construction" (*Language* 172). My presentation of "memory talk" and related issues relies heavily on Nelson's work. I like her balanced approach, her willingness to
draw upon an unusually wide array of theories from different disciplines in for-
mulating her own views.

vide "the primary organization of autobiographical memories" (194). He speculates, accordingly, that "one reason for the relatively late development of autobiographical memories in the form of personal histories may be children's limited opportunity to perceive extended events": "The construction of this knowledge may become possible only when children understand that extended events exist and that life can be viewed as a succession of such events." Interestingly, he notes that the new ability to organize autobiographical memories in the temporal framework provided by extended event time lines "may cooccur with an increased awareness of the cultural importance of developing a personal history" (235). The extended self emerges, then, during a peculiarly rich developmental phase in which newly acquired language and narrative skills combine with temporal awareness and a nascent sense of social accountability to lay the foundations of autobiographical memory.

Turning to the work of Catherine E. Snow and Dennie Palmer Wolf, I want to suggest how the development of autobiographical memory in early childhood prepares for the writing of autobiography—when it occurs—in adult life. The distance between little Emily's "narratives from the crib," studied by Katherine Nelson and her colleagues, and literary autobiography performed by adults is not so great as it might seem: both belong to a single, continuous, lifelong trajectory of self-narration.[16] Analyzing transcripts of parent-child conversations recorded over a period of several years, Snow distinguishes between "memories located in the parental mind, which are transferred to the child but not actually shared by the child before transferral, and memories which children have some access to, though they are undeniably enriched and structured by parental intervention" (227). "Ultimately," she concludes, "children become the authors of their

---

[16] The psychologist Daniel N. Stern implicitly confirms this point when, reviewing the Emily tapes, he identifies the "task" of her monologues as "the creation of her narrative self": "it is this self . . . that she will build upon for the rest of her life in explaining herself to herself and to others" ("Crib" 319).

own autobiographies and the repository of their own memories" (232).[17]

What, it is fair to ask at this point, does "memory talk" look like? Here is an example of an exchange between a twenty-four-month-old boy and his mother, which Nelson quotes to illustrate the dominant role of the parent in the memory work involved:

C: Mommy, the Chrysler building
M: The Chrysler building?
C: The Chrysler building?
M: Yeah, who works in the Chrysler building?
C: Daddy
M: Do you ever go there?
C: Yes, I see the Chrysler building, picture of the Chrysler building
M: I don't know if we have a picture of the Chrysler building. Do we?
C: We went to . . . my Daddy went to work
M: Remember when we went to visit Daddy? Went in the elevator, way way up in the building so we could look down from the big window?
C: big window
M: mmhm . . .

(Nelson, Language 166)

From such fragmentary beginnings as these, where the parent is doing most of the work, the balance of power will gradually shift until the child, having acquired the habit of reviewing autobiographical memories and mastered the narrative skills to organize

---

[17] The transfer of responsibility Snow traces from parent to child lends support to L. S. Vygotsky's theory of the developmental stages of speech and thought in the child from "social speech" to "egocentric speech" to "inner speech." For Nelson, Bruner, and many of the other child psychologists whose research I have been discussing, Vygotsky's work enjoys a central place. For more on Vygotsky, see Burkitt, *Social* 144–62; Nelson, *Language* 18–21, 82–84; and Wertsch.

them, can perform a self-narration of her own, such as this one by Emily in monologue at thirty-three months:

> We *bought* a baby.
> [*False starts*: cause, the, well because, when she, well]
> we thought it was for Christmas,
> *but when* we went to the store we didn't have our jacket on,
> *but* I saw some dolly,
> *and* I yelled at *my mother and* said
> I want one of those dolly.
> *So after* we *were finished* with the store,
> we *went* over to the dolly and *she* bought me *one*.
> *So* I have *one*.
>
> (Nelson, *Language* 204)

Study of this material, Nelson concludes, reveals children in the process of learning "to talk about—and to remember—their experience in specific ways": "They learn, that is, to 'narrativize' their experience" (*Language* 170).

In this formative phase of "memory talk," where parents are teaching the child how to work with autobiographical memories, parental styles of engagement can exert an enormous influence, transmitting both models of self and story. Thus Fivush, for example, finds "that females are being socialized into being more concerned about the past and about emotional aspects of the past [than males are]" ("Constructing" 153). Yet the role of gender as a factor proves to be quite complex. Nelson and Minda Tessler distinguish between "narrative" mothers and "paradigmatic" mothers (the terms are borrowed from Bruner). As in the example of the visit to the Chrysler building, the "narrative" mother actively coaches the child to create a micronarrative, supplying a simple story line, whereas the "paradigmatic" mother seeks to elicit from the child specific information about the past (the exchange is brought to closure when the child has answered the questions asked) (Nelson, *Language* 169–70). Peggy J. Miller and others have studied the ways in which storytelling is practiced in different communities, and preliminary cross-cultural research comparing Asian and American samples suggests that large-scale differences between cultures' models of self-concept significantly affect the date at which children are encouraged to construct an autobiographical memory system (Nelson, *Language* 171–72).

The child's growth toward what Snow terms "autonomous remembrances" (232) is investigated in fascinating detail by Dennie Palmer Wolf, who traces the emergence of what she terms "an *authorial self*" (185) between the ages of two and four. She documents the child's progressive ability to manipulate memories in a protoliterary fashion, rendering "the 'same' experience in a variety of formats" (185), playing with voices and versions of an event, becoming increasingly attracted to "fiction, with all of its selections, transformations, and distortions" (197). Of special note, as an anticipation of the autobiographer's stance, is the child's mastery in her "memory talk" of the double point of view that governs retrospect: "the person who identifies with the younger, distant person (the object of the memory) and the person who engages in recollection (the subject who currently has the memory)" (192). The child who has learned through "memory talk" "to speak as subject and object, author and critic, character and narrator" (208) is a budding autobiographer. Fivush, Snow, and Wolf link autobiographical memory to narrative forms, to the making of fiction, to the exercise of authorship, and Nelson has emphasized the dawning sense of audience, the pleasure-producing sociality, of these promptings.[18]

[18] I should acknowledge here the conceptual difficulty I struggled with in trying to sort out my exposition of the relational and narrative dimensions of self-hood, for the two are in fact inextricably intertwined. As my discussion of "memory talk" has suggested, narration is by definition a relational act, and the acquisition of narrative competence is transacted intersubjectively. I considered attempting to present both dimensions of selfhood simultaneously in a single chapter, but opted instead for separate treatment with a view to giving each a prominence that might otherwise have been compromised.

Children Using Stories

The child's early achievement of narrative competence in the preschool years ushers in a decisive phase of identity formation that lasts as long as the child remains within the family circle. Many factors contribute to the social construction of identity in this period; institutions such as the school and the church, for example, obviously play an important part in bringing home the lessons of social accountability.[19] I follow Jerome Bruner, however, and autobiographers themselves in placing special emphasis on the family's role in this process: the family serves, he writes, as the "vicar of the culture," indoctrinating the child in the received "genres of life-accounting" ("Invention" 32). From this perspective we can think of the child's sense of self as emerging within a crucible of family stories and cultural scripts. Because this phase is so familiar—it is often the primary subject of an autobiography—I will limit myself to a few observations about it to underline the connections autobiographers characteristically make between family narrative and identity. In a PBS broadcast, the poet Donald Hall observes, "The family stories you grow up with make you; they build you, they create you" ("Bill Moyers' Journal"). And who can forget the extraordinary figure of Maxine Hong Kingston's mother, Brave Orchid, in *The Woman Warrior* (1976), who "marked [Maxine's] growing up with stories" (6)? And then there are the stories adults tell one another when children are thought to be out of hearing. William Maxwell, John Updike, Henry James, and Eudora Welty are only a few of the autobiographers who remind us that children are always eavesdropping, lurking under the dining room table or listening in on the stairs, soaking up family stories. The importance of this phase of identity formation is often heightened by the structure of autobiographical narratives: typically, departure from the fam-

---

[19] Models of self and life story are transmitted to the child through various conduits. For further reflection on the transmission of cultural values to children, see Gullestad.

ily circle will mark at least a turning point in the narrative if not
its closure.

Having acquired narrative competence through "memory
talk," what does the child do with it? As far as I can make out, the
resources for tracking the child's experience with self-narration
during the school years are limited: autobiographical exercises
performed in school are ephemeral; and the project of keeping
a diary, usually not embraced until adolescence, is likely to remain private.[20] Occasionally, to be sure, adult autobiographers
include samples of early autobiographical writings in their narratives. If the written record of childhood self-narration is scant,
however, adult autobiographical retrospect helps to compensate
for this lack. Indeed, one of autobiography's great themes is the
child's awakening to the call of stories as they are performed
within the family circle and the larger community. The importance of this theme—I think, for example, of best-selling memoirs of the last couple of years, Mary Karr's *The Liars' Club* (1995),
Mikal Gilmore's *Shot in the Heart* (1994), and Frank McCourt's
Angela's Ashes (1996)—is hardly surprising, for the child's immer-
sion in a rich narrative culture of family storytelling doubtless informs the adult's autobiographical impulse. In Leslie Marmon
Silko's *Storyteller* (1981), as in Kingston's *The Woman Warrior*, the
telling of family stories and the writing of autobiography coalesce in a single act.

While many autobiographers instinctively document the
child's initiation into narrative practices, the historian Carolyn
Steedman has made this subject a focus of her research for more
than twenty years, notably in *The Tidy House: Little Girls Writing*
(1982) and in *Landscape for a Good Woman* (1986), which I dis-

---

[20] In the late 1980s, recognizing how little information was available about the
practice of keeping a diary among the French, Lejeune set out to gather data in
two different inquiries, publishing the results in "*Cher cahier . . .*": *Témoignages
sur le journal personnel* (1989) and *La pratique du journal personnel: Enquête* (1990).
Confirming that diary keeping is typically begun during adolescence, Lejeune
found that forty of the forty-seven respondents in the first study began keeping
a diary between the ages of ten and twenty ("*Cher cahier*" 228).

cussed in Chapter 2.[21] Like Bruner, who contends that narrative "operates as an instrument of mind in the construction of reality" ("Narrative" 6), Steedman also embraces a narrative epistemology, investigating children's engagement with story—their listening, their reading, their writing. As a historian, Steedman studies "the development of historical consciousness in children" ("History" 44): how do children achieve a quite specific knowledge of their social and economic circumstances? *That* they possess such knowledge is indisputable, as far as Steedman is concerned. Consider her favorite example of the knowing child, an eight-year-old watercress seller interviewed by Henry Mayhew in the winter of 1849–50 in preparation for his epochal study, *London Labour and the London Poor* (1851). Analyzing the girl's story, Steedman discerns the child's "economic vision," "the financial ordering of her household, and the way in which her labour was managed and controlled by her mother" (*Landscape* 135). *Children themselves*, Steedman argues, understand the process of identity formation as operating in a field of economic forces, in which selves function as commodities, "items of expenditure, investments, . . . objects of exchange" (*Landscape* 69).

How did Mayhew's little watercress seller—how did Steedman herself, and how do children today—acquire the kinds of historical knowledge that Steedman's studies have shown them to possess? Working as a teacher in a primary school classroom, observing "what it is that children *do* with history" ("True" 110), Steedman became persuaded that narrative functions as the medium through which children develop "the historical imagination" ("History" 44). In the summer of 1976, three of her working-class pupils, Carla, Melissa, and Lindie, composed a narrative they called "The Tidy House," a blunt and poignant story about "the getting and regretting of children" (*Tidy* 19). "They knew that children were longed for, materially desired," Steed-

---

[21] Steedman's book *Strange Dislocations: Childhood and the Idea of Human Interiority, 1780–1930* (1995) is the culmination of her lifelong concern with the historical study of childhood.

man comments, "but [they also knew] . . . that it would have been better had they never been born" ("Tidy" 74). Steedman traces the children's surprisingly shrewd grasp of the social and economic realities of their working-class family lives to long hours spent listening to adult women converse: "People talking to each other, and the effects that this talking had, was the most important and powerful event that the children ever witnessed" (*Tidy* 90).[22] The story the children write represents a further stage in their narrative formation, offering a window through which Steedman can witness their manipulation of symbolic forms—acquired through observing adult narrative practices— as they seek "to understand what set of social beliefs had brought them into being" (*Tidy* 25).

Complementing "The Tidy House" story, which illustrates the child's construction and use of an "interpretative device," is Steedman's account in *Landscape for a Good Woman* of her own experience at a similar age; the themes of the two narratives—the child's troubling realization that she is both product of and obstacle to her mother's desire—are identical. Reconstructing the process by which she achieved such knowledge, Steedman recalls herself for us as a working-class child reading fairy tales in her room in the summer of her seventh year. She was especially drawn to the gloomy violence of Hans Christian Andersen, drawn to the little mermaid who "must feel every step as if walking on the edge of knives" (*Landscape* 55) in order to enter the world of human love and adult sexuality, drawn to the little boy Kay in "The Snow Queen" who was wounded by a shard of glass from a troll's mirror that turns to a lump of ice in his heart.[23]

Fairy tales, Steedman's first "interpretative device," say to the

---

[22] Steedman's observation here confirms the findings of Fivush, Miller, and other child psychologists described earlier.

[23] Steedman's middle name is Kay. To my knowledge, Steedman as author signs her full name only in the case of *Landscape*. Interestingly, the only use of her middle name within the text occurs in a scene in which her mother charges her with being cold and "unfeeling" (*Landscape* 106), underlining the connection with the Kay of Andersen's "The Snow Queen."

child: "here are some kings and queens, a lost kingdom: use these figures to think about what you know" (*Landscape* 77). Using the story of the little mermaid, the seven-year-old girl replays an event she had witnessed when she was four, a scene that the adult historian identifies as her mother's "second seduction" of her father. Her mother had taken her down into the basement of the Hammersmith flat to see the dollhouse that the father was building for her: the moment seems mysteriously charged, her mother leaning back against a workbench, laughing; her father smiling, "a charmer charmed" (53). Now, three years later, lying on her bed reading, and imagining what her parents are doing downstairs, the seven-year-old girl conjures up a disturbing vision of her parents seated naked under the kitchen table, each drawing blood from the other with knives: "Downstairs I thought, the thin blood falls in sheets from my mother's breasts; she was the most cut, but I knew it was she who did the cutting. I couldn't always see the knife in my father's hands" (54). Reading fairy tales supplies the child's imagination with a set of symbols to express her intuitive knowledge of the sharp-edged necessities of working-class reality, "the mutilation involved in feeding and keeping us" (82).

Drawing on a feminist psychoanalytic perspective, the autobiographer supplies a second interpretation of the basement memory and its subsequent fantasy elaboration as a kind of primal scene. Although Steedman defends her mother as "good enough," given her endless struggle in the face of difficult economic circumstances, she holds her responsible nonetheless for Steedman's own refusal of motherhood. Following Nancy Chodorow, Steedman argues that "part of the desire to reproduce oneself as a body . . . lies in conscious memory of someone approving that body" (*Landscape* 95). Looking back, the adult historian believes that her seven-year-old self knew and expressed her mother's ambivalence toward her daughter's existence through the medium of her fairy-tale vision: "I knew this, I think, when I conjured her under the kitchen table, the thin wounds across her breasts pouring forth blood, not milk" (93). The yoking of milk and blood expresses the child's intuition of the mother's conflicted desire: the mother is hurt, and can bring hurt, wounding and deflecting the maternal principle in the daughter. Thus Steedman, like Kay in "The Snow Queen," grows up with a lump of ice in her heart, determined never to have children of her own.[24]

How did Steedman—even as a little girl—come to know her place in her mother's story? Through narrative, through the child's acquisition of an "interpretative device" that she could deploy to solve the riddles of her family experience. Steedman argues that although factual knowledge of her illegitimacy came to her late (in her early thirties, after the death of her father in 1977), she achieved an operative knowledge of her family's damaged affective structure by the time she was a child of seven or eight. Steedman projects the burden of the entire autobiography, stunningly compressed, in the temporal framing of this episode: the child of seven interpreting a memory from the time she was four; the adult autobiographer, some thirty years later on, reinterpreting the mind of her seven-year-old self. The autobiographer supplies the link among these frames, for she dates the decisive shift in her mother's attitude toward her from the birth of her sister ("the second seduction") when she was four.

Steedman claims, I repeat, that she acquired this knowledge through narrative, through the family stories she heard, through the fairy tales she read, and, drawing on these resources, through stories she learned to put together for herself. Even allowing for the distortions of retrospect, I think Steedman makes a compelling case for the role that fairy-tale narrative played in her early life. The child's imagination crystallizes her recogni-

---

[24] Yet it is also true that Steedman as historian and autobiographer extends a maternal solicitude to the little girls of working-class history, to Mayhew's watercress seller, to Carla, Lindie, and Melissa, and not least to her earlier self. For an illuminating reading of the fairy- tale material in *Landscape*—both feminist and psychoanalytic—see Abel.

tion that she was not a wanted child in a startlingly condensed image—the naked parents armed with knives under the kitchen table. Citing Freud's "Family Romances" and Bruno Bettelheim's *The Uses of Enchantment* ("True" 112–13), the autobiographer theorizes the interpretative resources that fairy tales provide as follows: "When children do confront daily the problems of poverty, sexual conflict between adults, love and hatred, despair and rejection, then fairy-tales can provide easily assimilable metaphors for children's social and personal feelings, confirming both that pain and the possibility of comfort are real, and that through action there may be resolution" (*Tidy* 141).

In *The Words,* Jean-Paul Sartre offers a much more elaborate instance of the way in which a child may come to view self and life story in terms supplied by narrative. Sartre would have us believe that reading a little book titled *The Childhood of Famous Men,* a collection of biographies for children, planted in him the prototype for the book of his own life, which he attempted to write in his living by aligning his own conduct with that of the great-man-as-child in the literary model.[25] No one has ever written a more devastating critique of the literatus and the literary life than Sartre in *The Words,* yet Sartre, like Steedman, confirms that we are always writing our lives in the act of living them, that we perform this life writing in narrative terms.

Narrative Disorders, Identity Disorders

I have been arguing that narrative plays a central, structuring role in the formation and maintenance of our sense of identity. Most of us, however, never give much thought to the place of self-

---

[25] Sartre claims that he became obsessed with *The Childhood of Great Men* when he was nine. Two years later, he reports, he had so completely internalized this literary model of self and life story that although it became the guiding principle of his existence, indeed the basis of his "neurosis," he didn't become conscious of it again until more than thirty years later.

narration in our lives; we run, as it were, on automatic narrative pilot. Only when the capacity to construct narrative is impaired (as in cases involving brain damage) or never acquired in the first place (as in severe cases of child abuse) are we apt to recognize that identity itself has been damaged as well. I want now to test this proposition, suggesting that narrative disorders and identity disorders go hand in hand.

"Dysnarrativia"

In their enormously suggestive paper "The Neurology of Narrative," Kay Young and Jeffrey Saver describe four types of *dysnarrativia*, "states of narrative impairment experienced by individuals with discrete focal damage in different regions of the neural network subserving human self-narrative." They believe that the various lesions they describe in the frontal lobe structures and in the amygdalohippocampal system point to "the inseparable connection between narrativity and personhood." In addition to global amnesia, which produces the familiar "arrested narrative" (autobiographical recall "up until, or a few years before" the injury), they describe other, subtler malfunctions that manifest themselves in a variety of narrative deformations—confabulation, "under-narration," "denarration." "Individuals who have lost the ability to construct narrative," they conclude, "have lost their selves."

Whether or not the capacity for making narrative should be regarded as the sine qua non of identity, however, should give us pause. As I suggested at the beginning of this chapter, Sacks takes a similarly strong position on the link between narrative and identity. By uncovering the neural substrate of the memory-narrative-identity connection, moreover, Young, Saver, and Sacks seem to confirm the notion of embodied selfhood I presented in Chapter 1. Yet other clinicians, equally disturbed by the profound, identity-altering loss of affect that seems to characterize patients suffering from Korsakov's syndrome, Alzheimer's disease, and other forms of massive memory loss, do not identify the narrative construction of autobiographical memory as the sole source of our operative sense of identity. Complementing Daniel L. Schacter's findings on the implicit memories of amnesiacs (*Searching* 163–76), for example, William Hirst argues that an individual "can have a dynamic changing self-concept even without personal narratives," for "memories may be implicit or stored in the social setting around us" (255).[26] Thus, guided by Hirst and Schacter, and recalling the many dimensions of self-experience that I presented in Chapter 1, I think it's a mistake to make narrative identity coextensive with the entire experience of selfhood. Instead, returning to Young and Saver's linkage of narrative capacity and selfhood, I would want to specify that the identity that is impaired by the failure of explicit memory is what Ulric Neisser terms the extended self, the self that emerges in "memory talk," the self that occupies so central a place in adult autobiography.

Nevertheless, for both Hirst (271) and Schacter (*Searching* 149–50, 160), there is no question that the self of the amnesiac is radically altered by the loss of explicit memory. Sacks registers the jolt such cases give to the sense of identity that we usually take for granted when, contemplating the ravages of Korsakov's syndrome on "Mr. Thompson's" personality, he asks, "has he been pithed, scooped-out, de-souled, by disease?" (*Man* 113). Would we be prepared, though, to follow Sacks in questioning whether "there is a *person* remaining" (115) in "Mr. Thompson"?[27] That we *do* instinctively ask such a question reveals the im-

---

[26] See also Neisser, who comments: "Selves are not supported by narrative alone": "amnesics have no current autobiographical memories and no ongoing self-narratives . . . . Nevertheless each of them has, and is aware of having, an obvious and distinct identity" ("Self-narratives" 14–15).

[27] Kerby asks a similar question with regard to autism: "Even to think of an autistic person as having a world similar to the language user's is begging the question. Language not only operates on the perceptually given, imbuing it with a meaning it would otherwise lack, but also goes a long way toward constituting what we mean by being a self, a person" (122 n. 2). In Chapter 4, on the

portance we attach to our identity conventions and narrative practices. How often have we said, or heard it said, for example, after visiting a friend or relative slipping into senility, "She was not herself today"—an arresting thing to say, on the face of it, yet we know what we mean when we say it. Even Schacter, who is careful to note that something of memory and identity survive even the most destructive amnesia, points in this direction. Concluding his discussion of "Gene," "Frederick," and his other amnesiac patients, he observes that "when we lose the capacity to travel in time, we are cut loose from much of what anchors our sense of who we are and where we are headed" (*Searching* 160).[28] That this particular mode of self-experience should be regarded by Young, Saver, and Sacks as equivalent to the whole of identity itself confirms the special status accorded to narrative identity in the child's initiation into "memory talk" that I considered earlier in this chapter. Social accountability, early and late, in "memory talk" exchanges between children and caregivers, between clinicians and their patients, conditions us to believe that our recognition as "persons" is to be transacted through the exchange of identity narratives—no narrative, no self.

Consider once more Saver and Young's statement: "Individuals who have lost the ability to construct narrative . . . have lost their selves." What, exactly, do we mean when we say such things? That such individuals literally have no selves? Or that we're not in a position to recognize them as such? Is there such a thing as an unstoried self? Shifting from a neurological to a cultural per-

---

ethics of life writing, I will have more to say about what it is that constitutes a *person*.

[28] When Schacter characterizes "Gene's" life as "psychologically barren—the mental equivalent of a bleak Siberian landscape" (*Searching* 149), the frozen identity he conjures up makes clear by contrast our working assumption that extended selfhood is changing and dynamic. Damasio makes a similar observation about the loss of affect in patients suffering from anosognosia: "The state of self that they are able to construct is thus impoverished because of their impaired ability to process current body states. It relies on old information, which grows older by the minute" (237). (Anosognosia "denotes the inability to acknowledge disease in oneself" [62].)

spective, I want to comment on a searching essay by Sidonie Smith in which she investigates the case of autistic individuals whose silence precisely tests the linkage of narrative and identity. "Perhaps," she observes, "autistics remain outside the linguistic, narrative, and communal circuits of autobiographical telling" ("Taking" 231). The examples cited by Saver and Young imply that the possession of narrative competence is indispensable for the formation and maintenance of identity. Perhaps this proposition needs to be amended, however, to read: "the formation and maintenance of identity *as we know it*," for Smith's inquiry into autism prompts her to entertain the possibility of a subjectivity different from anything we think we know. I say, "we think we know," because Smith's speculations about the unknowable interiority of the autistic might with good reason be extended to all subjectivity. It may well be the case that the narrative model of identity that forms the bedrock of interpersonal relations in human communities is more like a piece of necessary cultural equipment than an ultimate psychological reality, something we need in order to get on with the business of living as we have been socialized to understand it.[29] That is, there might be a sense in which the subjectivity of the ordinary individual, stripped of the cultural overlay of linguistic and narrative socialization, might not be so different from that of the autistic, but such a possibility is difficult to imagine precisely because it lies beyond the ground of our linguistically, narratively constituted knowing.

In introducing autism into this discussion of the "dysnarrativia" associated with amnesia, I am not implying that a similar neurological deficit is at work. In the case of autism it is not a question of lesions producing memory loss; instead, another form of brain malfunction seems to be involved that impedes the

---

[29] When I speak of the narrative model of identity as a "necessary" piece of cultural equipment, I mean to suggest that individuals within a particular culture may be conditioned to accept such a model as necessary. Although I suspect that the role of narrative in identity formation may indeed be something on the order of a transcultural universal, I don't wish to imply that judgment in my usage here.

establishment of autobiographical memory in the first place.[30] In
Mindblindness (1995), Simon Baron-Cohen identifies four developmental steps that normally result in the child's ability to engage in "mindreading," which he defines as the individual's strategy "to make sense of the actions of others" (21). Adopting the
perspective of evolutionary psychology, Baron-Cohen formulates
the adaptive task that "mindreading" solves as "the rapid com-
prehension and prediction of another organism's behavior"
(12). Autistic children, like normal children, share the ability to
detect intentionality and also, more specifically, the ability to
infer from eye movement that someone is looking at something.
They do not, however, acquire what Baron-Cohen terms the
"shared-attention mechanism," which builds triadic representations of the "she sees I see the object" sort, allowing the child to
attribute a perceptual state to another organism. As a result,
such children do not develop a "theory-of-mind mechanism"
that permits them to infer the "full range of mental states from
behavior" (51). Clinical observation of autistic children suggests
that they "lack a concept of the other person as an interested listener"; their behaviors "do not indicate a desire to share interest
with another person for its own sake" (69). Thus the autistic
child is not equipped to engage in "memory talk" and indeed
language acquisition itself is troubled in such cases. Baron-
Cohen concludes that if autistic children are "blind to their own
past thoughts and to other people's possibly different thoughts,
their world must be largely dominated by current perceptions
and sensations" (82). Extended selfhood, which I believe provides the structure for the self created in adult autobiographical

[30] The etiology of autism remains a subject of considerable controversy. Simon
Baron-Cohen, citing the work by A. Bailey "The Biology of Autism" (1993),
writes: "That there is brain damage in autism is no longer disputed, but the site
of this damage is unclear because of what can only be described as contradic-
tory evidence" (94). Sacks is somewhat more cautious in his evaluation of the
research to date. Referring specifically to the "theory-of-mind" thesis embraced
by Baron-Cohen and others, he comments, "no theory, as yet, encompasses the
whole range of phenomena to be seen in autism" (*Anthropologist* 246).

discourse, does not emerge, and, not surprisingly, autobiography by autistics is comparatively rare.

Even so-called "high-functioning" autistics like Donna Williams and Temple Grandin, who *have* written autobiographies, testify to the difficulties of participating in the interpersonal exchange that fosters narrative identity.[31] Because other people are perceived as unpredictable and hence potentially threatening, the autistic individual engages in what Sacks has tellingly characterized as "pseudosocial conduct" (*Anthropologist* 203), going through the motions of conversation, for example, without understanding the social dynamics involved. Commenting on the challenge of fathoming the interpersonal exchange of motive and intention, Grandin told Sacks that "much of the time I feel like an anthropologist on Mars" (259). Grandin paints herself as someone who has devoted a huge amount of self-conscious effort in order to learn the scripts of human behavior that others acquire in the course of early childhood socialization. What should we conclude as we look at Grandin and Williams struggling to decode the mysteries of interpersonal communication? Are they, as Sacks remarks of the child savant–artist Stephen Wiltshire, "defective precisely in that range of emotions and states of mind that defines a 'self' for the rest of us" (239)? I want to pause here to examine this suggestive comment. Certainly a continuing refrain in the clinical accounts of amnesiacs and autistics is the clinician's distress over the subject's apparent loss of affect, confirming that one of the important adaptive functions of narrative identity and the exchange of identity narratives is the enhancement of bonding and social solidarity. Sacks's remark testifies to the working of social accountability: to achieve a socially recognized identity, individuals need to display "that range of emotions and states of mind that defines a 'self'

---

[31] So convinced was Sacks that "the autistic mind . . . was incapable of self-understanding and understanding others," that he was initially "suspicious" of Grandin's autobiography, *Emergence: Labeled Autistic* (1986). "How *could* an autistic person write an autobiography?" he muses. "It seemed a contradiction in terms" (*Anthropologist* 253).

for the rest of us." But we should not be too quick to assume that individuals who fail the test are therefore unprovided with "self." Temple Grandin, one of the rare autistics to break through this identity-recognition barrier, is extremely proud of her *autistic* identity: "If I could snap my fingers and be nonautistic," she told Sacks, "I would not—because then I wouldn't be me. Autism is part of who I am" (291).

"Hypernarrativia"—Narrative as Pathology

Neurologists and psychologists supply ample evidence to justify the claim that narrative is deeply involved in the construction and maintenance of the extended self, that mode of self-experience that we are socialized to recognize as identity's core. Much of this research assumes—explicitly or implicitly—that the ability to construct narrative is in itself a good; it prompts us to acknowledge the adaptive value of narrative, associated with health, with functioning identity, with integration into social groups. Conditioned through social accountability to think of narrative's contribution to identity as life-enhancing in these ways, we may find it hard to accept that narrative capacity is, in fact, value neutral, for there is evidence that narrative can warp or even destroy identity. In making this claim, I need to make it clear that I am not referring to the contents of particular narratives—of race, of class, of gender—but rather to narrative making itself. My own recognition of the dark side of narrative identity stems from a reading of Melanie Thernstrom's *The Dead Girl: A True Story* (1990), a narrative about making narrative that leads to suicide and murder.

If Saver, Young, and Sacks evoke the loss of identity that afflicts those who suffer from narrative incapacity, Thernstrom makes us see, by contrast, that narrative, so necessary to the very existence of identity, may also turn pathological and destroy it. In a curious, hybrid text in which autobiography and biography are intercut with various forms of documentary fact, *The Dead Girl* reconstructs the murder of Thernstrom's best friend, Roberta Lee, in the fall of her junior year at Berkeley. Out for a run with her boyfriend, Bradley Page, and another woman in a park near San Francisco, Roberta mysteriously disappears. After a month of futile searching, her body is discovered in a shallow grave in the park. Suspicion falls on the boyfriend, who confesses to the murder, and then recants his confession. During the next three and a half years Brad Page is tried twice and eventually convicted. Thernstrom's account of these events, however, is not just another tale of true crime on the order of Truman Capote's *In Cold Blood* (cited in a blurb on the paperback cover). Narrative in *The Dead Girl* operates in three different registers: hermeneutic, in its attempt to solve Roberta's murder; commemorative, in its elegiac portrait of Melanie's dead friend; and therapeutic, in its working through of Melanie's traumatic loss to a posture of recovery and acceptance.[32] This intricate braid of narrative reflects, moreover, its author's intensely literary sensibility; if Saver and Young can speak of "dysnarrativia," we can speak in Thernstrom's case of "hypernarrativia," of a consciousness working overtime to make experience read like a story in a book.

If we can credit Thernstrom's characterization of her earlier self, the book's retelling is apparently only the latest installment of a story that Melanie lived *as story*, relating it endlessly along the way to her friends and her analyst. The elaborate packaging of the narrative into nine parts and thirty-six chapters, together with the many epigraphs, emphasizes the literary nature of Melanie's friendship with Roberta. Thernstrom recaptures their adolescent attitudinizing, their love of quotations and personas, as they try out identities in high school. In her letters to Melanie from Berkeley, which punctuate each chapter, Roberta Lee continues this play of identity, signing herself Bibi, Rosamunde, B.B., Mei-hua, and so forth, as the spirit moves her. Confirming Melanie's inveterate addiction to narrative, another friend complains to her, "I get really tired of you talking about everything in terms of reading and writing." In her reply, Melanie points to the

---

[32] I use *hermeneutic* in the sense proposed by Roland Barthes in *S/Z*: "Under the hermeneutic code, we list the various (formal) terms by which an enigma can be distinguished, suggested, formulated, held in suspense, and finally disclosed" (19).

heart of the matter: "I used to have this idea I would think about all the time: that there was a book somewhere where the story of my life was written down" (405).

Melanie instinctively formulates her experience in terms of stories; any kind of narrative is grist for her mill—fairy tales, Nancy Drew mysteries, *Anna Karenina*, Harlequin romances. Meaning for Melanie is narrative meaning: you know what will happen, she tells herself, "because you know the genre." "In books," she continues, "events are meaningfully ordered, and people are suited to their fates" (112). Particularly insidious in Melanie's case is her notion that character is narratively determined, for, given her intense identification with her murdered friend, a perverse narrative logic suggests that Roberta's fate will be her own. So primed is she to see herself as the victim of a similar fate, the young woman brutally violated and murdered, that when an older woman leading the search for Roberta's body draws the parallel, Melanie's intake of breath, her narrative *frisson*, is if anything overdetermined:

> "And such a sweet and innocent girl," Lena adds, . . . "Naive, young, vulnerable, helpless, you know the type—*the type these things happen to*—the type Bibi must have been—the type you are—"
> I catch my breath. (106)

Thernstrom lives this notion of life as narrative to the hilt, and it nearly costs her her life, as we shall see. But first I want to look at the murder itself, for—apparently—Roberta's killer was also motivated by a narrative impulse; and I should add that a narrative impulse—a desire to flee from present constraints into an "Absolute Elsewhere" (52) of freedom—may have prompted Roberta herself to run off into the forest on her own, thereby sealing her fate.[33]

---

[33] As if to confirm that the desire to escape is one of Roberta Lee's most characteristic and deep-seated impulses, Thernstrom includes in the opening pages a memory of her friend's sudden and apparently inexplicable decision to get

"He says he made it up" (203). These words jolt Melanie with the news that Brad Page, the prime suspect, has retracted his confession; it takes two trials to settle the case, for the first ends in a hung jury. Brad's claim that he had made up his confession not only cancels any hope of solving the crime definitively, it suggests a disturbing *likeness* between Melanie and the presumed murderer of her friend: both are given over—dangerously as it turns out—to the work of the imagination, to fabulation. Reading the report of the first trial, Melanie observes, "I'm so sympathetic to Brad's main argument—the argument that he imagined it" (238).

During the interrogation that takes place after Brad is first brought in for questioning, two detectives convince the young man that they possess independent evidence linking him to the scene of the crime, and so he cooperates by supplying a "scenario" for the murder. Closing his eyes, Brad produces a series of images—making love to Roberta, hitting Roberta—and from these story fragments, he and the detectives gradually piece together a narrative of the murder: that he hit Roberta and left the park; that he returned that night, made love to her dead body and buried it. The status of the images, however, is baffling, even to Brad. Consider this exchange between Brad and the detectives, as reported by Brad under questioning in the first trial:

> And they said, "What about what you told us earlier?" I said, "Those are images." And they said, "What happens if they are real?" and I said, "I'd be scared." (363)

Are the images fantasies, memories, or both? Was Roberta the victim of narrative, of Brad's diseased imagination? "There is just no way of knowing" (261)—this is the constant refrain in these pages.[34]

---

off a bus they are riding at a point where they are miles from their homes in Cambridge (13–15).

[34] Given the promptings of the detectives and the atmosphere of coercion they brought to bear on their interrogation of Brad, the reliability of his testimony is certainly problematic. See, e.g., Schacter's account of memory distortion in the

Consider now the impact of making stories on Melanie. Because of her intense identification with Roberta and her story—"our stories were *the same*," she insists (402)—Melanie comes to see herself as "doomed" to a similar fate, namely that something "bad" will happen to her at the hands of "strangers." In her fragile state after Roberta's murder and funeral, all it takes is her boyfriend's decision to break up with her to send her over the edge into a suicidal literary hysteria: "Darling, I think we should be ending," he tells her, and, always suggestible, she tells herself, "you must do something ending" (281). The subtitle to this grim section of *The Dead Girl* captures Thernstrom's surrender to a peculiar narrative compulsion: "How She Tried to Tell the Story of Her Life So That It Would Be Just Like a Story" (265). Believing herself friendless and alone, she identifies with Hans Christian Andersen's "little match girl" in the fairy tale she is obsessed with; heading into cold and darkness, all her matches gone, Melanie tries to kill herself.[35]

In the world of *The Dead Girl*, imagination, narrative imagination, can kill. Roberta, Brad, and Melanie are all victimized by narrative. Not only can narrative not get the story of Roberta's murder straight (despite all the forensic interrogations, the truth remains undecidable, unknowable), but narrative making—*above and beyond the content of particular narratives*—may have been to blame for what went wrong in these young lives in the first place. In the midst of her story of Roberta's murder, Brad's conviction, and her own attempted suicide, Thernstrom observes, ruefully:

---

case of Paul Ingram, who, when asked "to visualize the events he was trying to remember and to conjecture about what happened" (*Searching* 132), generated images and eventually "memories" which later almost certainly proved to be false.

[35] See Thernstrom 192–203 for an account of Melanie's preoccupation with this story. Even though she recognizes that Andersen's fairy tale is "forced," "a pathetic ugly story" (196), she allows it to guide her perception of her own life story. As her friend Bob, ever the realist trying to get her to shake free of her literary fantasies, observes, "You're choosing to see things Match Girl" (202).

I try not to wonder whether . . . if we had never thought life and literature and film had anything to do with each other, and that our lives could therefore be written as such—whether the ending, which would no longer have to be an ending since only stories have to have endings, would have ended as it ended after all. (263)

Melanie recognizes at the last how much she "fictionalized" her experience, "how much [she] read in all the time" (403). She disavows her presentation of Brad, Roberta, and herself as characters in a book: Roberta was not "doomed"—"Doomed is what characters are" (402), nor was Melanie herself "*the type these things happen to,*" and "even Brad didn't turn out precisely like *Brad*" (261). Her life, she concludes, is "not a story" (405): "Dear God, I say, I return the story. I return the story and the meaning of the story and the need to make meaning of the story" (427).

Recovering from the overdose of "story thinking" (310) that blocked her grief for Roberta for several years after her death, Melanie is able to feel her sorrow for the first time, and presently, in a transcendent, visionary moment she sees Roberta's face: "Not a word, her face. . . . before and after and there all along there was something besides the story; there was her face." Yet Melanie, sober, chastened, refuses any easy resolution of the conundrums her narrative has failed to solve. Thus, balancing this nonnarrative epiphany, which reveals "a place where everything is intact" (428), Thernstrom returns us to the world of narrative, of time, mutability, and mortality. She confides in a postscript that legal constraints have obliged her to invent the texts of all of Roberta's letters: "No one can write for another because no one's spirit is like another's. The loss is, as it was, irreparable" (431). Melanie Thernstrom's trajectory leads not from story to no story, finally, but, as it has to, from story to *new* story, to this book, to the writing of the unwriting of her life. Only the dead are free of story. "The absoluteness of absolute elsewhere," she muses, "is that it is elsewhere from imagination too. It doesn't matter what you think. She was dead" (115).

The Dead Girl is the work of a gifted young writer who has experienced the pain of adolescence and early maturity in a harsh and striking fashion. Thinking about Melanie's relation to Roberta, I am reminded of the portraits of friendship in Alain Fournier's *Le Grand Meaulnes* and William Maxwell's *The Folded Leaf*: lurking in these works about youth is a deep-seated resistance to the world of adult life, a repudiation of the dispiriting narrative of responsibilities and routines—taxes, fuses, storm windows—that Melanie attributes to the "Grownups." "Grownupness is *feeble*," she protests. "I'm not excited about it, I've never been excited about it, and I'm not going to do it—not now—not now" (167). Accompanying this resistance is a distinctly regressive retreat to a childlike perspective, such that Melanie, a bright young woman in college, surrenders in her suicidal, "doomed" phase to thinking of "bad men and scary places."[36] For all her addiction to narrative, Thernstrom shares with many another twentieth-century autobiographer—I think, for example, of Maxine Hong Kingston, Ronald Fraser, Roland Barthes, and Richard Rodriguez—a distinctly antinarrative, antiautobiographical desire. All self-narration is by definition a narrative of individuation, yet, as I have observed elsewhere, one frequently detects the presence in autobiography of "an impulse to undo the work of individuation altogether," "to return to an earlier mode of being released from the burden of self-reflexive autonomy" (*Touching* 137). Given the violent end that had overtaken her friend, no wonder that Melanie should dream of an alternative world where she could be free of the mortal burden of narrative experience; "*Heaven*," she hums at one point to keep her spirits up, "*is a place—a place where nothing—nothing—ever—happens*" (115). Melanie eventually relinquishes the escapist fantasies of her darkened youth, however, for "Absolute Elsewhere" proves to be no more satisfying than the wishful realm of Keats's nightingale and urn. Thernstrom's book mounts a powerful indictment of

---

[36] "Bad Men and Scary Places" is the title to chapter 1, part 7, and the subtitle reads "Which Tells How the Little Match Girl Came to Fall into Bad Hands." All of the chapters in part 7 carry similar Little Match Girl subtitles.

narrative's destructive powers, yet it is through narrative that she brings this truth home. The vision that informs the writing of *The Dead Girl* remains profoundly narrative in character, but tested.

Beyond Narrative?

Can we escape narrative in life writing? I mean escape consciously, deliberately, as opposed to being unable to perform self-narration because of various pathologies of the sort I described under the heading of "dysnarrativia." From time to time, in a spirit of formal innovation, critics have sought to free autobiography from its perennial allegiance to biography's concern with narrative chronology, as though narrative's primacy in self-accounting were merely a matter of literary convention.[37] As I have shown in this chapter, however, narrative's role in self-representation extends well beyond the literary; it is not merely one form among many in which to express identity, but rather an integral part of a primary mode of identity experience, that of the extended self, the self in time. If my reading of narrative's place in life writing is correct, to move beyond narrative would involve not merely a shift in literary form but a more fundamental change in the culturally sanctioned narrative practices that function as the medium in which the extended self and autobiographical memory emerge. Having said that, I would like nonetheless to look briefly at one autobiography, *Roland Barthes by Roland Barthes* (1975), which stands out in my mind from all of the life writing I can think of in the last twenty years as a text that does attempt to jettison narrative in a singular and striking fashion. I have been investigating the link between narrative and identity, and in this context *Roland Barthes* is doubly apt, for Barthes repudiates both, at least as conventionally conceived.

Barthes explicitly disavows any connection between the "I" of his text and any self anchored in an extratextual realm of biographical reference: "Do I not know that, *in the field of the subject,*

---

[37] See, e.g., John Sturrock's essay "The New Model Autobiographer."

there is no referent?" He reminds himself, accordingly: "I do not say: 'I am going to describe myself' but: 'I am writing a text, and I call it R.B.'" (56). In order to shed the convention of authorship, Barthes as author is incorporated into the title—*Roland Barthes by Roland Barthes*—as though the text were somehow its own author, spinning free of any referential constraints. Just as Thernstrom understood that character and events were defined by their place in a narrative structure ("you know what will happen because you know the genre"), Barthes sought to deflect this meaning-making process by organizing his autobiographical material in an aggressively nonnarrative format, a largely alphabetical sequence of brief entries (most less than a page in length) on an exceedingly heterogeneous array of topics. "Perhaps in places," he concedes, "certain fragments seem to follow one another by some affinity; but the important thing is that these little networks not be connected, that they not slide into a single enormous network which would be the structure of the book, its meaning" (148). As if to demonstrate his successful evasion of some overarching identity narrative, Barthes displays at one point a series of "anamneses," memory fragments he cherishes precisely for their "insignificance," their lack of meaning that permits them to escape incorporation into "the image-system" (109–10).

Barthes's programmatic refusal of the narrative chronology that conventionally structures autobiographical discourse founders finally on the rock of the experience it is meant to exclude. Not only do individual entries include many a micronarrative and microchronology of autobiographical retrospect, but the great structuring relationship of his life, his profound tie to his mother, threatens to breach the theoretical dike erected against narrative and identity, notably in the fragment titled "A memory of childhood" (121–22) and in the moving portfolio of photographs featuring his childhood in Bayonne that opens the volume. As if finally to speak the depth of feeling that he had displayed in the photographs of *Roland Barthes*, Barthes devotes the central pages of his last published work, *Camera Lucida* (1980), to his mother's final illness and death in 1977. Identity, narrative, autobiography preempt the book's ostensible focus on photography. If we place Barthes's autobiographical writing in the context of the child's initiation into "memory talk," the autobiographer's assertion that he wants "to side with any writing whose principle is that *the subject is merely an effect of language*" (*Roland Barthes* 79) takes on a meaning quite different from the daring refusal of reference he intended. "The subject" is indeed "an effect of language," of the interpersonal discourse with parent or caregiver that fosters the emergence of the extended self and its store of autobiographical memories.

Make no mistake—Barthes's autobiography is like no other; his concerted effort at defamiliarization has kept it fresh over the years. *Roland Barthes* is one of a rather small group of autobiographies in which narrative is not the dominant mode—Carolyn Steedman's *Landscape for a Good Woman* and Richard Rodriguez's *Hunger of Memory* would be others. Yet narrative is inevitably present in all of these works. While Barthes manages to maintain his principled refusal to supply the familiar narrative of identity formation that is central to the genre (if we except the opening portfolio of photographs that stand in for this absent story), it would be hard to say that he isn't engaging, first and last, in self-narration. If one opens the book at random, one invariably finds little personal stories, frequent memories, and especially ideas and opinions, for *Roland Barthes* is very much the self-portrait of an intellectual. If this is truly a postmodern autobiography, then postmodernism's break with tradition insofar as life writing is concerned is rather less radical than some have made out. Despite the postmodern appetite for all things *post, after,* and *beyond* (literary conferences today commonly feature these terms), I see no signs of anyone anywhere unendowed with a narratively constituted identity, except, of course, in the case of the disorders noted previously such as amnesia and autism.

By way of conclusion to this discussion of narrative identity, I want to consider the implications of the tendency I noted earlier to regard the unstoried self as an instance of pathology.[38] In speaking of amnesia and autism as pathologies, I want to get at the psychological rather than the neurological dimension of these phenomena, the strange absence or loss of affect in such individuals that in case after case makes so deep an impression on the clinicians who study them. This sense of something missing, an inner chill or deadness, seems to be associated with a "dysnarrativia" that bespeaks a damaged identity. Who can say for sure, however, that the identities in question are truly damaged? It is the fact that those who observe such individuals should think so that interests me, suggesting that we live in a culture in which narrative functions as the signature of the real, of the normal. (I should add that, given the opportunity for first-hand observation, I suspect that I would agree that identity has been damaged in these cases.) In a remarkable essay that I keep going back to, "The Value of Narrativity in the Representation of Reality," Hayden White makes this point in connection with history, whereas I want to apply it here in connection with identity. Social accountability requires identity narrative; in *The Woman Warrior*, Maxine Hong Kingston gives a nice rendering of a child's perception of this requirement: "I thought talking and not talking made the difference between sanity and insanity. Insane people were the ones who couldn't explain themselves" (216). It is revealing in this connection, moreover, that Roy Schafer, Donald Spence, and others have conceived of psychoanalysis as a narrative practice.[39]

I am less interested, finally, in demonstrating that there is a link between narrative disorders and identity disorders than I am

[38] Susanna Egan, who has been studying contemporary accounts of trauma, notes the potential of crisis to "disconnect the autobiographer from time and from place so radically that narrative ceases to function" (letter to the author). The "antinarrative" tendency she identifies in the literature of trauma is the product not of formal and theoretical considerations as in the case of Barthes but of the lived chaos of brutal experiences.

[39] Steven Marcus writes that Freud believed that "a coherent story is in some manner connected with mental health" (92).

in pointing out that both clinicians (psychologists and neurologists) and conventionally socialized laymen make this link. What I find striking in both Sacks's and Schacter's cases on the one hand and in Thernstrom's account of her friends' response to her own "case" on the other is the steady monitoring of narrative practices by these observers for familiar signs of healthy identity. Well before Melanie's attempted suicide, for example, her down-to-earth, sarcastic friend Bob condemns her morbid tendency to "see things Match Girl" (202): "I think, actually, the metaphor sucks," he tells her bluntly (272). And her boyfriend Adam, increasingly disturbed, joins Bob in attacking her Match-Girl self-characterization as "*the doomed kind*": "But this isn't a story. . . . And you aren't a kind. . . . You are you," he protests (278). Identity narratives generate identity judgments; the way we practice identity narrative makes a difference: is the display of affect appropriate, is it lacking? Either way, as we make such evaluations (and I grant that we often make them in what we consider another's best interests), we enter an ethical realm that deserves further investigation. After Foucault, we hardly need to be reminded of the potentially disciplinary dimension of this regulation of identity, especially when it is a question of labeling the individual as healthy or normal.

CHAPTER FOUR

"The Unseemly Profession": Privacy, Inviolate Personality, and the Ethics of Life Writing

Everyone thinks he is more or less the owner of his name, of his person, of his own story (and even of his image).

—Philippe Lejeune

The right of property in its widest sense, including all possession, including all rights and privileges, and hence embracing the right to an inviolate personality, affords alone that broad basis upon which the protection which the individual demands can be rested.

—Samuel D. Warren and Louis D. Brandeis

Selling Selves

Everyone knows that publishers today frequently ask authors to hit the road to promote their books, and so, willing or not, they do the book tour with its formulaic press interviews, television guest appearances, and bookstore signings. Given the technology for media exposure, the photo- and telegenic author inevitably proves to be an asset to sales, and commentators in the *New York Times*, *Lingua franca*, and *Vanity Fair* have remarked on the increasing importance of the author's looks to a book's success. Of Kathryn Harrison's *The Kiss* (1997), for example, Paul Bogaards, director of promotion at Knopf, comments, "If an unattractive woman were to write a book about sleeping with her father, it would not command the same media real estate as an attractive woman sleeping with her father" (quoted in Pogrebin).[1] It's Bogaards's job, of course, to treat Harrison and her book as commodities, but we may well wonder whether the current popularity of memoirs like Harrison's—the desire to write them and the appetite to consume them—is somehow connected to this impulse to trade on the author's flesh. Certainly the media personality Howard Stern is cashing in on the conflation of self and body when he titles his autobiography *Private Parts* (1993); self-revelation becomes a form of flashing.

While autobiographers are not literally going "the full monty," they are indeed increasingly revealing what many might regard as their most private thoughts and deeds, apparently making good on Rousseau's injunction to perform a total and uncensored act of self-disclosure: "I have displayed myself as I was" (17). In his essay "The Art of Self: Autobiography in an Age of Narcissism," William Gass castigates recent memoir writing for its indiscriminate confessions, its childish self-indulgence: "Why is it so exciting to say, now that everyone knows it anyway, 'I was born . . . I was born . . . I was born'? 'I pooped in my pants, I was betrayed, I made straight A's' " (46). When autobiographers relate the trivial and banal, we yawn—or we ought to, Gass suggests; we don't need to be told what we already know. Are memoirs, however, now courageously speaking hitherto unspeakable things, things that we have held in silence precisely because we have refused to accept them as a part of knowledge? Or is their speech in such cases culpable, compounding the original trespass with unseemly disclosure?

What *are* we to think, for example, of "an attractive woman" who writes about "sleeping with her father"? In an early review of *The Kiss* in the *Wall Street Journal*, Cynthia Crossen offers "two wise but widely ignored words of advice for Ms. Harrison and her brethren: Hush up." "Ms. Harrison *and her brethren*"—in making Harrison's case representative, Crossen strikes a characteristic note that was echoed by many others in the weeks and months

---

[1] See Emily Nussbaum, Pogrebin, Shnayerson, and Zalewski.

following the publication of *The Kiss* in the spring of 1997. Because Harrison's slim volume became a lightning rod for debate about what columnists are calling the "age of memoir," I will use it as a point of departure for my own discussion of the ethics of life writing. Before reviewing the fallout in the press, however, I will first consider the book itself, even though it's true that it was precisely the controversy about the book that brought it to my attention in the first place.

The Kiss is intensely focused on Harrison's incestuous affair with her father that lasted some four or five years, beginning when the author was a twenty-year-old junior in college, and concluding, apparently, with the death of her mother in 1985. During this period, Harrison surrendered to her father's demands for a sexual consummation of their love, eventually moving into his house for a time to live with the wife and children of his second marriage. The book makes a powerful case for the central importance of this episode in the author's identity formation: that is, if Harrison were to write her autobiography, *The Kiss* would have to be it.

Harrison's narrative is harrowing: in a stripped-down, clinical prose she relates a story of failed maturity, of relational identity gone pathologically wrong. In presenting relational identity in Chapter 2, I drew on Jessica Benjamin's work to formulate the crucial role that others play in the individual's achievement of autonomous selfhood, and I want to recall Benjamin's theory here, for Harrison's story seems to illustrate it in striking fashion. Stressing the "intersubjective dimension" (49) of individuation, Benjamin argues that "at the very moment of realizing our own independence, we are dependent upon another to recognize it" (33). As Harrison tells it, circumstances conspire to prevent this recognition in her case, paving the way for the incest into which she is propelled by the identity deficit that is the legacy of her loveless childhood: her parents divorce when she is six months old, her mother moves out and leaves her when she is six, and she is raised by her maternal grandparents until she is seventeen. Except for two brief visits (when she is five and again when she is ten), her father is entirely absent from her growing up, and her mother, wholly self-involved, might as well have been. The child hungers for the mother's love and acknowledgment, but her existence remains largely unconfirmed by the mother's gaze: "Her eyes, when they turn at last toward me, are like two empty mirrors. I can't find myself in them" (9).[2] Painfully, the child learns that her mother "will accept, acknowledge, *see* me only in as much as I will make myself the child who pleases her" (20), a price, however, that the child refuses to pay. And so the stage is set for the series of battles between the two that continues until the mother's early death when Harrison is twenty-four.

At fifteen, the daughter wins a round in her endless contest of wills with her mother, affirming her existence by starving it in a dangerous replay of the mother's withheld gaze and love: "*You want thin?* I remember thinking, *I'll give you thin. I'll define thin, not you*" (39). Losing weight provides the satisfaction—however perverse—of defining and loving herself. Looking in the mirror, she recalls: "Seeing myself is enough to make me gasp with pleasure . . . I am amazed by this body I've made" (40). The mother, however, brutal and controlling, wins the next round. In a scene of violation as sinister as anything in Faulkner's *Sanctuary*, the mother insists that the daughter be fitted with a diaphragm before she goes away to college, even if it means breaking her hymen; she watches while the gynecologist "deflowers" her daughter with "a series of graduated green plastic penises" (42–43). Here and throughout the book, rage—not love—is played out on Harrison's body.

As *The Kiss* unfolds, Harrison's thesis about her stunted identity becomes increasingly clear. Reunited with her father at age twenty, during the spring break of her junior year in college, bathed in her father's loving gaze, Harrison seems poised to reenact—belatedly—the child's passage into secure identity previously denied by the unseeing mother: "My father . . . has some-

---

[2] The pathos of the child's wish for recognition is haunting. Harrison recalls that when she was five, she pushed away her mother's sleep mask and attempted to open her mother's closed eyes (197–98).

how begun to *see* me into being. His look gives me to myself, his gaze reflects the life my mother's willfully shut eyes denied" (63). Their relationship, however, swiftly takes a dark, incestuous turn, revealing the dangerous underside of the identity transaction. Harrison spells out the terms: "From a mother who won't see me to a father who tells me I am there only when he does see me: perhaps, unconsciously, I consider this an existential promotion. I must, for already I feel that my life depends on my father's see-ing me" (89).[3] The father's ego, however, proves to be if anything even more unstable than the daughter's, and ego boundaries dis-solve between them: "He calls as many as three times a day," she writes, " 'How am I?' he says when he calls" (134). When they fi-nally yield to their mutual obsession, Harrison presents the in-cest as "an act that defines me, that explains who I am" (138–39), but it looks much more like an act of self-annihilation, to the ex-tent that the daughter can be said to have had a self to destroy. She is possessed by, incorporated into, the father: "I have no life or will apart from his" (160). It follows, then, that her memories of days, weeks, and months of this period are not "forgotten" but "lost," "because they were never lived" (169).

Thus, the incest that "defines" Harrison also, and more accu-rately, does not define her, although it inevitably defines the rep-utation of the book as the story of "an attractive woman sleeping with her father." The true axis of *The Kiss* is the daughter's rela-tionship not with her father but with her mother.[4] Interestingly, the father captures this deep truth about this hellish story in a se-ries of pictures he takes on the occasion of the fateful family re-union that was to throw Harrison's already fragile identity into crisis:

[3] Harrison insists on the logic of her obsession with her father in several places. E.g., "Because, if she won't love me, then the only way not to fall into the abyss of the unloved is by clinging to him" (99).

[4] In "Seeking Rapture: Lessons for an Apprentice Saint," an autobiographical sketch that Harrison published in 1994, Harrison presents her relationship with her mother as the primary, structuring armature of her life story. This version repeats the general outline of the story she tells in *The Kiss*, minus her incestu-ous affair with her father.

These pictures of my mother and me are the last I have of us together. As it turns out, they are overexposed; my father never
makes individual prints of them, so I have only the proof sheets
showing the two of us, our heads inclined, our bodies not touching. Behind my mother and me, visible between our shoulders,
are tongues of flame from the gas log. In certain of the poses the
fire looks as if it comes from our clothes themselves, as if the an-
guished expression we each wear is not the smile we intended but
the first rictus of pain. As if what my father caught with his camera was the moment when suddenly we knew we'd begun to burn.
(55)

The pictures, taken by the father whose own relationship with
the mother had also failed, disclose the failed relationship between mother and daughter. Animating the attraction between
father and daughter is their shared rage against the cold, refusing mother: they are "locked in the kind of sympathy for each
other that only two people spurned by the same woman could
feel" (78). It is only with the mother's death that the destructive
field of force loses its power to enslave (139, 147). Only after
viewing her mother's body a second time, to the annoyance of
the undertaker, is Harrison finally convinced that she is now free
to return to "my life" (199): "the spell is broken, her death has
released me" (200).

An identity so deeply wounded, however, cannot swiftly recover. All it takes is a brief meeting with her half-sister years
later to call up the destructive power of Harrison's past, confirming her continuing insecurity despite the fact that she has
married, had two children, and become a published novelist:
"Once upon a time I fell from grace," she confides to the
reader, "I was lost so deeply in a dark wood that I'm afraid I'll
never be safe again" (174). Harrison suggests, however, that she
did eventually achieve a sense of secure and autonomous selfhood, so long deferred. In the final pages of her narrative, she
records a memorable dream she had about her mother in 1995,
some ten years after her death. In the dream, as they never had

done in life, mother and daughter exchange a profound gaze of mutual recognition and reconciliation: "Nothing happens then, and yet everything transpires. . . . Our eyes don't move or blink, they are no more than a few inches apart. . . . In this dream, I feel that at last she knows me, and I her" (206–7). When her mother died, Harrison had left the space beneath the dates on her tombstone blank, "because . . . the only word that I could imagine carved in that blank struck me as one I didn't deserve to use, rather than the truth that it was. Is. Beloved" (204). Now, with *The Kiss*, she reburies the past, dedicating the book to her mother:

> Beloved
> 1942—1985

The aura of determinism that surrounds *The Kiss* stems from Harrison's rather schematic working out of the psychological forces that governed her growing up. She unfolds the triangular set of relations among father, mother, and daughter like necessary steps in a proof. This "Q.E.D." effect is heightened by the almost total absence of moral reflection in this resolutely psychological account. This exclusion of moral commentary is, moreover, apparently quite deliberate on Harrison's part, for she told one interviewer, "Personally, I've tried to strip judgment away" (St. John, "Saucy" 30). The very rigor and clarity with which the narrator solves the identity equations of her younger self, however, generate a new identity conundrum to take their place: namely, a curious discrepancy between the identity portrayed—weak, controlled, victimized—and the identity predicated by the act of writing this tight, austere memoir—strong, controlling, even manipulative.[5] The reader has no way of knowing how—or whether—the truth of the one could be squared with the truth of the other; the identity narrative that could connect them remains untold at present. The older Harrison prefers

---

[5] Is it a discrepancy of this sort that led a reviewer, Christopher Lehmann-Haupt, to comment that "the mystery of her healthy survival remains a flaw in her memoir"?

to see her younger self as shaped by others; in the words of the epigraph to *The Kiss* from François Mauriac, "We are, all of us, molded and remolded by those who have loved us, and though that love may pass, we remain none the less *their* work—a work that very likely they do not recognize, and which is never exactly what they intended."

"*Their* work"? While the epigraph accurately captures the world of *The Kiss*, a hermetic world of passion and dependency in which autonomy and choice are largely absent, in which responsibility, power, and authorship are assigned to others, it masks the obvious truth that Kathryn Harrison is the author of her younger self. As the writer of a *memoir*, of course, Harrison can claim to be merely the transparent medium through whom we witness her earlier self. Consonant with this posture, she presents the past of the incestuous affair in the present tense, generating an effect of "you are there" immediacy that conceals the present of the autobiographical act in which *The Kiss* is written, in which the earlier Harrison is "molded and remolded" by Harrison the writer.

We never really know why writers write what they write, and this very unknowability can make any inquiry into an author's intentions seem fruitless if not impertinent. Because self-proclaimed memoirs purport to tell the truth, however, not only about their authors' lives but about the lives of other people, the motives for that truth-telling are inevitably placed in question when the truth is unsavory, as it appears to be in this case. (I say "appears to be" because Harrison's father, traced by an enterprising reporter, has neither confirmed nor denied Harrison's account of their affair.)[6] When it comes to motive, some autobiographers choose to dramatize their relationships toward their material, while others, including Harrison, do not. The deterministic cast of *The Kiss* leaves us to infer that just as the incest had to be committed, so its story had to be told. The taboo nature of Harrison's subject, however, has inevitably shifted the assessment of her intentions from the psychological to the moral,

---

[6] See St. John, "Kathryn Harrison's Dad."

with commentators invariably defending or deploring her decision to write this book. In the light of the controversy that followed its publication, which I want to consider in a moment, it is
hard not to read the packaging of the hardcover edition as a pre-
emptive strike designed to cast Harrison's motives in the best
possible light.

The front cover of the dust jacket displays a photograph of a
man in dark suit and tie and (presumably) a woman standing on
a lawn posed in front of a house. We see this pair and we do not
see them: the head of the man at the top of the picture is
cropped, and a large white rectangle containing the title of the
book and the author's name is superimposed on the center of
the photograph, concealing the face of the second, shorter figure and the bodies of both except for their feet (the man is wear-
ing dress shoes; the woman's clothes are invisible, her legs and
feet are bare). Thus the cover both invites and obstructs our
gaze; it seems to have been censored, yet it suggests that the narrative it announces will reveal what we do not yet see. How did
the author look at the truth of this image, the cover seems to say,
and how should we?

To prime us, the publishers include nine different blurbs on
the rest of the dust jacket which serve collectively to characterize
Harrison's unstated intentions and to praise them. The first of
these, by Robert Coles, who is identified as the author of *The
Moral Intelligence of Children*, serves as the book's imprimatur, for
Coles interprets *The Kiss* as "an account of a moral victory," be-
stowing on the narrative a kind of Good Housekeeping Seal of
Approval. Most of the other blurbs come from writers of well-
reviewed memoirs—Tobias Wolff, Mary Karr, Mary Gordon, and
others—who honor Harrison for her courage, honesty, and
artistry in facing the truth about the most painful passage of her
experience.

What information is there about the story of the story that
could shed light on Harrison's reasons for writing this book? According to *The Kiss* itself, the father seems to have believed that
the incest once committed foreclosed the daughter's options,

binding her to him forever because the telling of their secret would drive anyone else away: "You've done what you've done, and you've done it with me. And now you'll never be able to have anyone else, because you won't be able to keep our secret. You'll tell whoever it is, and once he knows, he'll leave you" (188). The father was right that his daughter wouldn't be able to keep their secret, but he didn't reckon with the possibility that Colin Harrison, the young man she told it to in 1985, would not only marry her but support her in her decision some eleven years later to tell her untellable story to the world.

In one of several prepublication interviews and related stories about *The Kiss*, Kathryn Harrison told Warren St. John of the *New York Observer*, a weekly featuring news of the publishing industry, that she decided to write the story of the affair at the urging of her literary agent, Amanda Urban, and that she wrote it in a "white heat" ("Saucy" 30). When she met St. John, Harrison was on the defensive from an article in *Vanity Fair* that "portrayed me as calculating and mercenary" (1); "I was never trying to figure out what I was going to get from this book," she protested. "Really, I just wanted to write it" (30).[7] St. John was obviously skeptical: "By deciding to merchandise her pain," he comments, "Ms. Harrison surely knew what she was getting into" (1), and he reports that New York publishing circles characterized the Harrisons as self-promoting literary yuppies, as "the Colin and Kathryn Harrison Show" (30). (Colin Harrison is a novelist and also an editor at *Harper's*; they live in a brownstone in the "writerly Park Slope" [30] section of Brooklyn.) In a second, follow-up article on *The Kiss*, "Kathryn Harrison's Dad Responds to Her Memoir," St. John proposes a third, psychological motive for Harrison's project, in addition to the creative necessity claimed

[7] The article to which Harrison refers, "Women Behaving Badly," is by Michael Shnayerson and appeared in *Vanity Fair* in February 1997. Describing Harrison's career as having reached a plateau, Shnayerson suggests that Harrison exploited the memoir genre to give her sales a boost. "Off-the-book-page coverage—meaning news stories and author profiles, in addition to the usual book reviews—is, indeed," Shnayerson observes, "one reason publishers have scooped up memoirs as eagerly as they have" (60).

by Harrison, her husband, and her agent, and the commercial opportunism alleged by their detractors. Noting that Harrison's father is "a retired Protestant minister, living in a small Southern city" (1), St. John speculates, "If her father is correct that there are many people capable of connecting him to his daughter, and that she is aware of that fact, *The Kiss* seems, in part, a calculated act of revenge" (9).

Whatever her motives may have been, it is nonetheless true that Harrison has been active in publicizing her book: according to St. John, she appeared on "national television programs like *Dateline* and the *Today* show" ("Kathryn" 9). Particularly pertinent in connection with the ethical ramifications of her decision to go public with her story is St. John's account of an Authors Guild forum he attended in Manhattan on "The Memoir Explosion" on April 8, 1997, in which Harrison's response to a question concerning "the memoirist's responsibility to his or her family" struck him as "cavalier": " 'All's fair in love and war, in this case,' she said" (9). St. John notes that Frank McCourt, also on the panel, took a more conservative stance about his disclosure of sensitive family material in his own memoir, *Angela's Ashes* (1996): "I could not write about my mother and her affair with her cousin until she was dead, because she couldn't live through it" (9). Apparently on this occasion Harrison left the impact of her revelations on her children entirely out of account. Interestingly, St. John reports that Robert Coles " 'recanted' a blurb he provided for the book, saying he had not realized Ms. Harrison had young children of her own who would have to cope with her public revelations" (9).

So why *did* she write the book? Of the many pieces that came out in the spring of 1997, one in particular captures the disturbing mix of motives that clouds any attempt to read the ethics of the situation clearly: an article by Colin Harrison titled "Sins of the Father" in the April issue of *Vogue*. Here the husband echoes the main lines of the wife's account given to St. John: in writing her story, Kathryn Harrison answered to an imperative of the creative imagination, an artistic "necessity" overriding any other consideration—he "could only wonder what might happen to my wife if she did not write her book." Should he have been wondering what might happen to her if she did? Colin Harrison relates that, in fact, writing the book nearly cost Kathryn her life: the "inordinate stress" triggered a collapse from Graves' disease—"she was dying" (376). This extraordinary tale of suffering is accompanied by a full-page color portrait of the Harrisons: he seated, rather homely and scruffy, gazing up at her; she, svelte, statuesque, strikingly attired in a stunning, cream-colored pinstripe suit, looking out at us. What exactly, I wondered, were the Harrisons and their burden of incest doing in the glossy world of fashion and luxury presided over by *Vogue*'s editor and style setter, Anna Wintour? I found myself thinking again of St. John's phrase, "merchandising pain."[8]

Kathryn Harrison's interview with St. John, Colin Harrison's piece in *Vogue*, the packaging of the book itself by Random House—all these moves seem to have anticipated the storm that would break once *The Kiss* was out, and I want to survey rapidly the commentary in the *New York Times* to suggest the tenor of the reception the book received in the spring of 1997.[9] On February 27, Christopher Lehmann-Haupt praises Harrison's writing, but wonders whether "a memoir can ring too artistic for the truth." In her op-ed column for March 15, Maureen Dowd notes the explosion of memoir writing—"out of the top 11 books on The New York Times nonfiction best-seller list, 9 are autobiographical"—and she dismisses this literature as an exhibitionist display

---

[8] Margo Jefferson's reaction to Colin Harrison's "mini-memoir" in *Vogue* is similar to my own: the conjunction of story and photograph is inescapably troubling. See "Facing Truth about Incest, in Memoir and Novel."

[9] St. John reports that "Ms. Harrison said she and Random House decided against a book tour: 'They thought there was something inherently exploitative about sending me to go to a bookstore and have me be accosted by whoever wanted to accost me,' she said" ("Saucy" 30). And Colin Harrison writes, "The book, I feared, would expose Kathryn to all manner of criticism, name-calling, cheap psychologizing, yellow journalism, ridicule, even hate" (376).

of "dirty laundry" for cash—"publishers are frantically signing up the hampers." She brands *The Kiss* as characteristic, an instance of "creepy people talking about creepy people."[10]

On March 30, a glowing review by the memoirist Susan Cheever appears in the *New York Times Book Review*. Cheever bestows high praise for the way *The Kiss* "brilliantly, heartbreakingly lays out the helplessness of being a young woman." On the same date, the *Times* runs a feature story by Karen De Witt titled "Incest as a Selling Point." De Witt sees *The Kiss* as symptomatic of a surge of interest in the incest theme in contemporary film and memoir—"Incest is the plat du jour in the '90s marketplace," she quips, and she quotes one authority who associates this trend with "ambush television and mid-afternoon shame programs."

On April 5, Doreen Carvajal echoes the drift of the De Witt piece in a front-page story headlined "Book Publishers Are Eager for Tales of True Torment." Probing the motives for tell-all memoirs, she suggests that they represent "the print version of the television anxiety show circuit" (1). In this vein she cites the memoir anthologist Laurie Stone's division of contemporary memoirs into "two categories, victim stories and shame narratives," but she also points out that at least for some of the best-selling memoirists, moral issues are decisive. Thus she notes that Mary Karr, author of *The Liars' Club* (1995), told her that "what's happened is that we're looking for some sort of moral compass," and she concludes by reporting Frank McCourt's reservations about *The Kiss*. The author of *Angela's Ashes* comments, "I thought she should have waited till he was dead. . . . In some ways, there's a feeling of a subconscious vendetta and it makes me queasy." In her defense, Harrison told De Witt that she took "a great deal of trouble" not to expose her father, stressing instead her own "great compulsion" to confess: "I wanted . . . to really vivisect myself" (23).

[10] Mary Anne Sacco, writing in the letters column on March 21, agrees with Dowd that memoir is a "hot genre," but she defends its power to "transform" the writer's life and the lives of others—she has conducted a memoir workshop for second-graders.

In an op-ed article the following day, on April 6, Tobias Wolff, author of *This Boy's Life* (1989), strikes a blow in Harrison's defense. Citing bad reviews of *The Kiss* by Michael Shnayerson in *Vanity Fair* ("squalid grab for publicity and sales"), by Jonathan Yardley in the *Washington Post* ("personal gain and talk-show notoriety"), and James Wolcott in the *New Republic* ("narcissistic act . . . intended to invite misery and humiliation on her children"), Wolff accuses Harrison's detractors of using her "as a target of convenience for their animus against the genre she's working in—the memoir." Championing memoir, Wolff places Harrison in the company of some of its most admired twentieth-century practitioners, including George Orwell, Mary McCarthy, Frank Conroy, and Mary Karr. Brent Staples, author of *Parallel Time* (1994), makes a similar case for memoir against charges of opportunism and literary inferiority in the Editorial Notebook for April 27, under the heading "Hating It Because It Is True: The Backlash against the Memoir."

The outlines of the controversy become increasingly clear with each new salvo, such that Margo Jefferson, writing under the headline "Facing Truth about Incest, In Memoir and Novel" in the Critic's Notebook for May 29, attempts to provide an overview. Opening with excerpts from three twentieth-century incest narratives, by Virginia Woolf, Edna O'Brien, and Kathryn Harrison, Jefferson observes that with the last "we enter a vehement, even hysterical debate about the literary, social and psychological propriety of publishing such stories." Summarizing, she identifies three primary responses to *The Kiss*: "media condemnation" (Harrison ignored the consequences for her father and her children), "media congratulation" (Harrison demonstrated courage and artistry), and "cultural handwringing and lamentation" (the book is a sign of moral decay and social decline). Addressing "the memoir backlash," Jefferson believes that the "problem" of memoir is "figuring out how to examine and dramatize ourselves without forgetting to pay the same attention to the larger historical and spiritual forces that have made us." This, she argues, *The Kiss* does not do. Harrison's book, she concludes, is of a piece with the publicity surrounding it: "In the end, you have to treat 'The Kiss' as if it were performance art, with the book, the reviews, the interviews, the editorials and the readers' responses all spread across some vast media gallery."[11]

I've already noted Harrison's claim that she "sought to strip judgment away" in writing *The Kiss*, but judgment is clearly the hallmark of all the commentary I have described, not only judgment of the book and its author but judgment of memoir as a kind of writing and judgment of the society in which such work is produced and consumed. What I hear as I reread these clippings from the *Times* is a note of vehemence, of intensity, that seems to exceed the admittedly extreme circumstances of Harrison's case. In piece after piece the Harrison example is grouped with others to provide a springboard for sweeping cultural critique. It is the grounds for this critique that I want to explore in the rest of this chapter, and I think that Cynthia Crossen's early review of *The Kiss* in the *Wall Street Journal* provides an important lead when she censures the book for its assault on privacy: "Today's memoirists have yanked away the last veil of privacy that protected the sanctity of the individual from the mindless tittle-tattle of the masses." The memoirist's urge to confess, she observes, however therapeutic, necessarily entails a cost to others: "Their children, their friends, perhaps society itself may pay a terrible price for the writers' solace." As some of the commentators paused to ask, what are the consequences for those whose lives touched—and touch—Harrison's, the father, the husband, the children? No one is likely to feel any special solicitude for the abusive father, but is there a sense in which life writers themselves can be said to be abusive?

In *Secrets: On the Ethics of Concealment and Revelation* (1982), Sissela Bok reminds us that "no one lives in complete isolation" (85), and she pursues the ethical questions involved when we disclose others' secrets in the act of disclosing our own. Two recent

---

[11] Jefferson's article is by no means the last word in the debate about memoir stirred up by the publication of *The Kiss*. I think, however, that the leading positions are clear.

developments have made these questions even more pressing. First, as I suggested in Chapter 2, if identity is increasingly understood in relational terms, then it follows that the lives of others are centrally implicated in the telling of any life story. Second, the public appetite for life stories of all kinds seems to be voracious: witness the phenomenal success of McCourt's *Angela's Ashes* and the regularity with which memoir is featured in the "Personal History" and "Brief Lives" formats of the *New Yorker* and the *Atlantic*, not to mention the popularity of the television talk shows, which offer the security of a nonjudgmental format to the endless parade of victims who provide their stock-in-trade. In "The Shameless World of Phil, Sally and Oprah," Vicki Abt and Mel Seesholtz argue that "television is rewriting our cultural scripts" (172), undermining the traditional foundations of moral behavior in both the "guests" and the viewing audience. "The talk show ideology" trains those who confess to see themselves as " 'victims' rather than possibly . . . irresponsible, weak people," with the result that "traditional boundaries between very private matters and public discussions are continuously breached" (178). For Abt and Seesholtz, the talk show confessional is socially, because morally, dangerous: "The split between the televised action and the concomitant social effects in real life situations must be eroding our collective ability to make causal connections between actions and consequences" (187–88). And is memoir equally dangerous? Is it one more sign of a decadent culture of disclosure?

I have been using the reception of *The Kiss* to capture the climate of the so-called age of memoir in which we live, but is this example a reliable indicator of the larger cultural and ethical concerns posed by memoir writing? *The Kiss*, after all, is an extreme case, although the insistent references in the reviews to television talk shows suggest that personal extremity has become our daily fare. Even so, lest the particulars of the book place a limit on its value as a representative instance of contemporary memoir, I'd like to conclude this section by discussing briefly another case—less charged but nonetheless highly revealing—in which the ethical issue involved turns precisely on the individual's right to privacy, a right that the author of this sketch explicitly and pointedly violated.

In the October 1997 issue of the *Atlantic*, under the rubric "Brief Lives," Phyllis Rose published a portrait of her brother-in-law, Alain de Brunhoff, "legendary in Paris for his talent, looks, and charm, and the glamorous life he had led before abruptly retiring from the world and becoming a monk at the age of forty" (44). Rose's account of Alain's withdrawal from the world is absorbing, so much so that the reader experiences a jolt when she announces in the final paragraph that "Alain disapproves completely of my having written this and asked me not to publish it." She goes on to say that she has changed his name and certain details "to protect his privacy," but, she notes, "I will never get him to see my having written what he told me as anything but a violation of a confidence."[12] And so she concludes, "By profession and national temperament, I believe in making things known; by profession and national temperament, he believes in keeping them quiet" (48).

Clearly readers of the piece were not satisfied by Rose's breezy appeal to stereotypical notions of "profession and national temperament," and they wrote to the magazine to protest. In the January 1998 issue, the editors of the *Atlantic* published four letters, all making essentially the same point about Rose's failure to respect her subject's privacy. As one writer puts it, "Phyllis Rose . . . should consider the possibility that the reason 'I will never get [my subject, Alain] to see my having written what he told me as anything but a violation of a confidence' is that that is precisely what it was." Moreover, by withholding acknowledgment of her subject's objection to the piece until the final paragraph, she obliged readers to be unwittingly complicit in her project: "At

---

[12] Rose opens the sketch by saying that she has married into "an extraordinary family" (44). She states that her husband is the son of Jean de Brunhoff, author of the Babar books; his brother Mathieu is a pediatrician, and "Alain," the youngest brother, is the concert pianist turned monk. If she had taken the privacy issue as seriously as she claims, she would have had to suppress all allusions to the de Brunhoff family; she did not do so.

that point," one of the letter writers comments, "I felt as if I had been duped into invading this man's privacy" ("Letters" 9).

Rose's reply to her critics is surprisingly lame. She opens by repeating her notion that it is the writer's professional "responsibility to testify." Always? I suspect that even Rose could see that such a sweeping claim does not bear scrutiny, and so she goes on to raise "a real dilemma: how can I be truthful about my own life without infringing on somebody else's?" Like Kathryn Harrison, Rose confides that a kind of psychological necessity drove her to write:

> The piece demanded to be written because of my mental involvement with my brother-in-law. Both as a member of my family and as someone who had great worldly success and turned his back on it, he figures large in my imagination, putting into perspective the way I live. His withdrawal is an envied possibility, a moral pole. In speaking truthfully about this for myself, I expect in some way to be speaking for others. A writer has no other justification. ("Letters" 9–10)

The only problem with Rose's second line of defense, her claim that her brother-in-law's withdrawal from the world put her own life choices into perspective, is that this high-sounding rationale doesn't fit the piece she wrote: there is nothing in the sketch to sustain such a reading; her own life choices are not mentioned. Because our own lives never stand free of the lives of others, we are faced with our responsibility to those others whenever we write about ourselves. There is no escaping this responsibility, as Rose belatedly acknowledges, and I want to explore in the rest of this chapter the ethical consequences for life writing that stem from the way we live our privacy.

Privacy and Inviolate Personality

Is there harm in life writing? A good deal of the commentary on *The Kiss*, for example, as well as the letters criticizing Rose's piece in the *Atlantic* suggest that there is. But aside from writing something libelous, what exactly is the harm? Initially, I found this question disturbing, for I had conditioned myself for many years to think rather of the good of life writing, of its natural place in a lifelong process of identity formation. Moral issues, of course, the rightness of a subject's acts or motives, frequently constitute a primary content of biographical and autobiographical narrative. But I want instead to focus this inquiry on the moral consequences of the act of writing itself. What is right and fair for me to write about someone else? What is right and fair for someone else to write about me? I discovered the beginnings of an answer to these difficult questions in legal and philosophical treatments of the individual's right to privacy.

I want to note at the outset that a distinctly individualist bias colors this discussion. Philosophers and jurists characteristically posit the capacity for action in an autonomous, free-standing model of selfhood—a distinct and clearly defined person who acts and is acted upon. Defining agency in this way helps both to identify the individual in whom privacy is vested and to assign responsibility for violations of that privacy.[13] Ethical determinations become more complex, however, if we conceptualize identity as relational rather than autonomous, for such a model makes it more difficult to demarcate the boundaries of the self upon which a privacy-based ethics of the person can be founded.[14] Against the autonomous moral agent posited by ethical theory I want to set the relational self that is frequently portrayed in contemporary autobiography and memoir. Speaking of her relation with her mother, for example, Carolyn Kay Steedman writes, "She made me believe that I was her" (*Landscape* 141); similarly,

---

[13] Robert Young observes, "Autonomy is commonly held to be a presupposition of moral agency and hence of responsibility, dignity, and self-esteem" (77). See also the essays collected in the Christman and Schoeman volumes.

[14] In opposing relational and autonomous models of identity here, I simplify for the purpose of laying out the issues involved. As I suggested in my discussion of the work of Jessica Benjamin in Chapter 2, the relational and the autonomous dimensions of identity formation are more usefully conceived as complementary.

recalling his relation with his father, Philip Roth evokes a period when their lives were "intermeshed and spookily interchangeable" (225). As these examples suggest, in contrast to the supposedly self-determining model of identity that autonomy predicates, a relational concept of selfhood stresses the extent to which the self is defined by—and lives in terms of—its relations with others. If, as I contended in Chapter 2, we are relational selves living relational lives, an ethics of privacy needs to address that fact.

Jeffrey H. Reiman argues that privacy is "a precondition of personhood," "*a social ritual by means of which an individual's moral title to his existence is conferred*" (310). Moreover, theorists of privacy seem to agree that space or social distance is a precondition of privacy. If we accept these hypotheses, ethical problems will arise in life writing when space is transgressed, when privacy is abridged, with the result that the integrity of the person is breached or violated. I investigate this link between privacy and personhood first in the philosophical and juridical literature and then in various kinds of life writing.

The American press seized upon the death of the late Jacqueline Kennedy Onassis in 1994 to mourn the passing of an ideal of privacy that this beloved public figure had, paradoxically, come to represent. No one needs reminding that we live in an age of intrusiveness, where each innovation in communications technology seems to create some new threat to the possibility of being left alone: we read daily about eavesdropping on the eaveless virtual space of cellular phones, about call screening, caller identification, and scrambling devices. It is surely a sign of the times that *access* is newly empowered as a transitive verb. The hunger of the public for the private lives of the rich and famous has spawned a breed of professional privacy-busters—gossip columnists and paparazzi—and Onassis became the chosen prey of self-styled paparazzo Ronald E. Galella. Photographer Galella's single-minded pursuit of Onassis resulted in more than a decade of litigation, culminating in a Federal Superior Court judgment in 1982 that upheld Onassis's "constitutional right of privacy" (*Galella* 1106). A particularly interesting feature of the case, and one that gives it special symbolic value for my purposes here, was that the series of judgments against Galella prohibited the photographer from approaching "within 100 yards of the home of Mrs. Onassis and her children; 100 yards from the children's school; and at all other places 50 yards from Mrs. Onassis and 75 yards from the children" (1081). Space is the prerequisite of privacy, that "right to be left alone" which Galella, in the judge's finding, had "relentlessly and shockingly invaded" (1106).[15]

The legal history of the right to privacy invoked in this case dates from the publication in 1890 of a celebrated article by Samuel D. Warren and Louis D. Brandeis titled, precisely, "The Right to Privacy." The article was occasioned by Warren's exasperation with intrusive coverage of his family's social life by the popular press of the period; revolutions in printing technology and photography exposed anyone deemed to be a celebrity—the Warrens were wealthy, socially prominent Bostonians—to the gaze of a mass-circulation audience.[16] Brandeis and Warren argued for "a general right to privacy for thoughts, emotions, and sensations . . . whether expressed in writing, or in conduct, in conversation, in attitudes, or in facial expression" (82), a right so comprehensive and fundamental, in fact, that we might call it the right to personhood. Their own formulation, however, as we shall see, has proved peculiarly memorable, "the right to an inviolate personality" (85).

The subsequent legal history of privacy is rich and complex, turning especially on challenges to Brandeis and Warren's positing of a single, all-embracing right.[17] William Prosser, for ex-

---

[15] As Susanna Egan points out (letter to the author), contemporary legislation in the United States concerning stalking and access to abortion clinics reflects a growing public awareness that physical privacy is under attack.

[16] See Pember 23–25 for an account of the circumstances that led to the publication of the Warren and Brandeis article.

[17] My own abbreviated account of the legal history of the right to privacy has been guided by Schoeman's illuminating introduction to this thorny subject ("Privacy").

ample, reviewing seventy years of cases in 1960, found that "the law of privacy comprises four distinct kinds of invasion of four different interests of the plaintiff." I quote his description of these four torts to suggest something of the complex of issues with which the right to privacy has been associated in the law:

1. Intrusion upon the plaintiff's seclusion or solitude, or into his private affairs.
2. Public disclosure of embarrassing private facts about the plaintiff.
3. Publicity which places the plaintiff in a false light in the public eye.
4. Appropriation, for the defendant's advantage, of the plaintiff's name or likeness. (107)

Countering the apparent reductiveness of Prosser's four-part analysis, however, is Edward J. Bloustein's "Privacy as an Aspect of Human Dignity: An Answer to Dean Prosser" (1964), a defense of the distinctiveness of the right to privacy claimed by Brandeis and Warren. Bloustein discerns in all of the manifold transgressions against the right to privacy "an interference with individuality, an interference with the right of the individual to do what he will." His portrait of the person deprived of privacy, moreover, is chilling: "Such a being, although sentient, is fungible; he is not an individual" (188).

How did we come to possess the privacy that the Warrens and Jacqueline Onassis felt was being violated, the privacy that Warren and Brandeis and their followers would protect with the law? In *Home: A Short History of an Idea*, Witold Rybczynski has traced the outline of the history of privacy in the West, and as an architect himself, Rybczynski highlights the connection between privacy and physical space. The seventeenth century, especially in the Protestant bourgeois culture of Holland, marks the appearance of "privacies," "rooms to which the individual could retreat from public view"; before that, "houses were full of people, . . .

and privacy was unknown" (18). Citing John Lukacs's "The Bourgeois Interior," Rybczynski links this shift in the design of domestic space to "the emergence of something new in the human consciousness: the appearance of the internal world of the individual, of the self, and of the family" (35).[18]

Are these concepts of privacy and the individual peculiar to Western culture? Certainly Rybczynski's analysis suggests that they are by-products of a bourgeois capitalist society in which it has seemed natural to associate person and privacy with the notion of property. We don't need to look far, moreover, to find large-scale twentieth-century counterexamples, totalitarian societies whose state apparatuses of gulags and secret police are specifically designed to destroy the individual's "right to an inviolate personality"; the very term *brainwashing*, which we instinctively associate with the Orwellian state, captures perfectly the antithesis of the ideal Warren and Brandeis sought to defend.

Some anthropologists, however, taking the longer view, regard the need for privacy and the physical space required to achieve it as transcultural universals of human behavior. Thus, concluding his analysis of the veil as a "distance setting mechanism" among Tuareg males, Robert F. Murphy writes:

> I have argued, following [Georg] Simmel, that social distance pervades all social relationships though it may be found in varying degrees in different relationships and in different societies. . . . The privacy and withdrawal of the social person is a quality of life in society. That he withholds himself while communicating and communicates through removal is not a contradiction in terms but a quality of all social interaction. ("Social" 51)

Confirming Murphy's views, the law professor Alan Westin traces the origins of the human need for privacy back to the territorial imperative that Robert Ardrey posits as a governing principle of

---

[18] For further discussion of the emergence of the modern concept of the self, see Taylor and Trilling.

animal behavior. While Westin acknowledges that "modern industrial societies . . . provide greater situations of physical and psychological privacy" (69) than do so-called "primitive" cultures, he proceeds nevertheless to formulate the key features of privacy "which apply to men living together in virtually every society that has been systematically examined" (61).

Having considered privacy briefly from legal, sociological, and anthropological perspectives, I want to return to Reiman's hypothesis that privacy is "a precondition of personhood" and ask this question: how can the practice of life writing be said to infringe on the individual's "right to an inviolate personality"? In order to answer this question, however, we need to answer another one first, asking with Robert C. Post, "What does it mean to violate personality" ("Rereading" 650)? Post observes that when Warren and Brandeis describe "the space that is supposed to buffer personality from the world, the language is less that of empirical distance than of moral characterization. . . . So conceived, privacy does not refer to an objective physical space of secrecy, solitude, or anonymity, but rather to the forms of respect that we owe to each other as members of a common community" (651). In distinguishing this "normative" model of privacy from a "descriptive" one, Post provides an important clue to the ethical problems posed by life writing in particular communities: "Normative privacy . . . lends itself to a straightforward account of why a person socialized to certain forms of respect would experience harm when those forms of respect are disregarded" (653).[19]

[19] See Post, "Social Foundations," for an illuminating account of privacy which balances "the interests of individuals against the demands of community" (959). Especially striking is his invocation of Erving Goffman's "The Nature of Deference and Demeanor." Goffman's articulation of the rules governing social interrelations posits a model of the person that is established through a dynamic of mutual recognition: "Each individual is responsible for the demeanor image of himself and the deference image of others, so that for a complete man to be expressed, individuals must hold hands in a chain of ceremony, each giving deferentially with proper demeanor to the one on the right what will be received deferentially from the one on the left. While it may be true that the individual has a unique self all his own, evidence of the possession is thoroughly a product of joint ceremonial labor, the part expressed through the individual's

Post offers further clarification of the ethical dimensions of privacy when he probes Brandeis and Warren's determination to found privacy "within a regime of personal rather than property rights" (667). In much of the thinking about copyright and publicity, the person is commodified as data or information, whereas "the personal right of privacy advocated by Warren and Brandeis . . . attaches personality firmly to the actual identity of a living individual" (668).[20] The distinction between person and property strikes me as crucial, for the extent to which integrity of person rather than security of property is at stake in a given situation would provide a basis for assessing the comparative gravity of an ethical violation; moreover, to flout the distinction altogether, to treat the person *as* property, would carry denial of privacy to an absolute degree. Following Post, then, the ethical questions would be these: Is the life writer guilty of a fundamental lack of respect for the other? Has the life writer transformed the other "into a *thing* or an object" (Post 667)?

Note, however, that there is a persistent and troubling ambiguity—an ambiguity, moreover, with important ethical consequences for the life writer—about the distinction between person and property, for many of the formulations of privacy, person, and autonomy are couched precisely in the language of property. Thus Reiman writes that "to be a person . . . presupposes that [the individual] believes that the concrete reality which he is, and through which his destiny is realized, belongs to him in a moral sense" (310), and Brandeis and Warren construe "the right of property in its widest sense" as the only possible basis for "the right to an inviolate personality" (85).[21] Nevertheless, in placing person ("the actual identity of a living individ-

---

demeanor being no more significant than the part conveyed by others through their deferential behavior toward him" (quoted in Post 963).

[20] See Coombe on the "infinite" possibilities for commodification of "the human persona" (103).

[21] Historians of Western individualism trace its "possessive" element back to seventeenth-century political theory, which posits the individual "as an owner of himself" (Macpherson 3).

ual") rather than property (various alienable possessions—data, information) at the center of their thinking about privacy, Warren and Brandeis, Reiman, and Bloustein suggest the potential gravity of infractions of privacy. As a measure of the harm that lack of respect or commodification can visit upon the "inviolate personality," consider the consequences of the total deprivation of privacy. Positing privacy as "a condition of the original and continuing creation of 'selves' or 'persons' " (310), Reiman cites Erving Goffman's work on asylums as evidence that the programmatic elimination of the inmate's privacy can lead to "destruction of the self"—can "literally . . . kill it off" (311).

James Rachels and William Ruddick take Reiman's hypothesis a step further, making liberty itself a precondition of personhood.[22] Distinguishing between "*being alive*" (a "biological notion") and "*having a life*" (a "notion of biography"), they hold that "only persons have lives" (226, 228). To the person they attribute what I would characterize as a distinctly *autobiographical* consciousness, a set of "self-referring attitudes" that "presuppose a sense of oneself as having an existence spread over past and future time" (227). Paralleling Reiman's testing of privacy by evoking its deprivation, Rachels and Ruddick consider the consequences of the deprivation of liberty for the distinguishing mark of the person—"having a life"—and conclude that "victims of dire poverty, illness, and slavery" "might retain the capacity for social responses and yet have none of the intentions, plans, and other features of will and action that define a life" (228).[23]

While Rachels and Ruddick's concern is with liberty rather than privacy, I introduce it here because of the suggestiveness of their concept of "having a life" for any attempt to formulate the ethics of life writing. When it comes to texts, to life stories, the law tends to adopt a commodified notion of personality, gravitating to questions of ownership and copyright, but if we regard the

[22] Brandeis eventually linked the right to privacy to the pursuit of happiness (Bloustein 186–87).
[23] See especially their discussion of the question, Can a slave have a biography? (228–30).

possession of "a life"—and, by extension, "having" a life story—as a defining attribute of the individual, then, once again, violations of privacy could be construed as committed against person rather than property.[24] The conclusion from this style of reasoning—in Post, in Reiman, in Rachels and Ruddick—is clear: life writing that constitutes a violation of privacy has the potential to harm the very self of the other.

Before turning to the practice of life writing to test these findings, I want to repeat that all of the preceding discussion assumes an autonomous, discrete model of identity that makes it possible to distinguish clearly between one self and the next, between the boundaries of your life and mine. Much of this discussion also assumes that autonomous individuals in their status as persons stand free of questions of property. But what if individual identity is relational rather than autonomous in formation? What if individual agency is limited by the function of the person as property?

Carolyn Kay Steedman's *Landscape for a Good Woman: A Story of Two Lives* (1986), which I discussed in Chapter 2, illustrates the problems posed by a relational model of identity for a privacy-ased ethics of life writing. In writing her autobiography, Steedman tells the story of two lives because she believes that her mother's self and story provide the key to her own. Steedman argues that her dawning recognition of the circumstances of her conception—her realization that she was neither a wanted nor a legitimate child—determined the very structure of her personality. *Landscape for a Good Woman*, then, is a *relational life* in which the story and self of the author are shown to be intimately and inextricably linked to the story and self of another person. The illusory nature of autonomy is brought home to Steedman as a girl when she lingers one day after school to try out for a part in a radio program. Arriving home late, she finds her mother "waiting on the doorstep":

[24] See Post, "Rereading" 667–70.

I withered, there was nothing I could say. She'd wanted me to go down the road to fetch a bunch of watercress for tea, and I ought to have known she couldn't go, couldn't leave my sister. . . . In this way, you come to know that you are not quite yourself, but someone else: someone else has paid the price for you, and you have to pay it back. (105)

From a relational perspective, then, the boundaries between self and other are hard to determine, and, as the economic figure Steedman employs here suggests, the boundaries between person and property as well. In Steedman's view, women especially function in both registers simultaneously, operating willy-nilly in an intricate web of agency and commodity that challenges the simplifying vision of the law. Thus she portrays her working-class mother as "both bargain and bargainer" (69) in a patriarchal system of exchange, an individual who sought to exploit her status as a commodity for purposes of her own: "Under particular social circumstances, people may come to understand that whilst they do not possess any*thing*, they possess themselves, and may possibly be able to exchange themselves for something else" (68). Steedman's "story of two lives," then, makes us ask another question: in what way can the relational self be said to "have" a life—and a life story—in Rachels's sense? As Lejeune reminds us, "private life is almost always a co-property" (*Moi aussi* 55, my trans.).

"Bloodsport" Biography

I began by delineating an ethics of privacy centered on the sanctity of the "inviolate personality," which turns precisely on the notion of boundaries that may not be transgressed with impunity; Steedman's story, however, suggests the difficulty of drawing the line between self and other, person and property. With these reservations in mind, I want to proceed nevertheless to test the Brandeis and Warren model by taking up first the cases of biography and ethnographic and as-told-to collaborative autobiography; it is the ethical implications of these kinds of life writing that have received the most scrutiny to date.

Despite Janet Malcolm's claim that "the transgressive nature of biography is rarely acknowledged" (9), the ethics of biography has never been more widely and heatedly discussed than at present.[25] In "Biography as a Blood Sport" (May 1994) the *New York Times* book reviewer Michiko Kakutani indicts the turpitude of contemporary biographical practice, while the biographer James Atlas defends his vocation against such charges in a similarly titled essay for the *New York Times Magazine*, "The Biographer and the Murderer" (December 1993). And Malcolm's own unflinching anatomy of the biographer's art in the case of Sylvia Plath quotes Ted Hughes's scathing condemnation of biography's reading public. Defending his embattled privacy, Hughes writes to the biographer Anne Stevenson in November 1989:

> I preferred [remaining silent], on the whole, to allowing myself
> to be dragged out into the bull-ring and teased and pricked and
> goaded into vomiting up every detail of my life with Sylvia for the
> higher entertainment of the hundred thousand Eng Lit Profs and
> graduates who—as you know—feel very little in this case beyond
> curiosity of quite a low order, the ordinary village kind, popular
> bloodsport kind, no matter how they robe their attentions in Lit
> Crit Theology and ethical sanctity. (141)

When we survey with Kakutani the sleaziness and nastiness of many current biographies, hardcover cousins of the supermarket tabloids, this imagery of blood and guts may not seem farfetched; we may need to be reminded that biography isn't by definition an unethical practice, that its origins can be traced back to a venerable tradition of gospels, hagiography, and exemplary

---

[25] The extensive national coverage in 1991 of Jeffrey Masson's libel suit against Malcolm for her biographical profile of him in the *New Yorker* has doubtless contributed to the current visibility of this issue. For astute commentary on the legal issues involved in this trial, see de Grazia.

lives which sought to contribute to the public good. Allowing for journalistic hyperbole, the drift of the imagery is telling nonetheless: all parties to the biographical enterprise seem to concede that biography has the potential to assault—symbolically—the very person of its subject.

Fictions about biography, from Henry James's *The Aspern Papers* to A. S. Byatt's *Possession*, focus on struggles for ownership, and Malcolm likens "the biographer at work" to "the professional burglar" (9).[26] Yet Malcolm undercuts this judgment when she challenges the notion that, in Ted Hughes's words, "each of us owns the facts of her or his own life." Malcolm contends that "we do not 'own' the facts of our lives at all. This ownership passes out of our hands at birth, at the moment we are first observed" (8).[27] Certainly this is true of the dead, and Warren and Brandeis would seem to concur in limiting the right of privacy, of "inviolate personality," to the living individual, as we have seen.[28]

Certain living subjects, however, refusing to concede the truth of Malcolm's view of ownership, have doggedly resisted the attempts of enterprising biographers to transform their identities into text for gain. Ironically, their defensive strategies have played into the very commodification of the person that they seek to defy. I am thinking of reclusive figures such as J. D. Salinger and Howard Hughes—Salinger, who placed many of his unpublished letters under copyright in order to prevent their

---

[26] Malcolm's image of the burglar here confirms the linkage of person, privacy, and space discussed previously.

[27] Stanley I. Benn argues that this condition of being observed by others is instrumental in creating *self*-consciousness: "Finding oneself an object of scrutiny, as the focus of another's attention, brings one to a new consciousness of oneself, as something seen through another's eyes. According to Sartre, indeed it is a necessary condition for knowing oneself *as* anything at all that one should conceive oneself as an object of scrutiny" (227). If scrutiny by the other possesses the potential to violate inviolate personality, it also—paradoxically—plays a decisive part in constituting it in the first place.

[28] I have chosen to concentrate on the living because their litigation promotes the visibility of the issues I have been dealing with. Absent Ted Hughes's "perpetual" struggle with Plath "over the ownership of his life" (Malcolm 140), for example, and the whole Hughes-Plath biographical saga is greatly diminished.

use in Ian Hamilton's "unauthorized" biography of him; and Hughes, who, outdoing Salinger, "tried mightily to copyright his life" (Couser, *Altered* 5).[29] These attempts to literally possess one's life story seem to confirm Richard A. Posner's economic theory of privacy, which pits privacy and prying against each other as two competing "economic goods" in a world where "few people want to be let alone" (338); in a commodity culture the individual's right to privacy becomes "the right to control the flow of information about [oneself]" (334), while others claim the right to obtain "the information necessary to verify or disprove these claims" (338)—the right to produce and consume biographies, for example, whether they are "authorized" or not.

Still, to characterize biography as "bloodsport" suggests that it does possess the potential to harm its subjects; text can harm a person because the person-property axis runs both ways. To begin with, the very existence of life writing requires the fiction that persons and their lives be susceptible to the commodification involved in textual representation. But this fiction creates not only the possibility of disrespecting the person, treating the person as a thing; it also allows for the assault on the person's "inviolate personality" precisely because privacy's protective space has been breached—the person, embodied in text, made thing, is accessible to harm. One can strike at a textualized body.

Ethnographic Autobiography: "We are using *them* for *our* books"

I have been addressing "bloody," "unauthorized," adversarial biographies because these are the ones that have been censured. Accordingly, if we turn to collaborative autobiography, we might not expect to encounter ethical problems, for the collaborative relation is presumably and by definition entered into voluntarily. The first-person narrative products of such relations, however, turn out to be as ethically complex as they are rhetorically am-

---

[29] For an account of the Salinger case, see Hamilton and Hoban.

biguous, for these first-person narratives largely—often completely—conceal the collaborative mediation, the interlocutive role of a second person, on which they are founded. The peculiarity of the central rhetorical feature of these texts, an "I" that refers to two different individuals, is nicely captured by G. Thomas Couser when he observes that all collaborative autobiography "speaks with a cloven tongue . . . because it conflates two consciousnesses . . . in one undifferentiated voice" (*Altered* 208). As a result, from the perspective of the reader, the rhetorical ambiguity is compounded by a generic one: these mediated texts purport to be autobiographies but are in many cases closer to biography, given the decisive role played by the writer/editor in their creation.

Philippe Lejeune identifies two major varieties of collaborative autobiography: ethnographic accounts prepared by anthropologists and oral historians, and "as-told-to" lives of celebrities written by "ghosts."[30] The latter variety is characteristically "ghostly," for ghostwriters usually neither claim the full status of authorship, accepting a "with" or "with-the-assistance-of" tag, nor discuss the details of the collaborative relation.[31] I focus, instead, on the ethnographic variety, for ethnographers not only sign on the title page as author but also discuss—in varying degrees—the collaborative relation, and occasionally even reflect on the ethical implications of their intervention into the lives of their subjects.[32] The details of the collaborative process, however, and the exact nature of the contribution of each member of the pair to the jointly created text, are usually masked.

All students of the ethnographic life story regard power rela-

[30] Lejeune's pioneering attempt to classify this huge and various literature, "The Autobiography of Those Who Do Not Write," has been extremely helpful to me in my own thinking about it.
[31] Alex Haley, who served as "ghost" to Malcolm X, represents an important exception. In the remarkable epilogue to the narrative, written after Malcolm's death, Haley reveals the conflicts between the two men—"Whose book is this?"—that lurk behind the seemingly seamless "I" of the narrative we read.
[32] "As-told-to" autobiographies also differ from the ethnographic variety with regard to consent: in the case of the former, the conventional assumption is that the ghost is employed by the celebrity, whereas in the case of the latter the initiative usually comes from the ethnographer and not from the informant.

tions as central to the dynamic of textual production. Lejeune and Daphne Patai stress the asymmetry of the relationship between informant and (typically) academic author, assigning dominance to the latter, who belongs to the class that controls the production and consumption of such texts (Lejeune, "Autobiography" 209). Two studies of collaborative autobiography, however, by Anne E. Goldman and Mark A. Sanders, make a case for the resisting informant, who manages to withstand the editor's control. It is impossible to adjudicate with any certainty the truth of these differing interpretations of collaboration, but obviously such works are published to serve the purposes of the ethnographer who signs as author (Marjorie Shostak, for example, or Paul Radin). Moreover, because the informant, often distanced by language, class, and culture, can have little or no conception of these purposes, any mitigating notion of "consent" is problematical, and the potential for exploitation—for colonization—is inevitable.[33] Patai, who has researched the ethical problems of collaboration extensively, states the central issue bluntly: "The fact remains that it is we who are using *them* for *our* books" (21). Her conclusion may be applied to life writing generally: "A person telling her life story is, in a sense, offering up her self for her own and her listener's scrutiny. . . . Whether we *should* appropriate another's life in this way becomes a legitimate question" (24–25).[34]

---

[33] In a lecture at Indiana University on March 25, 1994, titled "Ethnography as Responsible Discourse: Is a Collaborative Narrative Ever Possible?" Elaine Lawless argued that the anthropologist could proceed in such a way that she could be "authorized" by her informants to tell their story. While I honor the attempt to respect the integrity of her informants, I remain skeptical that they could sufficiently understand her purposes to validate such an authorization.

[34] Patai sent a letter to sixty-five colleagues who have made extensive use of oral history or personal narratives in their research, asking them to respond to a series of questions about the ethical implications of such work. The nineteen who replied present a revealing picture of the dilemmas involved. See Patai, "Ethical Problems." Lejeune formulates the central issue of such research as follows: "Can one enter into a relation of friendship and trust with someone in order to get him to relate the story of his life, and then go on to publish this life together with a critical analysis conducted from a point of view that is altogether foreign to that person and which reduces him to the status of an object?" (*Moi aussi* 285, my trans.).

Thus Patai argues that to author the informant, as ethnographic collaboration necessarily entails, is to incur a moral obligation that not every researcher is prepared to acknowledge. Lejeune reports, for example, that Adélaïde Blasquez, the author of *Gaston Lucas, serrurier* (1976), was prepared to appropriate the self and life story of her subject without batting an eye. When Lejeune proposes to her that Lucas be interviewed as part of the publisher's promotion for the book, she repudiates the suggestion, replying that in the context of the book, what the living Gaston has to say is without value; he doesn't exist in himself, for it is the written Gaston that counts, an individual who has acquired, thanks to her art, the consistency and truth of a character in a novel.[35] Ironically, even writers who are ostensibly sensitive to the integrity of their informants may do them harm. Couser, for example, suggests that the homage that John G. Neihardt intended to express to Black Elk in writing *Black Elk Speaks* (1932) eventuated in an act of betrayal; in misrepresenting the truth of the Sioux chief's vision, Neihardt may have compromised him in his very being, in what he stood for.[36]

Collaborative Autobiography: "She had taken over, or been taken over by, the voice I had created for her"

If Ted Hughes, J. D. Salinger, Gaston Lucas, and even Black Elk begin to look like casualties of bloodsport life writing, why don't we just shut up the biographical shop, give up writing about other people as a bad—if well-paying—business, as none of our business at all? From the perspective of an ethics of privacy, the ethnographer and literary biographer begin to resemble the gossip columnist and paparazzo: all are engaged in exploiting other people's lives for their own purposes and profits. Even Warren and Brandeis, however, properly recognize the necessity of limiting the "right to an inviolate personality," conceding, among other limitations, that protection of privacy must be balanced

[35] I paraphrase Lejeune's account in *Moi aussi* 283–84.
[36] See Couser, *Altered* 189–209; and Krupat, *For* 126–35.

against the public's right to be informed about persons who "have assumed a position which makes their doings legitimate matters of public investigation" (88). In turning to consider relational autobiography, I want to ask whether there isn't also a private good, even a private necessity, to be weighed against the other's right to privacy. If we assume a relational model of identity, as Carolyn Steedman does when she speaks of children as "episodes in someone else's narrative," then other people's selves and lives may become our business just as, reciprocally, ours become theirs. In these cases of what I call the *proximate* other—a parent, a child, a sibling, an intimate—it is difficult not only to determine the boundaries of the other's privacy but indeed to delimit the very otherness of the other's identity.

In proximate collaborative autobiography, the story of the self is constructed through the story told *of* and *by* someone else. These collaborative texts feature two first-person speakers, the "I" of the proximate other's story and the "I" of what I term *the story of the story*, the narrative of the self's recording of the other's story. Because identity is conceived as relational in these instances, such narratives defy the distinctions we try to establish between genres, for they are autobiographies that offer not only the autobiography of the self but the biography *and* the autobiography of the other. This indeterminacy of form points to the psychological ambiguity of the collaborative situation and the narratives it generates, for these texts suggest that the identity of the self who writes and signs as author includes and is included in the identity of the other whose story she presents. The signature on the title page, moreover, reflects the necessarily unequal distribution of power in situations of this kind: once the narrative has been published, whatever the terms of the collaboration may have been, an act of appropriation has occurred, and the self who signs may well be led to reflect on the ethical responsibilities involved.

Art Spiegelman's *Maus: A Survivor's Tale*, published in two volumes in 1986 and 1991, offers a peculiarly instructive example of proximate collaboration because the graphic medium of the text prompts us to visualize the collaborative process involved in its creation. We see the cartoonist Spiegelman recording and translating into comic strip form his father Vladek's astonishing tale of his survival at Auschwitz. Troubled by the success of the first volume, Spiegelman opens the second chapter of the second volume with a disturbing self-portrait. The cartoonist depicts himself at his drawing board perched on a heap of bodies that we have been primed to recognize as the paramount symbol of those who perished in the Holocaust; shady entrepreneurs and reporters armed with mikes and videocameras are shown walking on the bodies as they bombard Spiegelman with questions and deals. Is the artist's representation of his father and his father's story somehow complicit, then, with his father's Nazi persecutors? Is he in effect trampling on his father's body, exploiting his life for gain?

Other images confirm this notion that the collaboration is somehow lethal, that the son's dogged determination to get his father to tell his story contributes to the father's death. Suffering from heart disease, Vladek is shown pedaling on his life cycle as he tells his harrowing tale. The initial session of dictation begins with Vladek mounting his bike—"It's good for my heart, the pedaling"—and another ends, characteristically, with Vladek too exhausted to pedal and talk any more (1:12, 91). And in the final images Vladek calls a halt to all the talking—"Let's stop, please, your tape recorder"—and dies (2: 136). The father's existence is, in the son's retelling, intimately linked to narration; the end of the one is the end of the other. Was telling his story life-sustaining, or did the collaboration finish him off? It's hard to say. In any case, *Maus* is particularly compelling in its unsparing evocation of the dark underside, the murderous impulses and guilt, of the son's attempt to restore an intimate bond with the father, a bond that may never have existed in the first place. The yoking of Holocaust tale and bedtime story is violent and unsettling, to say the least.[37]

[37] For the bedtime story motif, see the final panels on 2:136, and also a related image (designed by Spiegelman) on the back cover of the first volume.

Collaborative autobiographies of this kind inevitably probe the self's responsibility to the proximate other. Is the act of writing about the other a violation of that responsibility? As its title suggests, this is the question that preoccupies the novelist John Edgar Wideman as he attempts in *Brothers and Keepers* (1984) to reconstruct the personal and family history that led to his brother Robby's life imprisonment for murder. As in Spiegelman's *Maus*, Wideman's rendering of the story of his story offers an elaborately detailed account of the collaborative process that leads him to question the ethics of his project. Focusing on the interpersonal dynamics of his visits with his brother in prison, visits during which he gathers Robby's story, the novelist observes, "I had to root my fiction-writing self out of our exchanges. I had to teach myself to listen . . . tame the urge to take off with Robby's story and make it my own" (77). Curiously, in Wideman's view, the "fiction-writing self," despite its predatory nature, is drawn helplessly and irresistibly to inhabit the penal interior of the other—"That boundless, incarcerating black hole is another person" (77–78). The imagination's out-of-the-body travel into the private territory of another's identity leaves the novelist feeling "slightly embarrassed, guilty because I've been trespassing and don't know how long I've been gone or if anybody noticed me violating somebody else's turf" (78).

Yet, listening to Robby and listening to himself listen, Wideman traces the origins of his brother's tangled history and his own to a family tradition of walled privacy that had kept them apart—"He's been inside his privacy and I've been inside mine" (80). Wideman's intricate, acutely self-conscious inquiry displays the ambiguities of privacy, at once the family's guarantee of Robby's integrity and autonomy yet implicated in his downfall because it fostered a dangerous, self-destructive isolation. Is the sanctuary of inviolate personality one more prison in this narrative of prisons and prisoners? Privacy may be a right, but is it a good? And is the act of representing the other and the other's story an exploitative invasion or a self-transcending attempt at empathy—as Wideman puts it, "a way of seeing out of another person's eyes" (78)?

It is one of the defining paradoxes of proximate collaborative autobiography that such narratives both confirm and resist the reality of relational identity. The very title of Kim Chernin's autobiography, *In My Mother's House: A Daughter's Story* (1983), attests to Chernin's belief—like Steedman's—that mothers and daughters are so intimately bound in the process of identity formation that to tell the story of the one is necessarily to tell the story of the other. For Chernin, in fact, relational identity must be understood in generational perspective, for every mother has also been a daughter. Instinctively grasping the interconnectedness of her own life to her mother's, Kim Chernin initially resists when her mother Rose asks her to write the story of her tumultuous career as a tireless organizer for the Communist Party. To write her mother's story, Kim fears, would be to lose herself "back into the mother" (12), reversing the quest for autonomy that had driven her to break away from her mother and especially from the communist ideology that anchored her mother's identity. But Chernin persuades herself that in surrendering to her mother's wish she is initiating a therapeutic process that will heal the rift of the years between them.

In the foreword to the second edition of *In My Mother's House* (1994), Chernin traces the origin of the book and her own formation as a writer to the "stories my mother told me when I was a small child" (vii). When she proceeds to comment on her representation of her mother's voice, however, Chernin inverts this reading of the source of her narrative and identity, presenting herself as the author of her mother in a very expansive sense. Readers of her narrative, she reports, have mistakenly assumed that she had merely "recorded and transcribed my mother's stories, that her voice in my book was the voice in which she had told the stories to me" (ix). In fact, Chernin claims, in the interests of verisimilitude—"to get my mother to sound like my mother on a page"—she was obliged to create a voice that had

"something of her in it but something of me as well" (x). But
then this collaborative version of the book's creation gives way to
a more distinctly imperialistic interpretation in which the domi-
neering personality of the mother has been colonized by the resisting daughter. At a bookstore promotion the mother is presented as "simultaneously the Rose Chernin she had always been,
as well as, now, the central character of a book her daughter was
proudly signing." The shift in power relations between the two is
completed when Kim overhears Rose telling one of her own stories *but in Kim's words*: "after that, my mother never, to my knowledge, told her stories again in her own voice. From that moment
in the bookstore she had taken over, *or been taken over by*, the voice
I had created for her" (xii–xiii, emphasis added).[38]

In "Sanctioning Voice: Quotation Marks, the Abolition of Torture, and the Fifth Amendment," Margreta de Grazia suggests
the momentousness of such an appropriation of voice. De
Grazia's analysis of the Supreme Court's decision in the celebrated Jeffrey Masson–Janet Malcolm case (*Masson v. New Yorker
Magazine*) argues that "lurking behind the Court's dread of misquotation is . . . a long history of the gruesome inquisitorial pro-
cedures deployed in Europe and England to exact self-incrimi-
nating testimonies" (286)—the *peine forte et dure* prescribed to
force speech from prisoners who refused to enter a plea before
the bar (295). Misquotation and torture, de Grazia concludes,
"produce the same effect: the takeover of another's voice" (286),
a takeover protected by the Fifth Amendment. But what, it is reasonable to ask, have torture and the Fifth Amendment to do with
a mother-daughter story like Chernin's that is drenched in sen-
timent, that becomes, at the last, a veritable love fest? Namely
this: legal protection of an individual's voice and words places
them at the center of the culture's definition of the integrity and
liberty of the person; thus, in a culture centered on individualism, representation of the self and voice of the other acquires a

[38] For additional commentary on mother-daughter power relations in
Chernin's narrative, see Neuman, "Your" 60–62.

special power. How that power is exercised becomes the central problem of the ethics of life writing, for there is no getting around the fact that ventriloquism, making the other talk, is by definition a central rhetorical phenomenon of these narratives. Proximate collaborative autobiography seems to embrace, conceptually, the reality of relational identity, the structuring bond between self and other, but the desire for autonomy, for mastery of one's origins, for authorship, persists. Children *may be* "episodes in someone else's narrative," as Carolyn Steedman proposes, whether they like it or not; when children turned adults become the authors of such a narrative, however, it is a different story, and the tables are turned. Rhetorically, Spiegelman Wideman, and Chernin become self-determining and more: they make someone else into "episodes" in their own narratives.[39] The ambivalences of these writers toward their projects express an unresolved tension between relational and autonomous modes of identity.

"Bury him naked": The Legitimacy of Life Writing

The ethics of privacy as traditionally conceived requires the drawing of boundaries, but how do we delimit the person? Relational identity confounds our familiar literary and ethical categories; both need to be stretched to accommodate the fluidity of selves and lives. The currency of hybrid forms in contemporary life writing points up the limitations of generic classifications focused on individual selves and lives as discrete entities. An ethics of life writing founded on the inviolate personality becomes similarly problematic. How do we sort out the legitimacy of life writing, how can we specify its responsibilities, if we cannot say for sure where the "I" begins and ends? The status of privacy is

---

[39] Spiegelman gives a graphic representation of this split role—child / adult author—in numerous images in *Maus* (see especially 2:41–47), and both Spiegelman and Chernin stress the importance of the parent telling a story to the child as the prototype of the autobiographical acts they perform.

fraught with contradictions. Inviolate personality may be protected in the courts, but it is routinely violated in the practice of life writing—witness the scale and scope today of biographers, autobiographers, and their readers.

Lest I seem to have mounted a case against the propriety of writing lives, I want to conclude by considering Philip Roth's *Patrimony* (1991), a relational life modeling a relational concept of identity, which demonstrates that transgression of privacy is not incompatible with the most profound respect for the integrity of the person. Roth himself, however, seems to have had a bad conscience about his narrative of his father's last years and illness, for he ends the book with a harrowing dream in which the dead father reproaches his son for having buried him not in the business suit of his lifelong vocation but in a shroud. "I had dressed him for eternity in the wrong clothes" (237), Roth observes, whereas his instinct had been to say to the mortician, "Bury him naked" (234). He had, in effect, buried Herman Roth naked in a memoir of *apparently* total candor—this is the heart of the dream—and he interprets the father's "rebuke" as an allusion to "this book, which, in keeping with the unseemliness of my profession, I had been writing all the while he was ill and dying" (237). *Patrimony* sets the son's "unseemly" practice of life writing on a collision course with the father's right to privacy.[40]

The content of the memoir is as transgressive as its telling, and the figure of nakedness points, moreover, to the bodily nature of the boundary crossed between father and son.[41] Roth spares neither himself nor the reader the progressive intimacy with his father's body that the circumstances of the father's debilitation require. In an early moment in the narrative Roth contemplates the MRI scan of the tumor in his father's brain: "I had seen my

[40] The other's right to privacy is frequently assumed to terminate at death. It is worth noting that for Roth this is emphatically not the case—hence the disquieting dream.

[41] Nancy K. Miller notes the "permeable borders between . . . fathers and sons" in *Patrimony*, and her comments on embodiment, on Roth's insistent preoccupation with the body of his father, are especially illuminating (*Bequest* 26).

father's brain, and everything and nothing was revealed" (17). In a late episode, helping his father bathe, he studies his father's penis: "I don't believe I'd seen it since I was a small boy" (177). Gradually the taboo of the body of the other is eroded. "Taking [his] dentures, slimy saliva and all, and dumping them in my pocket, I had, quite inadvertently, stepped across the divide of physical estrangement that, not so unnaturally, had opened up between us once I'd stopped being a boy" (152).

In the most remarkable sequence in the narrative, an extended and detailed account of the father's exploding bowels after days of postoperative constipation, Roth explores every last crevice of a humiliating experience his father regards as the depth of shame and disgrace. " 'I beshat myself,' he said" (172). Cleaning up the befouled bathroom—"the shit was everywhere . . . even on the tips of the bristles of my toothbrush . . . there was a little shit in my hair" (172–75), Roth is never closer to his father's body; mapping every inch of the interpersonal space they share, he works his way through to a stance of acceptance, coming into his own through the body of the other. "So *that* was the patrimony. . . . not the money, . . . but the shit" (176). And as for privacy, that, too, is exploded with the shit. His father had pleaded with him never to tell anyone, whereas Roth pursues a policy of total disclosure—if he is holding anything back, what could it be?

This penetration of the territory of the other is not only physical but psychological. Roth recalls that if his college education deepened "the mental divide" between him and his father, it also curiously involved a "sense of merging" (160) with him, and when Roth undergoes a quintuple bypass operation in the months just before the father's death, he recalls this experience of identification. "Not since college . . . had our lives been, if not identical, so intermeshed and spookily interchangeable" (225). This interchangeability extends to a reversal of roles between the two men, for "the little son" displays a parental solicitude—"like a mother," "like a father" (181)—toward his father in his final dependency; indeed, in writing *Patrimony*, Roth proposes to father the father who had created him. Although we don't know exactly when Roth began this commemorative project, he dedicates himself to it solemnly when he helps his father bathe the night after the episode of the shit. Observing the size and surprising youth of his father's penis, the son vows "to fix it in my memory for when he was dead": " 'I must remember accurately,' I told myself, 'remember everything accurately so that when he is gone I can re-create the father who created me.' *You must not forget anything*" (177).

Despite this display of filial piety, Roth's thoughts about his father in this scene and others are colored by Oedipal conflict. Citing Freud's theory of "the primal horde of sons who . . . have it in them to nullify the father by force," Roth identifies himself as another kind of son, "from the horde that can't throw a punch": "When we lay waste, . . . it isn't with raging fists . . . but with our words" (159). And his words, his weapons, Roth recognizes, in a further twist of the Freudian paradigm, are part of his paternal legacy. "He taught me the vernacular. He *was* the vernacular, unpoetic and expressive and point-blank, with all the vernacular's glaring limitations and all its durable force" (181).

The father is, then, the source of the son's creative power, yet this recognition does not seem to trigger a Bloom-style patricidal anxiety of influence. For all its unsparing display of his privacy, the portrait of Herman Roth reads not as an act of violation but of respect. Fearing an absolute autonomy—in the penultimate passage Roth dreams of himself as "a small, fatherless evacuee" unwilling "to be expelled" (237) from the body of the dead father (the father displaces the mother in this fantasy birth)—the son presents his memoir in the final lines of the narrative as a restoration of filial relation in obedience to paternal law:

> The dream [of having buried his father in the wrong clothes] was telling me that, if not in my books or in my life, at least in my dreams I would live perennially as his little son, with the conscience of a little son, just as he would remain alive there not only

as my father but as *the* father, sitting in judgment on whatever I
do.
　You must not forget anything. (237–38)

By repeating here the command he formulated earlier in the
episode in which he observes his father's penis, Roth enhances
its phallic authority: the son is under his father's orders to write
this "unseemly" book!

I want to return to the episode of the shit because it poses so
starkly the ethical dilemmas of life writing. The father's position
is absolutely clear: "Don't tell the children," and the son replies,
"I won't tell anyone" (176). Yet Roth not only persists in publishing these private things, but even seeks to put an obedient face
on this act of disobedience. Thus for the paternal command—
"don't tell"—he substitutes another of his own design—"You
must not forget anything"—which he attributes ultimately to *"the
father, sitting in judgment on whatever I do"* (238). Which command should be observed? Should fidelity to the truth of the
son's experience take precedence over the father's right to privacy?

To obey the father, to omit the episode of the shit, is to deny
the son the climax of his story, by which I mean not only the
rhetorical narrative he is writing but also the psychological narrative of identity formation it recounts. "His story"? Isn't there a
legitimate sense, as *Patrimony* boldly asserts, in which the episode
of the shit is inextricably relational, belonging at once to father
and son alike? Or does the episode merely confirm our misgiv-
ings about life writing of any kind, prompting us to recognize
that the confessional drive behind life writing that draws us to
it—our desire to penetrate the mystery of another person—may
also constitute its primary ethical flaw? Philippe Lejeune formulates the issue precisely when he observes, "In confessing ourselves we inevitably confess those who have shared our life intimately. . . . The attack on private life, which the law condemns, is
the very basis of autobiographical writing" ("L'atteinte" 17, my

trans.). When Roth claims his father's shit as his "patrimony," he calls on us, in effect, to acknowledge that the circumstances of relational identity challenge our familiar notions of privacy and ownership. The public/private dichotomy to which Ted Hughes appeals in judging the biographer's ethical responsibilities does not conveniently structure the relation between life writer and subject in a relational life like *Patrimony*, where the author shares the private world of his subject (and in some potentially compromising respects).

"Really, universally, relations stop nowhere," Henry James observed, "and the exquisite problem of the artist is eternally but to draw, by a geometry of his own, the circle within which they shall happily *appear* to do so" (*Theory* 171–72). James was referring to the problem of closure in the novel, but the comment applies with equal point to the dilemma of the ethicist who would draw the circle within which the individual is sacrosanct and may not be touched. If our identities and lives are more entangled with those of others than we tend to acknowledge in the culture of individualism, then existing models of privacy, personhood, and ethics may have to be revised. I would be the first to admit, however, that this is easier said than done, for in questioning the boundaries that secure the rights of individual subjects we may place in jeopardy the boundaries that define the moral responsibilities of those who write about them. I take heart, nonetheless, in Roth's brave negotiation of the difficulties posed by relational identity, in the seemliness of his practice of the "unseemly" profession.

Works Cited

Abel, Elizabeth. "Race, Class, and Gender in Psychoanalysis." In *Conflicts in Feminism*, ed. Marianne Hirsch and Evelyn Fox Keller. New York: Routledge, 1990. 184–204.

Abt, Vicki, and Mel Seesholtz. "The Shameless World of Phil, Sally and Oprah: Television Talk Shows and the Deconstructing of Society." *Journal of Popular Culture* 28 (1994): 171–91.

Andrews, William L. *To Tell a Free Story: The First Century of Afro-American Autobiography, 1760–1865*. Urbana: University of Illinois Press, 1986.

Angelou, Maya. Foreword to *Dust Tracks on a Road*, by Zora Neale Hurston. New York: HarperPerennial, 1991. vii–xii.

Atlas, James. "The Biographer and the Murderer." *New York Times Magazine*, 12 December 1993, 74–75.

Auster, Paul. *The Invention of Solitude*. 1982. New York: Penguin, 1988.

Baron-Cohen, Simon. *Mindblindness: An Essay on Autism and Theory of Mind*. Cambridge: MIT Press, 1995.

Barsalou, Lawrence W. "The Content and Organization of Autobiographical Memories." In *Remembering Reconsidered: Ecological and Traditional Approaches to the Study of Memory*, ed. Ulric Neisser and Eugene Winograd. New York: Cambridge University Press, 1988. 193–243.

Barthes, Roland. *Camera Lucida: Reflections on Photography*. 1980. Trans. Richard Howard. New York: Hill and Wang, 1981.

——. *Roland Barthes by Roland Barthes*. 1975. Trans. Richard Howard. New York: Farrar, 1977.

——. *S/Z*. 1970. Trans. Richard Howard. New York: Hill and Wang, 1974.

Benhabib, Seyla. "Feminism and the Question of Postmodernism." In *Situating the Self: Gender, Community and Postmodernism in Contemporary Ethics.* New York: Routledge, 1992. 203–41.

Benjamin, Jessica. *The Bonds of Love: Psychoanalysis, Feminism and the Problem of Domination.* New York: Pantheon, 1988.

Benn, Stanley I. "Privacy, Freedom, and Respect for Persons." 1971. In Schoeman, *Philosophical* 223–44.

Benveniste, Emile. *Problems in General Linguistics.* Trans. Mary Elizabeth Meek. Coral Gables, Fla.: University of Miami Press, 1971.

Bérubé, Michael. *Life As We Know It: A Father, a Family, and an Exceptional Child.* New York: Pantheon, 1996.

Bloustein, Edward J. "Privacy as an Aspect of Human Dignity: An Answer to Dean Prosser." 1964. In Schoeman, *Philosophical* 156–202.

Bok, Sissela. *Secrets: On the Ethics of Concealment and Revelation.* New York: Pantheon, 1982.

Brée, Germaine. "Autogynography." 1986. In *Studies in Autobiography,* ed. James Olney. New York: Oxford University Press, 1988. 171–79.

Brodzki, Bella, and Celeste Schenck. Introduction to *Life/Lines: Theorizing Women's Autobiography,* ed. Bella Brodzki and Celeste Schenck. Ithaca: Cornell University Press, 1988. 1–15.

Brown, Chip. "I Now Walk into the Wild." *New Yorker,* 8 February 1993, 36–47.

Bruner, Jerome. *Acts of Meaning.* Cambridge: Harvard University Press, 1990.

———. "The Invention of Self: Autobiography and Its Forms." Paper presented at the conference "Autobiography and Self-Representation," University of California–Irvine, 3–4 March 1990.

———. "Life as Narrative." *Social Research* 54 (1987): 11–32.

———. "The Narrative Construction of Reality." *Critical Inquiry* 18 (1991): 1–21.

Bruss, Elizabeth. *Autobiographical Acts: The Changing Situation of a Literary Genre.* Baltimore: Johns Hopkins University Press, 1976.

Burkitt, Ian. "The Shifting Concept of the Self." *History of the Human Sciences* 7 (1994): 7–28.

———. *Social Selves: Theories of the Social Formation of Personality.* London: Sage, 1991.

Butler, Judith. *Bodies That Matter: On the Discursive Limits of "Sex."* New York: Routledge, 1993.

———. "Contingent Foundations: Feminism and the Question of 'Postmodernism.' " In *The Postmodern Turn: New Perspectives on Social Theory,* ed. Steven Seidman. Cambridge: Cambridge University Press, 1994. 153–70.

Cadava, Eduardo, Peter Connor, and Jean-Luc Nancy, eds. *Who Comes after the Subject?* New York: Routledge, 1991.

Carlson, E. Mary. " 'In Dixieland where I was born . . . ' The Role of Autobiography in the Shaping of Southern Cultural Identity, 1920–1954." Ph.D. diss., Indiana University, 1994.

Carvajal, Doreen. "Book Publishers Are Eager for Tales of True Torment." *New York Times*, 5 April 1997:1.

Cheever, Susan. "Innocence Betrayed." Review of *The Kiss*, by Kathryn Harrison. *New York Times Book Review*, 30 March 1997, 11.

Chernin, Kim. *In My Mother's House: A Daughter's Story.* 1983. 2d. ed. New York: HarperCollins, 1994.

Chodorow, Nancy. *The Reproduction of Mothering: Psychoanalysis and the Sociology of Gender.* Berkeley: University of California Press, 1978.

Christman, John, ed. *The Inner Citadel: Essays on Individual Autonomy.* New York: Oxford University Press, 1989.

Claridge, Laura, and Elizabeth Langland. Introduction to *Out of Bounds: Male Writers and Gender(ed) Criticism*, ed. Laura Claridge and Elizabeth Langland. Amherst: University of Massachusetts Press, 1990. 3–21.

Cohen, Anthony P. *Self-Consciousness: An Alternative Anthropology of Identity.* London: Routledge, 1994.

Coombe, Rosemary J. "Author/izing the Celebrity: Publicity Rights, Postmodern Politics, and Unauthorized Genders." In Woodmansee and Jaszi 101–31.

Couser, G. Thomas. *Altered Egos: Authority in American Autobiography.* New York: Oxford University Press, 1989.

——. *Recovering Bodies: Illness, Disability, and Life-Writing.* Madison: University of Wisconsin Press, 1997.

Coward, Rosalind, and John Ellis. *Language and Materialism: Developments in Semiology and the Theory of the Subject.* London: Routledge, 1977.

Crossen, Cynthia. "Know Thy Father." Review of *The Kiss*, by Kathryn Harrison. *Wall Street Journal*, 4 March 1997, A16.

Dahlberg, Edward. *Because I Was Flesh: The Autobiography of Edward Dahlberg.* London: Methuen, 1965.

Damasio, Antonio R. *Descartes' Error: Emotion, Reason, and the Human Brain.* 1994. New York: Avon, 1995.

de Grazia, Margreta. "Sanctioning Voice: Quotation Marks, the Abolition of Torture, and the Fifth Amendment." In Woodmansee and Jaszi 281–302.

Dennett, Daniel C. *Consciousness Explained.* Boston: Little, Brown, 1991.

——. "The Self as a Center of Narrative Gravity." In *Self and Consciousness: Multiple Perspectives*, ed. Frank S. Kessel, Pamela M. Cole, and Dale L. Johnson. Hillsdale, N.J.: Lawrence Erlbaum, 1992. 103–15.

Descartes, René. *Discourse on Method* and *The Meditations*. Trans. F. E. Sutcliffe. Harmondsworth, England: Penguin, 1968.

Descombes, Vincent. "Apropos of the 'Critique of the Subject' and of the Critique of this Critique." In Cadava, Connor, and Nancy 120–34.

Dessaix, Robert. *A Mother's Disgrace*. Sydney: Angus & Robertson, 1994.

De Witt, Karen. "Incest as a Selling Point." *New York Times*, 30 March 1997, sec. 4, p. 6.

Dowd, Maureen. "Banks for the Memories." *New York Times*, 15 March 1997, A19.

Eakin, Paul John. *Fictions in Autobiography: Studies in the Art of Self-Invention*. Princeton: Princeton University Press, 1985.

——. "Malcolm X and the Limits of Autobiography." 1976. In Olney, *Autobiography* 181–93.

——. *Touching the World: Reference in Autobiography*. Princeton: Princeton University Press, 1992.

Edelman, Gerald M. *Bright Air, Brilliant Fire: On the Matter of the Mind*. New York: Basic, 1992.

Egan, Susanna. "Encounters in Camera: Autobiography as Interaction." *Modern Fiction Studies* 40 (1994): 593–618.

——. *Mirror Talk: Genres of Crisis in Contemporary Autobiography*. Chapel Hill: University of North Carolina Press, 1999.

Elias, Norbert. *The Society of Individuals*. Ed. Michael Schröter. Trans. Edmund Jephcott. Oxford: Basil Blackwell, 1991.

Fivush, Robyn. "Constructing Narrative, Emotion, and Self in Parent-Child Conversations about the Past." In Neisser and Fivush 136–57.

——. "The Functions of Event Memory: Some Comments on Nelson and Barsalou." In *Remembering Reconsidered: Ecological and Traditional Approaches to the Study of Memory*, ed. Ulric Neisser and Eugene Winograd. New York: Cambridge University Press, 1988. 277–82.

Fivush, Robyn, and Elaine Reese. "The Social Construction of Autobiographical Memory." In *Theoretical Perspectives on Autobiographical Memory*, ed. Martin A. Conway, David C. Rubin, Hans Spinnler, and Willem A. Wagenaar. Dordrecht, The Netherlands: Kluwer Academic Publishers, 1992. 115–32.

Foucault, Michel. *Discipline and Punish: The Birth of the Prison*. Trans. Alan Sheridan. New York: Pantheon, 1977.

Fox-Genovese, Elizabeth. "My Statue, My Self: Autobiographical Writings of Afro-American Women." In *The Private Self: Theory and Prac-*

tice of Women's Autobiographical Writings, ed. Shari Benstock. Chapel Hill: University of North Carolina Press, 1988. 63–89.

Frank, Arthur W. *At the Will of the Body: Reflections on Illness.* Boston: Houghton, 1991.

Fraser, Nancy. "False Antithesis: A Response to Seyla Benhabib and Judith Butler." *Praxis International* 11 (1991): 166–77.

Friedman, Susan Stanford. "Women's Autobiographical Selves: Theory and Practice." In *The Private Self: Theory and Practice of Women's Autobiographical Writings*, ed. Shari Benstock. Chapel Hill: University of North Carolina Press, 1988. 34–62.

Gagnier, Regenia. *Subjectivities: A History of Self-Representation in Britain, 1832–1920.* New York: Oxford University Press, 1991.

Galella v. Onassis. 533 F.Supp.1076 (1982).

Gardner, Howard. *The Mind's New Science: A History of the Cognitive Revolution.* 1985. New York: Basic, 1987.

Gass, William. "The Art of Self: Autobiography in an Age of Narcissism." *Harper's,* May 1994, 43–52.

Gates, Henry Louis, Jr. "Afterword: Zora Neale Hurston: 'A Negro Way of Saying.' " In *Dust Tracks on a Road,* by Zora Neale Hurston. New York: HarperPerennial, 1991. 257–67.

———. *Colored People: A Memoir.* 1994. New York: Vintage, 1995.

Gergen, Kenneth J. "Mind, Text, and Society: Self-Memory in Social Context." In Neisser and Fivush 78–104.

Gibson, Eleanor J. "Ontogenesis of the Perceived Self." In *The Perceived Self: Ecological and Interpersonal Sources of Self-knowledge*, ed. Ulric Neisser. New York: Cambridge University Press, 1993. 25–42.

Gilligan, Carol. *In a Different Voice: Psychological Theory and Women's Development.* Cambridge: Harvard University Press, 1982.

Gilmore, Mikal. *Shot in the Heart.* New York: Doubleday, 1994.

Goldman, Anne E. "Is That What She Said? The Politics of Collaborative Autobiography." *Cultural Critique* 25 (Fall 1993): 177–204.

Gordon, Mary. *The Shadow Man.* New York: Random, 1996.

Gornick, Vivian. *Fierce Attachments: A Memoir.* New York: Farrar, 1987.

Gosse, Edmund. *Father and Son; A Study of Two Temperaments.* London: Heinemann, 1907.

Granel, Gérard. "Who Comes after the Subject?" In Cadava, Connor, and Nancy 148–56.

Grealy, Lucy. *Autobiography of a Face.* 1994. New York: HarperPerennial, 1995.

Grene, Marjorie. "The Primacy of the Ecological Self." In *The Perceived Self: Ecological and Interpersonal Sources of Self-knowledge*, ed. Ulric Neisser. New York: Cambridge University Press, 1993. 112–17.

Grosz, Elizabeth. *Volatile Bodies: Toward a Corporeal Feminism.* Bloomington: Indiana University Press, 1994.

Gubrium, Jaber F., and James A. Holstein. "Grounding the Postmodern Self." *Sociological Quarterly* 35 (1994): 685–703.

Gullestad, Marianne. *Everyday Life Philosophers: Modernity, Morality, and Autobiography in Norway.* Oslo: Scandinavian University Press, 1996.

Gunther, John. *Death Be Not Proud: A Memoir.* New York: Harper, 1949.

Gusdorf, Georges. "Conditions and Limits of Autobiography." 1956. In Olney, *Autobiography* 28–48.

Haizlip, Shirlee Taylor. *The Sweeter the Juice: A Family Memoir in Black and White.* New York: Simon & Schuster, 1994.

Hale, Janet Campbell. *Bloodlines: Odyssey of a Native Daughter.* New York: Random, 1993.

Hall, Donald. "Bill Moyers' Journal: A Life Together [Donald Hall and Jane Kenyon]." PBS. 17 December 1993.

Hamilton, Ian. "J. D. Salinger *versus* Random House, Inc." *Granta* 23 (Spring 1988): 197–218.

Hampl, Patricia. *A Romantic Education.* Boston: Houghton, 1981.

Harris, Grace Gredys. "Concepts of Individual, Self, and Person in Description and Analysis." *American Anthropologist* 91 (1989): 599–612.

Harrison, Colin. "Sins of the Father." *Vogue,* April 1997, 328ff.

Harrison, Kathryn. *The Kiss.* New York: Random, 1997.

——. "Seeking Rapture: Lessons for an Apprentice Saint." *Harper's,* September 1994, 64–72.

Hawkins, Anne Hunsaker. *Reconstructing Illness: Studies in Pathography.* West Lafayette, Ind.: Purdue University Press, 1993.

Heller, Agnes. "Death of the Subject?" In *Constructions of the Self,* ed. George Levine. New Brunswick, N.J.: Rutgers University Press, 1992. 269–84.

Hellman, Lillian. *Maybe: A Story.* Boston: Little, Brown, 1980.

——. *Pentimento: A Book of Portraits.* Boston: Little, Brown, 1973.

Henry, Michel. "The Critique of the Subject." In Cadava, Connor, and Nancy 157–66.

Hirst, William. "The Remembered Self in Amnesics." In Neisser and Fivush 252–77.

Hite, Shere. *The Hite Report on Male Sexuality.* New York: Knopf, 1981.

Hoban, Phoebe. "The Salinger File." *New York,* 15 June 1987, 36–42.

Hogan, Rebecca. "Engendered Autobiographies: The Diary as a Feminine Form." In *Autobiography and Questions of Gender,* ed. Shirley Neuman. London: Frank Cass, 1991. 95–107.

Hooton, Joy. "Individuation and Autobiography." In *Left, Right or Centre? Psychiatry and the Status Quo,* ed. Harry Heseltine. Occasional

Paper No. 19. Canberra: University College, University of New South Wales, 1990. 59–79.

Howard, Maureen. *Facts of Life.* Boston: Little, Brown, 1978.

Howells, William Dean. *My Mark Twain; Reminiscences and Criticisms.* New York: Harper, 1910.

Hull, John M. *Touching the Rock: An Experience of Blindness.* 1990. New York: Vintage, 1992.

Hurston, Zora Neale. *Dust Tracks on a Road.* 1942. New York: Harper-Perennial, 1991.

James, Henry. *Notes of a Son and Brother.* New York: Scribner's, 1914.

——. *A Small Boy and Others.* New York: Scribner's, 1913.

——. *Theory of Fiction: Henry James.* Ed. James E. Miller, Jr. Lincoln: University of Nebraska Press, 1972.

Jefferson, Margo. "Facing Truth about Incest, in Memoir and Novel." *New York Times,* 29 May 1997:B1.

Jelinek, Estelle C. "Introduction: Women's Autobiography and the Male Tradition." In *Women's Autobiography: Essays in Criticism,* ed. Estelle C. Jelinek. Bloomington: Indiana University Press, 1980. 1–20.

Juhasz, Suzanne. "Towards a Theory of Form in Feminist Autobiography: Kate Millett's *Flying* and *Sita;* Maxine Hong Kingston's *The Woman Warrior.*" In *Women's Autobiography: Essays in Criticism,* ed. Estelle C. Jelinek. Bloomington: Indiana University Press, 1980. 221–37.

Kakutani, Michiko. "Biography as a Blood Sport." *New York Times,* 20 May 1994:B1.

Karr, Mary. *The Liars' Club: A Memoir.* New York: Viking, 1995.

Kazin, Alfred. *A Walker in the City.* New York: Harcourt, 1951.

Keller, Helen. *The Story of My Life.* 1903. New York: Doubleday, 1949.

——. *Teacher: Anne Sullivan Macy; A Tribute by the Foster-child of Her Mind.* Garden City, N.Y.: Doubleday, 1955.

——. *The World I Live In.* 1908. New York: Century, 1910.

Kerby, Anthony Paul. *Narrative and the Self.* Bloomington: Indiana University Press, 1991.

Kingston, Maxine Hong. *China Men.* New York: Knopf, 1980.

——. *The Woman Warrior: Memoirs of a Girlhood among Ghosts.* 1976. New York: Random, 1977.

Kleinman, Arthur. *The Illness Narratives: Suffering, Healing, and the Human Condition.* New York: Basic, 1988.

Krakauer, Jon. "Death of an Innocent." *Outside,* January 1993, 38–45, 90–92.

——. *Into the Wild.* 1996. New York: Anchor, 1996.

Kramer, Peter D. *Listening to Prozac.* New York: Viking, 1993.

Krupat, Arnold. *For Those Who Come After: A Study of Native American Autobiography.* Berkeley: University of California Press, 1985.
———. "Native American Autobiography and the Synecdochic Self." In *American Autobiography: Retrospect and Prospect*, ed. Paul John Eakin. Madison: University of Wisconsin Press, 1991. 171–94.
———. *The Voice in the Margin: Native American Literature and the Canon.* Berkeley: University of California Press, 1989.
Lakoff, George, and Mark Johnson. *Metaphors We Live By.* Chicago: University of Chicago Press, 1980.
Larcom, Lucy. *A New England Girlhood, Outlined from Memory.* Boston: Houghton, 1889.
Lawless, Elaine. "Ethnography as Responsible Discourse: Is a Collaborative Narrative Ever Possible?" Public lecture, Indiana University, 25 March 1994.
Lehmann-Haupt, Christopher. " 'The Kiss' Recounts Incestuous, Soul-Deadening Affair." Review of *The Kiss*, by Kathryn Harrison. *New York Times Book Review*, 27 February 1997, C18.
Lejeune, Philippe. "L'atteinte à la vie privée." *La Faute à Rousseau* (Bulletin de l'Association pour l'Autobiographie et le Patrimoine Autobiographique) 3 (June 1993): 17–20.
———. "The Autobiographical Pact." In Lejeune, *On Autobiography* 3–30.
———. "The Autobiographical Pact (bis)." In Lejeune, *On Autobiography* 119–37.
———. *L'Autobiographie en France.* Paris: A. Colin, 1971.
———. "The Autobiography of Those Who Do Not Write." In Lejeune, *On Autobiography* 185–215.
———. *"Cher cahier . . . ": Témoignages sur le journal personnel.* Paris: Gallimard, 1989.
———. *Je est un autre: l'autobiographie de la littérature aux médias.* Paris: Seuil, 1980.
———. *Moi aussi.* Paris: Seuil, 1986.
———. *On Autobiography.* Ed. Paul John Eakin. Trans. Katherine Leary. Minneapolis: University of Minnesota Press, 1989.
———. *La Pratique du journal personnel: Enquête. Cahiers de Sémiotique Textuelle* 17 (1990).
"Letters." *Atlantic Monthly*, January 1998, 9–10.
Levine, George. "Introduction: Constructivism and the Reemergent Self." In *Constructions of the Self*, ed. George Levine. New Brunswick, N.J.: Rutgers University Press, 1992. 1–13.
Levy, Steven. "Dr. Edelman's Brain." *New Yorker*, 2 May 1994, 62–73.
Lionnet, Françoise. *Autobiographical Voices: Race, Gender, Self-Portraiture.* Ithaca: Cornell University Press, 1989.

Lively, Penelope. *Oleander, Jacaranda: A Childhood Perceived.* 1994. New York: HarperCollins, 1995.

Loewenstein, Era A. "Dissolving the Myth of the Unified Self: The Fate of the Subject in Freudian Analysis." *Psychoanalytic Quarterly* 63 (1994): 715–32.

Macpherson, C. B. *The Political Theory of Possessive Individualism: Hobbes to Locke.* Oxford: Clarendon Press, 1962.

Malcolm, Janet. *The Silent Woman: Sylvia Plath & Ted Hughes.* 1993. New York: Knopf, 1994.

Malcolm X. *The Autobiography of Malcolm X.* New York: Grove, 1965.

Malouf, David. "12 Edmondstone Street." In *12 Edmondstone Street.* 1985. Ringwood, Victoria, Australia: Penguin, 1986. 1–66.

Marcus, Steven. "Freud and Dora: Story, History, Case History." *Partisan Review* 41 (1974): 12–23, 89–108.

Mason, Mary G. "The Other Voice: Autobiographies of Women Writers." In Olney, *Autobiography* 207–35.

Maxwell, William. *Ancestors: A Family History.* New York: Knopf, 1971.

McBride, James. *The Color of Water: A Black Man's Tribute to His White Mother.* New York: Riverhead, 1996.

McCarthy, Thomas. *Ideals and Illusions: On Reconstruction and Deconstruction in Contemporary Critical Theory.* Cambridge: MIT Press, 1991.

McCourt, Frank. *Angela's Ashes: A Memoir.* New York: Scribner's, 1996.

McNee, Lisa. "Autobiographical Subjects." *Research in African Literatures* 28 (1997): 83–101.

Miller, Nancy K. *Bequest and Betrayal: Memoirs of a Parent's Death.* New York: Oxford University Press, 1996.

——. "Facts, Pacts, Acts." *Profession 92* (New York: Modern Language Association, 1992): 10–14.

——. "Representing Others: Gender and the Subjects of Autobiography." *differences* 6 (1994): 1–27.

Miller, Peggy J., Randolph Potts, Heidi Fung, Lisa Hoogstra, and Judy Mintz. "Narrative Practices and the Social Construction of Self in Childhood." *American Ethnologist* 17 (1990): 292–311.

Modjeska, Drusilla. *Poppy.* Ringwood, Victoria, Australia: Penguin, 1990.

Morgan, Sally. *My Place.* South Fremantle, Australia: Fremantle Arts Centre Press, 1987.

Morrison, Blake. *And When Did You Last See Your Father? A Son's Memoir of Love and Loss.* New York: Picador, 1993.

Murphy, Robert F. *The Body Silent.* 1987. New York: Norton, 1990.

——. "Social Distance and the Veil." 1964. In Schoeman, *Philosophical* 34–55.

Naipaul, V. S. *The Enigma of Arrival.* 1987. New York: Vintage, 1988.

Neisser, Ulric. "Five Kinds of Self-knowledge." *Philosophical Psychology* 1 (1988): 35–59.

———. "Self-Narratives: True and False." In Neisser and Fivush 1–18.

Neisser, Ulric, and Robyn Fivush, eds. *The Remembering Self: Construction and Accuracy in the Self-Narrative.* New York: Cambridge University Press, 1994.

Nelson, Katherine. "Introduction: Monologues in the Crib." In Nelson, *Narratives* 1–23.

———. *Language in Cognitive Development: Emergence of the Mediated Mind.* New York: Cambridge University Press, 1996.

———. "Monologue as the Linguistic Construction of Self in Time." In Nelson, *Narratives* 284–308.

———. "The Ontogeny of Memory for Real Events." In *Remembering Reconsidered: Ecological and Traditional Approaches to the Study of Memory,* ed. Ulric Neisser and Eugene Winograd. New York: Cambridge University Press, 1988. 244–76.

———, ed. *Narratives from the Crib.* Cambridge: Harvard University Press, 1989.

Neuman, Shirley. " 'An appearance walking in a forest the sexes burn': Autobiography and the Construction of the Feminine Body." *Signature* 2 (1989): 1–26.

———. " 'Your Past . . . Your Future': Autobiography and Mothers' Bodies." In *Genre * Trope * Gender: Essays by Northrop Frye, Linda Hutcheon, and Shirley Neuman.* Ottawa: Carleton University Press, 1992. 51–86.

Nussbaum, Emily. "The Mirror Stage." *Lingua franca,* August 1997, 7–8.

Nussbaum, Felicity A. *The Autobiographical Subject: Gender and Ideology in Eighteenth-Century England.* Baltimore: Johns Hopkins University Press, 1989.

Olney, James. "Autobiography and the Cultural Moment: A Thematic, Historical, and Bibliographical Introduction." In Olney, *Autobiography* 3–27.

———. "Some Versions of Memory / Some Versions of *Bios*: The Ontology of Autobiography." In Olney, *Autobiography* 236–67.

———, ed. *Autobiography: Essays Theoretical and Critical.* Princeton: Princeton University Press, 1980.

Olshen, Barry N. "Subject, Persona, and Self in the Theory of Autobiography." *a/b: Auto/Biography Studies* 10 (1995): 5–16.

Ondaatje, Michael. *Running in the Family.* New York: Norton, 1982.

Padilla, Genaro M. *My History, Not Yours: The Formation of Mexican American Autobiography.* Madison: University of Wisconsin Press, 1993.

Patai, Daphne. "Ethical Problems of Personal Narratives, or, Who Should Eat the Last Piece of Cake?" *International Journal of Oral History* 8 (1987): 5–27.

Pember, Don R. *Privacy and the Press: The Law, the Mass Media, and the First Amendment.* Seattle: University of Washington Press, 1972.

Peterson, Linda H. "Institutionalizing Women's Autobiography: Nineteenth-Century Editors and the Shaping of an Autobiographical Tradition." In *The Culture of Autobiography: Constructions of Self-Representation,* ed. Robert Folkenflik. Stanford: Stanford University Press, 1993. 80–103.

Pile, Steve, and Nigel Thrift, eds. *Mapping the Subject: Geographies of Cultural Transformation.* London: Routledge, 1995.

Pillemer, D. B., and S. H. White. "Childhood Events Recalled by Children and Adults." In *Advances in Child Development and Behavior,* vol. 21, ed. H. W. Reese. New York: Academic, 1989. 297–340.

Pogrebin, Robin. "The Naked Literary Come-On." *New York Times,* 17 August 1997, sec. 4, p. 2.

Porter, Roger J. "Figuration and Disfigurement: Herculine Barbin and the Autobiography of the Body." *Prose Studies* 14 (1991): 122–36.

Posner, Richard A. "An Economic Theory of Privacy." 1978. In Schoeman, *Philosophical* 333–45.

Post, Robert C. "Rereading Warren and Brandeis: Privacy, Property, and Appropriation." *Case Western Law Review* 41 (1991): 647–80.

———. "The Social Foundations of Privacy: Community and Self in the Common Law Tort." *California Law Review* 77 (1989): 957–1010.

Prosser, William L. "Privacy." 1960. In Schoeman, *Philosophical* 104–55.

Proust, Marcel. *Remembrance of Things Past.* Trans. C. K. Scott Moncrieff. 2 vols. New York: Random, 1934.

Rachels, James, and William Ruddick. "Lives and Liberty." In *The Inner Citadel: Essays on Individual Autonomy,* ed. John Christman. New York: Oxford University Press, 1989. 221–33.

Reiman, Jeffrey H. "Privacy, Intimacy, and Personhood." 1976. In Schoeman, *Philosophical* 300–16.

Ricoeur, Paul. *Oneself as Another.* Trans. Kathleen Blamey. Chicago: University of Chicago Press, 1992.

Rodriguez, Richard. *Hunger of Memory: The Education of Richard Rodriguez.* Boston: Godine, 1981.

Rorty, Amelie Oksenberg. "A Literary Postscript: Characters, Persons, Selves, Individuals." In *The Identities of Persons,* ed. Amelie Oksenberg Rorty. Berkeley: University of California Press, 1976. 301–23.

Rose, Phyllis. "The Music of Silence." *Atlantic Monthly,* October 1997, 44–48.

Rosenfield, Israel. *The Invention of Memory: A New View of the Brain.* New York: Basic, 1988.

———. *The Strange, Familiar, and Forgotten: An Anatomy of Consciousness.* New York: Knopf, 1992.

Roth, Philip. *Patrimony: A True Story.* 1991. New York: Simon & Schuster, 1992.

Rousseau, Jean-Jacques. *The Confessions of Jean-Jacques Rousseau.* 1781. Trans. J. M. Cohen. Harmondsworth, England: Penguin, 1953; reprint 1988.

Rybczynski, Witold. *Home: A Short History of an Idea.* New York: Viking, 1986.

Rymer, Russ. *Genie: An Abused Child's Flight from Silence.* New York: HarperCollins, 1993.

Sacco, Mary Anne. "Ask 7-Year-Old Memoirists about Wisdom." *New York Times,* 21 March 1997, A18.

Sacks, Oliver. *An Anthropologist on Mars.* 1995. New York: Random, 1996.

———. *Awakenings.* London: Duckworth, 1973.

———. Foreword to *Touching the Rock: An Experience of Blindness,* by John M. Hull. New York: Vintage, 1992.

———. *A Leg to Stand On.* 2d ed. with "Afterword." 1993. New York: HarperPerennial, 1994.

———. "Making up the Mind." *New York Review of Books,* 8 April 1993, 42–49.

———. *The Man Who Mistook His Wife for a Hat and Other Clinical Tales.* 1985. New York: Harper, 1987.

———. "Neurology and the Soul." *New York Review of Books,* 22 November 1990, 44–50.

Sampson, Edward E. "The Deconstruction of the Self." In *Texts of Identity,* ed. John Shotter and Kenneth J. Gergen. London: Sage, 1989. 1–19.

Sanders, Mark A. "Theorizing the Collaborative Self: The Dynamics of Contour and Content in the Dictated Autobiography." *New Literary History* 25 (1994): 445–58.

Sarraute, Nathalie. *Childhood.* 1983. Trans. Barbara Wright. New York: Braziller, 1984.

Sartre, Jean-Paul. *The Words.* Trans. Bernard Frechtman. New York: Braziller, 1964.

Sass, Louis A. "The Self and Its Vicissitudes in the Psychoanalytic Avant-Garde." In *Constructions of the Self,* ed. George Levine. New Brunswick, N.J.: Rutgers University Press, 1992. 17–58.

Schacter, Daniel L. "Memory Distortion: History and Current Status." In *Memory Distortion: How Minds, Brains, and Societies Reconstruct the*

Past, ed. Daniel L. Schacter. Cambridge: Harvard University Press, 1995. 1–43.

——. *Searching for Memory: The Brain, the Mind, and the Past.* New York: Basic, 1996.

Schafer, Roy. "Narration in the Psychoanalytic Dialogue." *Critical Inquiry* 7 (1980): 29–53.

Schoeman, Ferdinand David. "Privacy: Philosophical Dimensions of the Literature." In Schoeman, *Philosophical* 1–33.

——, ed. *Philosophical Dimensions of Privacy; An Anthology.* Cambridge: Cambridge University Press, 1984.

Scot, Barbara J. *Prairie Reunion.* New York: Farrar, 1995.

Searle, John R. "The Mystery of Consciousness: Part II." *New York Review of Books*, 16 November 1995, 54–61.

Sedgwick, Eve Kosofsky. *Between Men: English Literature and Male Homosocial Desire.* New York: Columbia University Press, 1985.

Sheringham, Michael. "The Otherness of Memory." In *French Autobiography: Devices and Desires.* Oxford: Clarendon Press, 1993. 288–326.

Shnayerson, Michael. "Women Behaving Badly." *Vanity Fair*, February 1997, 54–61.

Shotter, John. "Social Accountability and the Social Construction of 'You.' " In *Texts of Identity*, ed. John Shotter and Kenneth J. Gergen. London: Sage, 1989. 133–51.

Silko, Leslie Marmon. "Landscape, History, and the Pueblo Imagination." *Antaeus* 57 (1986): 83–94.

——. *Storyteller.* New York: Arcade, 1981.

Smith, Paul. *Discerning the Subject.* Minneapolis: University of Minnesota Press, 1988.

Smith, Sidonie. "The [Female] Subject in Critical Venues: Poetics, Politics, Autobiographical Practices." *a/b: Auto/Biography Studies* 6 (1991): 109–30.

——. *Subjectivity, Identity, and the Body: Women's Autobiographical Practices in the Twentieth Century.* Bloomington: Indiana University Press, 1993.

——. "Taking It to a Limit One More Time: Autobiography and Autism." In *Getting a Life: Everyday Uses of Autobiography*, ed. Sidonie Smith and Julia Watson. Minneapolis: University of Minnesota Press, 1996. 226–46.

Snow, Catherine E. "Building Memories: The Ontogeny of Autobiography." *The Self in Transition: Infancy to Childhood.* Ed. Dante Cichetti and Marjorie Beeghly. Chicago: University of Chicago Press, 1990. 213–42.

Spence, Donald P. *Narrative Truth and Historical Truth: Meaning and Interpretation in Psychoanalysis.* New York: Norton, 1982.

Spiegelman, Art. Interview by Robert Siegel. "All Things Considered."
National Public Radio, Washington, D. C., 12 November 1991.

———. *Maus I: A Survivor's Tale: My Father Bleeds History*. New York: Pantheon, 1986.

———. *Maus II: A Survivor's Tale: And Here My Troubles Began*. New York: Pantheon, 1991.

Sprinker, Michael. "Fictions of the Self: The End of Autobiography." In Olney, *Autobiography* 321–42.

Squire, Larry R. "Biological Foundations of Accuracy and Inaccuracy in Memory." In *Memory Distortion: How Minds, Brains, and Societies Reconstruct the Past*, ed. Daniel L. Schacter. Cambridge: Harvard University Press, 1995. 197–225.

Stanton, Domna C. "Autogynography: Is the Subject Different?" 1984. In *The Female Autograph: Theory and Practice of Autobiography from the Tenth to the Twentieth Century*, ed. Domna C. Stanton. Chicago: University of Chicago Press, 1987. 3–20.

Staples, Brent. "Hating It Because It Is True." *New York Times*, 27 April 1997, sec. 4, p. 14.

———. *Parallel Time: Growing Up in Black and White*. 1994. New York: Avon, 1995.

Steedman, Carolyn Kay. "History and Autobiography: Different Pasts." In Steedman, *Past Tenses* 41–50.

———. *Landscape for a Good Woman: A Story of Two Lives*. 1986. New Brunswick, N.J.: Rutgers University Press, 1987.

———. *Past Tenses: Essays on Writing, Autobiography and History*. London: Rivers Oram Press, 1992.

———. *Strange Dislocations: Childhood and the Idea of Human Interiority, 1780–1930*. London: Virago, 1995.

———. "The Tidy House." In Steedman, *Past Tenses* 65–89.

———. *The Tidy House: Little Girls Writing*. London: Virago, 1982.

———. "True Romances." In Steedman, *Past Tenses* 109–15.

Stern, Daniel N. "Crib Monologues from a Psychoanalytic Perspective." In Nelson, *Narratives* 309–19.

———. *The Interpersonal World of the Infant: A View from Psychoanalysis and Developmental Psychology*. New York: Basic, 1985.

Stern, Howard. *Private Parts*. New York: Simon & Schuster, 1993.

St. John, Warren. "Kathryn Harrison's Dad Responds to Her Memoir." *New York Observer*, 21 April 1997:1.

———. "The Saucy, Literary Harrisons Pucker Up." *New York Observer*, 10 February 1997:1.

Sturrock, John. "The New Model Autobiographer." *New Literary History* 9 (1977): 51–63.

Taylor, Charles. *Sources of the Self: The Making of the Modern Identity.* Cambridge: Harvard University Press, 1989.

Thernstrom, Melanie. *The Dead Girl: A True Story.* 1990. New York: Pocket Books, 1991.

Toth, Susan Allen. *Blooming: A Small-Town Girlhood.* Boston: Little, Brown, 1981.

Trillin, Calvin. *Messages from My Father.* New York: Farrar, 1996.

Trilling, Lionel. *Sincerity and Authenticity.* Cambridge: Harvard University Press, 1972.

Tulving, Endel. "Episodic and Semantic Memory." In *Organization of Memory,* ed. Endel Tulving and W. Donaldson. New York: Academic, 1972. 381–403.

Updike, John. *Self-Consciousness: Memoirs.* New York: Knopf, 1989.

Warren, Samuel D., and Louis D. Brandeis. "The Right to Privacy." 1890. In Schoeman, *Philosophical* 75–103.

Watson, Julia. "Toward an Anti-Metaphysics of Autobiography." In *The Culture of Autobiography: Constructions of Self-Representation,* ed. Robert Folkenflik. Stanford: Stanford University Press, 1993. 57–79.

Weintraub, Karl J. *The Value of the Individual: Self and Circumstance in Autobiography.* Chicago: University of Chicago Press, 1978.

Welty, Eudora. *One Writer's Beginnings.* Cambridge: Harvard University Press, 1984.

Wertsch, James V. "From Social Interaction to Higher Psychological Processes: A Clarification and Application of Vygotsky's Theory." *Human Development* 22 (1979): 1–22.

Westin, Alan. "The Origins of Modern Claims to Privacy." 1967. In Schoeman, *Philosophical* 56–74.

White, Hayden. "The Value of Narrativity in the Representation of Reality." 1980. In *The Content of the Form: Narrative Discourse and Historical Representation.* Baltimore: Johns Hopkins University Press, 1987. 1–25.

Wideman, John Edgar. *Brothers and Keepers.* 1984. New York: Penguin, 1985.

——. *Fatheralong: A Meditation on Fathers and Sons, Race and Society.* New York: Pantheon, 1994.

Wolf, Christa. *Patterns of Childhood.* 1976. Trans. Ursule Molinaro and Hedwig Rappolt. New York: Farrar, 1980.

Wolf, Dennie Palmer. "Being of Several Minds: Voices and Versions of the Self in Early Childhood." In *The Self in Transition: Infancy to Childhood,* ed. Dante Cichetti and Marjorie Beeghly. Chicago: University of Chicago Press, 1990. 183–212.

Wolff, Tobias. "Literary Conceits." *New York Times,* 6 April 1997, sec. 4, p. 19.

———. *This Boy's Life: A Memoir.* New York: Atlantic Monthly, 1989.

Woodmansee, Martha, and Peter Jaszi, eds. *The Construction of Authorship: Textual Appropriation in Law and Literature.* Durham, N.C.: Duke University Press, 1994.

Woolf, Virginia. "A Sketch of the Past." In *Moments of Being,* ed. Jeanne Schulkind. 2d ed. New York: Harcourt, 1985. 64–159.

Young, Kay, and Jeffrey L. Saver. "The Neurology of Narrative." Paper presented at a session on "Autobiography and Neuroscience," Modern Language Association Convention, New York, 29 December 1995.

Young, Robert. "Autonomy and the 'Inner Self.'" 1980. In *The Inner Citadel: Essays on Individual Autonomy,* ed. John Christman. New York: Oxford University Press, 1989. 77–90.

Zalewski, Daniel. "Nature Boys." *Lingua franca,* February 1996, 25.

Index